MBA
Guelph Public Library
327.1092 MUKBI
Mukbil, Huda.
Agent of change my life fig
June 28, 2023   Oct
33281021961211

AGENT
OF
CHANGE

AGENT OF CHANGE

My Life Fighting Terrorists, Spies, and Institutional Racism

HUDA MUKBIL

McGill-Queen's University Press
Montreal & Kingston | London | Chicago

© McGill-Queen's University Press 2023

ISBN 978-0-2280-1655-7 (cloth)
ISBN 978-0-2280-1656-4 (ePDF)
ISBN 978-0-2280-1657-1 (ePUB)

Legal deposit second quarter 2023
Bibliothèque nationale du Québec

Printed in Canada on acid-free paper that is 100% ancient forest free (100% post-consumer recycled), processed chlorine free

We acknowledge the support of the Canada Council for the Arts.

Nous remercions le Conseil des arts du Canada de son soutien.

Library and Archives Canada Cataloguing in Publication

Title: Agent of change : my life fighting terrorists, spies, and institutional racism / Huda Mukbil.
Names: Mukbil, Huda, author.
Description: Includes bibliographical references.
Identifiers: Canadiana (print) 20220437289 | Canadiana (ebook) 20220437432 | ISBN 9780228016557 (cloth) | ISBN 9780228016564 (ePDF) | ISBN 9780228016571 (ePUB)
Subjects: LCSH: Mukbil, Huda. | LCSH: Canadian Security Intelligence Service—Officials and employees—Biography. | LCSH: Intelligence officers—Canada—Biography. | LCSH: Muslims, Black—Canada—Biography. | LCSH: Race discrimination—Canada. | LCSH: Terrorism—Prevention. | LCGFT: Autobiographies.
Classification: LCC JL86.I58 M85 2023 | DDC 327.1092—dc23

Set in 11/14 Sina Nova with Uniform Extra Condensed
Book design & typesetting by Garet Markvoort, zijn digital

This book is dedicated to my parents, Zeinab and Abdulsalam, who taught me how to trust my moral compass, independent of others, and for their continued love. It is also dedicated to Ali, my husband, for taking my untested musical talent seriously and buying me an oud, an Arabic musical instrument. Kids, your mom is thankful for your forgiveness for skipping story time so that I could write the night away.

I also want to dedicate this book to Krista Carle, one of the first women of the Royal Canadian Mounted Police who stepped forward to shine light on sexual harassment and bullying in the organization. It is in her footsteps, fighting for greater equity in national security and a better future for Canada, that I follow. Rest in peace, Krista.

Author's Note: The views and sentiments expressed in this book are mine and reflect my interpretation of events. I am deliberately vague about specific events and the people that work in national security in Canada and globally. Much of what occurs behind the walls of the Canadian Security Intelligence Service must remain classified to protect personnel and intelligence work methods and techniques. To protect the identities of Canadian and British security and intelligence professionals, I use pseudonyms and change the descriptive details of those I mention, except executive managers and directors who are already in the public record. These views do not necessarily reflect any government organization's official policy or position.

CONTENTS

Abbreviations   ix
Prologue   xi

1 Exile   3
2 A Thousand Minarets   11
3 Remembrance Day   21
4 Rebel Girl   26
5 The Pitch   34
6 Recruitment   43
7 Raison d'être   59
8 Officer in Training   64
9 Sunni Islamic Extremism   79
10 First through the Door   98
11 Operation Crevice   102
12 Loyalty   116
13 London   129

14 The Canadian Spy   136

15 Toronto Region   145

16 Marital Status   156

17 Common Ground   165

18 Official Complaints and Repercussions   176

19 Lean In   184

20 Security Screening   188

21 Fight-or-Flight   200

22 Don't Be a Martyr   210

Afterword   229

Acknowledgments   231

Notes   233

ABBREVIATIONS

Those in government tend to speak in shorthand when referring to other branches and departments. In this book, I minimize abbreviations, acronyms, and initialisms so that the reading is always clear, plain, and free of "government speak." However, to protect and maintain the accuracy of the speech of others, I've left their use of abbreviations and so forth intact. The following is a list of the shorthand common to CSIS culture or often used by those in this book.

CBSA	Canadian Border Security Agency
CHRC	Canadian Human Rights Tribunal
CI	Counter Intelligence [CSIS]
CP	Counter Proliferation [CSIS]
CSE	Communications Security Establishment (Canada)
CSIS	Canadian Security Intelligence Service
CT	Counter Terrorism [CSIS]
EA	Employee Association [CSIS]
IO	Intelligence Officer
IOET	Intelligence Officer Entry Training [CSIS]
IOIC	Intelligence Officer Investigator Course [CSIS]
IRCC	Immigration, Refugees and Citizenship Canada
MI5	The British Security Service
RAP	Research Analysis and Production [CSIS]
RCMP	Royal Canadian Mounted Police
SIRC	Security Intelligence Review Committee
SSB	Security Screening Branch [CSIS]

PROLOGUE

The British Security Service, MI5, had sent out an urgent request for an intelligence officer matching my exact profile – someone with top-secret and signals intelligence security clearance and knowledge of East African languages and cultures. They wanted help with their investigations into what had become London's 9/11: the 7 July and 21 July 2005 terrorist attacks on the London transit system.

CSIS's international languages team leader called me to eagerly confirm my availability and linguistic profile: "Oh my God, Huda, you may be asked to go to London. Wouldn't that be something?"

I received my order to depart at a meeting with the deputy director general of Counter Intelligence, Jeff Yaworski. He was intimidating – a tall, heavy CSIS executive with glasses, a buttoned-down upper lip, and an inflexibly thick grey moustache. As the national decision maker for Counter Intelligence operations concerning Russia, China, North Korea, and other countries of interest, he was privy to Canada's most sensitive security operations.

"C'mon in, Huda," he said in a deep voice.

I walked in, nervous and self-conscious for not having dressed more formally – I hadn't known that I'd be called to his office. I sat. The expansive desk between us provided just the right distance for my comfort. His large paintings and memorabilia from Canadian intelligence, security partners, and international security agencies left me breathless.

"Hi, Jeff," I said solemnly. Silence followed. I was, by then, a seasoned intelligence officer and no longer the uninhibited, unreserved young woman who was quick to speak her heart and mind. I'd learned to demonstrate calm and that trust must be earned. I knew what Jeff wanted, and I'd already made my decision. Still, I wanted to show respect for the hierarchy and its decision-making culture. He'd have to ask.

"Huda, I spoke with David, our head-of-station in London. It appears MI5 has an urgent need for your specific linguistic skills and operational experience. The director, Jim Judd, has approved your deployment to that organization for an undetermined amount of time – upon your acceptance, of course. I called you in here today to ask if you'd be available to assist the British in their investigations into the terrorist attacks of the last weeks. There's news today that they've managed to arrest some of the terrorists, but there's a wider network and other emerging threats."

If I seemed calm before, he now, surely, saw through it. My eagerness and purpose had got the best of me. I was officially being offered an opportunity of a lifetime – what a moment! I'd be joining MI5 on an international investigation, searching for the terrorists who'd committed this heinous act. For an intelligence officer worth their salt, there's no higher calling.

Then suspicion clouded my elation. Was I back in the circle of the "trusted"? Was I again considered loyal, no longer an insider threat for being Muslim? Was I, once again, valuable as an intelligence officer and multilingual internationalist? I'd been trying, tiredly, for months to demonstrate my loyalty to queen and country. I'd been through unspeakable and painful isolation. I was seemingly being given a chance to prove that a Muslim could be faithful to her religion and Canada at the same time. With this assignment, I could demonstrate that I stood against those who called themselves Muslims but who worked to murder innocent people for illusory political gain. I'd get to show colleagues that my childhood spent in civil-war-torn countries had taught me to revere life, liberty, and democracy. I'd get to prove to CSIS that there was value to diversity and that diversity translates to saved lives.

I told Jeff that I'd be honoured to go and was immediately available – I had my passport ready. "Great, Huda," he replied. I could sense his relief as he leaned back. "We'll issue you a special passport and prepare work orders for your departure. Please remain in communication with David in London. He'll be your direct supervisor, and the staff at the Canadian High Commission will support your deployment by reserving your accommodation and covering your expenses." All this was standard operating procedure for any overseas mission. He looked at me as though he had more to say.

An awkward silence welled between us. *Is this my cue to thank him and walk away?* I resisted the urge to shift uncomfortably in my seat. Then he asked, with hesitation, "Would you like a family member or significant other to accompany you to London?" *Weird. Since when does the service cover expenses of accompanying family members? Are they offering me this because I'm a woman? Or are they trying to make up for how they hurt me? Do they think I need emotional support after all the suspicion and mistrust I've experienced?* Sigh. These were questions that a white man would never have to answer. *Stay optimistic, Huda.* I told Jeff that I'd be travelling alone. I thanked him for the offer and walked back to my office.

The Canadian Security Intelligence Service (CSIS) operates with absolute power and the iron shield of national security. For fifteen years, I worked within the orbit of that power fighting terrorists and spies. As a senior intelligence officer and a Black Muslim woman, I held a unique position as both an insider and a target of harassment at the service. The conflict between my reality working for a national security organization in a post-9/11 context and my identity as a practising Muslim meant that the high-profile status of my exit from CSIS was inevitable. In 2017, I launched a lawsuit with four of my colleagues that attracted international and Canadian media attention. At the time, one Global News headline read, "Canada's Spy Agency Faces $35-Million Lawsuit over Allegations of Islamophobia, Homophobia."[1] Prime Minister Justin Trudeau called the alleged harassment and discrimination within CSIS unacceptable,[2] and the New Democratic Party (NDP) released a statement: "Liberals Must End the 'Old Boys' Club' Culture of CSIS."[3]

Agent of Change is not a spy thriller. This memoir is my dedication and contribution to Canadian and international security and my fight for equity in the corridors of power at CSIS. Forcing the service to publicly acknowledge systemic racism was something no review body, public inquiry, or court was ever able to do. But I found a way to do it and followed through for my love of and duty to Canada. Now the ball is in their court to change and modernize. Equity, diversity, and inclusion (EDI) are necessary parts of the equation for modern intelligence work, described as "mission-critical" by Rep. Terri Sewell of Alabama, a member of the United States House Intelligence Committee.[4] British security agencies have also openly recognized the importance of EDI and have begun reckoning with their historic exclusion of racialized subjects.[5] In Canada, a multicultural country, we have not yet begun our own reckoning, and the trends of misogyny, sexism, and racism in our military, federal, provincial, and municipal police forces are pervasive and very worrisome realities.

It was in 2002, after a rigorous and lengthy security screening process, that I joined Canada's spy service as an intelligence officer. In so doing, I became a member of an exclusive and elitist organization that demanded absolute loyalty in exchange for exposure to the inner workings of Canada's security and intelligence community. I signed on knowing that I'd have to lead a secret life. My friends, neighbours, and acquaintances couldn't know what I did for a living. I understood that the service would scrutinize my activities, associations, financial records, and personal secrets and that CSIS would test my reliability and loyalty with filmed polygraphs. I accepted this transparency as necessary to belong to an organization that fought spies, terrorists, and traitors. I also understood that as a CSIS officer, I could become a target of a foreign counterintelligence agency or a terrorist group. Going public with my story was never my intention nor something I ever thought I'd have to do. From day one, I counted on CSIS to protect me and my family as I progressed at my job. I was convinced that being a spy and working towards the CSIS mission were more significant and meaningful than anything I could fathom – and they were. The post-9/11 world needed CSIS, and I felt that it needed me, too. I was young, educated, confident, unattached, and multilingual, *and I was desperate to belong* – my fatal flaw. Back then, security and intelligence organizations were shifting their focus, resources, and might to fight Islamist extremism. I had no loyalty to any country besides Canada, and I'd lived in a Muslim-majority country for many years. I was what every international and national security and federal law enforcement agency wanted and needed.

For more than fifteen years, along with other dedicated, brilliant colleagues, I safeguarded Canada and the public from internal and external threats. During the first four years of my service, I was the only intelligence officer in the Counter Terrorism branch at headquarters who spoke

Arabic. This positioned me in the front seat of CSIS operations, decision making, and the egos of the men who ran the organization. As an officer, I analyzed and advanced investigations that tracked down Canadians supposedly linked to Al Qaeda and other international terrorist groups. Later, in my counterproliferation work, I helped prevent countries like Iran from weaponizing. I worked as a liaison officer for CSIS at the Communications Security Establishment (CSE) – equivalent to the American National Security Agency – and the Integrated Terrorist Assessment Centre (which is equivalent to the Department of Homeland Security).

As an investigator at CSIS's Toronto office, I was at the heart of some of the service's most sensitive investigations. I ran and led Counter Terrorism source operations and contributed to CSIS's community outreach efforts. I coordinated with other national security and law enforcement agencies. I travelled overseas to represent the service and Canada at allied security intelligence agencies – the CIA, the FBI, MI5, and others. I'm most proud of my work at MI5, with whom I investigated and helped bring to justice the terrorists involved in the 7/7 and 21/7 London attacks.

My career as a CSIS spy was exhilarating and unique. I was passionate about my work, which was enticing, overwhelming, and addictive. This work will always be a part of who I am. Once you've trained and lived as an intelligence officer, the job becomes part of your identity. But as a racialized woman, my journey had challenges that nearly destroyed me, and sadly, my experience as the first hijab-wearing Muslim woman intelligence officer in the service came to a crashing end in December 2017. After many months of deliberations with CSIS's internal grievance mechanisms, I and four colleagues filed a civil lawsuit for harassment and discrimination against CSIS. In the subsequent court proceedings, I was identified as Bahira, a pseudonym, as CSIS directed. I served my country with pride until I could no longer do so, not through any fault of my own but because sexism, racism, and discrimination made it impossible for me to get my work done. Facing this fact was the most painful moment of my life.

Going public with my story, even under a pseudonym, was almost as soul-crushing. It ran counter to the instincts CSIS had cultivated in me. I'd taken a vow of secrecy when I joined CSIS to serve my country from the shadows with countless others who pledged the same. I had trained, worked, and lived to not be noticed. After we filed the lawsuit, anxiety plagued me: *What if the media figures out who I am? What if my name is published? Is my family safe? What about the sensitive operations I worked on? What if dangerous people come after me?*

No intelligence officer, or human being for that matter, should ever have to go through the bullying and harassment I did. At CSIS, I faced intimidation, isolation, exclusion, unfair scrutiny, a toxic work environment, and gender, racial, and religious discrimination. I was prevented from advancing my career by systemic racism and barriers meant to deny me opportunities. I often felt alone in my struggle. It took me many years to learn and acknowledge that CSIS was perpetuating systemic biases against women, Muslims, racialized minorities, Indigenous peoples, and LGBTQ2S+ people. I had tried to be the voice of reform on the inside, speaking out against bias and Bill 59, which gave more police-like power to CSIS. For many years, I watched as politics, race, and biases were rendered invisible in the operations and science of intelligence work. Publicly, discrimination was, and still is, evident in the way politicians demand answers, cough up resources, and change laws to increase surveillance powers only when the threat is from racialized groups. This discrimination is readily accepted and left unquestioned by most Canadian communities within and outside of the political sphere. Ultimately, working for the service unveiled to me the discriminatory ways in which national security providers perceive and prioritize threats.

When a Canadian Human Rights Commission employment equity audit report later revealed that visible minorities occupied 0 per cent of managerial roles and were underrepresented in professional CSIS positions, I became convinced, beyond any doubt, that my experience of systemic racism was one of many. It also underscored to me the importance of recognizing that change would have to be pushed from outside of the organization. Only by going public with colleagues whose commitments and contributions to national security equalled mine did I feel protected.

Sharing my story is a natural part of my service, an extension of my mission to stand up for Canada's values of democracy, equality, justice, and freedom – as one of the few women of colour and the first veiled Muslim woman at CSIS, it's my way of shining a necessary light on the systemic barriers that persecuted minorities face within the organization. These barriers threaten our national security efforts by preventing talented people of diverse backgrounds from serving their country. They also foster mistrust in government and in democracy. Systemic racism is not limited to CSIS but is a persistent challenge across national security in Canada.

Today, I am somewhat encouraged by the conversation we're having in Canada about the need for equity-based reforms in the intelligence community. However, while the American intelligence community is making positive equity-based changes, including open annual public hearings on diversity and inclusion, Canada has not yet begun to address the gender, race, and religious biases that prevail in our intelligence community. A 2019 report released by the National Security Intelligence Committee of Parliamentarians (NSICOP) indicates that the recruitment and retention of racialized Canadians is a challenge, and sadly, at the time of the report's publication, the numbers were continuing to decrease.[6] The NSICOP report is also critical of widespread harassment, violence, and discrimination, which it states are unacceptably high, with limited accountability for perpetrators. I believe that works, like my memoir, that seek to inform and engage the public are necessary to force positive change in the intelligence community. Stories linger in and shape our consciousness, providing context that is often missing from media reports, vetted surgical inquiries, and other findings. My journey was not one I had planned to take, but it was inevitable and humbling, exposing me to gaps in the intelligence community that I hope will start to be filled once my story and others like mine are shared.

More broadly, Canada and CSIS, as well as other national security organizations like the Royal Canadian Mounted Police (RCMP) and Canada Border Service Agency (CBSA), need to address the devastating militant and securitized post-9/11 policies and culture that have amplified Islamophobia and destroyed the lives of people in marginalized communities. Canada has had one of the highest rates of terrorist attacks against the Muslim community in the past five years in comparison to other G7 countries.[7] Examples include the 2017 Quebec City mosque attack that killed six Muslim worshippers, the 2021 London, Ontario, attack against a Muslim family on an evening walk, and Mohammed Aslim Zafis, the community volunteer who was stabbed to death outside a mosque in Rexdale, Ontario. The perpetrators of these deadly attacks all accessed far-right, white supremacist, and/or neo-Nazi material, according to media reports.[8] And while the Department of Public Safety did add several far-right organizations to its terrorist entities list, the Canadian government and national security organizations, including CSIS and the RCMP, proved to be slow in their response to protect the Canadians most vulnerable to far-right extremist violence, in part because of biases embedded in the organization and a total fixation on Islamist-inspired extremism. The first attack in 2017 should have set the alarm to shift resources to the ever-growing far-right threat – but it didn't. According to Global News, documents obtained under the Access to Information Act revealed discussions that took place in 2018 between CSIS, RCMP, Public Safety Canada, and the minister of public safety's office, which were aimed at toning down the discourse on the far-right threat.[9] This is in sharp contrast to the types of discussions I was privy to when the threat theatre was Islamist extremism. After an Islamist terrorist attack in Canada or abroad, the conversations and attitudes within national security focused on ensuring that no stone was left unturned to uncover the next threat. This justified widespread harassment and profiling within the Muslim community, for example, unannounced visits from CSIS officials in people's places of work, use of information obtained under torture, and the exchange of information with countries that have a history of dodgy human rights policies.

The double standard and lack of political will to tackle the growing threat posed by the far right was finally brought to public attention during the 2022 Freedom Convoy. Canada made international headlines for its inability to take back the streets of our capital city for weeks. Several US–Canada border crossings were closed, not only damaging our country's reputation but also bringing considerable financial loss to the Canadian economy. The comparatively lax attitude of national security organizations towards the far-right threat is a serious public safety concern that should lead to further policy changes and reforms in national security.

In this very personal memoir, I keep to my story and do not discuss any classified information as per my legal and ethical obligations under the Security of Information Act and CSIS Act. I use information that CSIS has declassified through the Access to Information Act, Security Intelligence Review Committee reports, parliamentary hearing reports, public inquiries, and court and regulatory body proceedings. To protect the identities of service employees, I use pseudonyms and change the descriptive details of those I mention, except executive managers and directors who are already in the public record. I also use pseudonyms for family and friends to protect their identities from danger should anyone want to target me for having worked within the intelligence community.

Finally, I want to make clear that I hold the CSIS mandate and my hardworking, committed colleagues in the highest esteem. They do important work, and I will never forget the overwhelming feeling of pride that came with working alongside Canada's national security professionals, regardless of how my story played out and the persistent challenges of systemic racism in my chosen field.

My CSIS work anniversary pins are to the right side of the frame, beside which (far right) is my pin from the Integrated Terrorism Assessment Centre. Second from the left is my award from the British Security Service, MI5, for my contributions to terrorist attack investigations, and to the far left, my CSIS badge, framed in clear glass. My second award from MI5 and a badge clip from the Communication Security Establishment are in the foreground.

(*left*) My family, sometime before 1977, when my youngest sister was born. We then had no plans to leave Ethiopia, as my father was a well-established businessman. Little did my parents know that my father would become a political prisoner, my mother a driver for family and friends through military-imposed checkpoints between Dire Dawa and Addis Abbas.

(*right*) Leaning forward, second from the right, with mischievous eyes, I am on a summer night cruise on the Nile River in Cairo, with my brothers and sisters.

(*opposite*) Proudly standing in front of Carleton University following my graduation ceremony in June 2000. I was the first in my family to graduate with a bachelor of arts honours degree in law; my siblings opted to study engineering and information technology, preferred career paths amongst many first-generation immigrants.

(*opposite*) Assistant director Jack Hooper arrives to testify at the Arar Inquiry in 2005. Hooper was a former RCMP Security Service officer who transferred to CSIS when the organization began. He led as deputy director of operations during 9/11 and was called upon to answer for the service's decisions with regards to the destruction of the Air India tapes, Maher Arar's rendition, interviews at Guantanamo Bay, and the illegal extradition of Mohamed Jabarah, a Canadian arrested in Oman for alleged Al Qaeda membership. Credit: REUTERS/Alamy Stock Photo

(*above*) Jim Judd was appointed CSIS director in 2004. Here, two years later, he prepares to testify before the House of Commons Committee on Public Safety and National Security on Parliament Hill. His leadership at CSIS saw an increase in diversity hires and in intelligence officers' salaries, as well as a movement away from the post-9/11, military-like culture of the service. During our last encounter, he called me into his office to thank me for representing CSIS at MI5. Credit: REUTERS/Alamy Stock Photo

(*opposite, top*) Enjoying an early autumn walk in London in 2005. I was thrilled to be on a foreign assignment, working for MI5 to keep all Londoners safe from the threat of terrorist attacks. I also got to work closely with the British Secret Intelligence Service (MI6), the legendary home of James Bond. The two awards I received for my service were icing on the cake.

(*opposite, bottom*) This 2005 Metropolitan Police sign captures the intense fear that gripped London following the 7/7 and 21/7 terrorist attacks. Fifty-two people were murdered, igniting the largest manhunt in the city's history. Members of the Muslim community, like others, were victims, though they also suffered from a 600 per cent increase in faith-based hate crime rates in the aftermath. Credit: amer ghazzal/Alamy Stock Photo

(*above*) While I was working for MI5, CSIS rented me a flat on Baker Street, close to Westminster Parliament. It was a quick stroll, both from the tube station for my morning commute and from the Sherlock Holmes Museum (pictured here). During this time, I received many suggestions to open a security consulting business, along the lines of the fictitious detective's. This exciting prospect was swept away by promise of work as an investigator in Toronto.

Elizabeth Lydia Manningham-Buller was the director general of the British Security Service when I was in London. I had an opportunity to meet her at the Canada House Christmas party where she made a short, but spectacular, appearance. I felt very inspired. Courtesy of the House of Lords, UK Parliament, CC BY 3.0, https://creativecommons.org/licenses/by/3.0/.

(*opposite*) A letter from Elizabeth Lydia Manningham-Buller, routed through my supervisor at MI5, thanking me for my "highly effective" contribution to the 7/7 investigations.

RESTRICTED & PERSONAL **THE SECURITY SERVICE**
LONDON

Eliza Manningham-Buller
DIRECTOR GENERAL

18 August 2005

Dear Huda

I write to thank you for the support you have given the Service's International Counter Terrorist effort in the weeks following 7 July. Your contribution to what has proved to be a highly effective team effort has been greatly appreciated by A2A. These are demanding times and I am grateful to you.

Yours,

Eliza

E L Manningham-Buller

Huda Mukbil

RESTRICTED & PERSONAL

(*opposite, top*) Posing next to the famous Niagara Falls in the spring of 2006, after a day roaming the streets as an investigator in CSIS's Toronto Region office.

(*opposite, bottom*) In Toronto, I met Ali Elbeddini and quickly fell in love. Our wedding was on 11 August 2007, in Gatineau. The parliament buildings can be seen in the background.

(*overleaf, top*) CSIS director Richard Fadden waits to testify before the Commons Public Safety and National Security Committee in 2010. Fadden was an appointee of Prime Minister Stephen Harper and later became his national security advisor. He was director when I returned to work in Ottawa. Credit: REUTERS/Alamy Stock Photo

(*overleaf, middle*) CSIS director Michel Coulombe waits to testify before the Commons Public Safety and National Security Committee in 2014. Also a Harper appointee, Coulombe was the first CSIS intelligence officer to head the organization. He led the service through the Islamic State in Iraq and Syria foreign fighters surge and the Parliament Hill shootings. Following my group's internal complaints, he called for the third-party investigation of the Toronto Region. Credit: REUTERS/Alamy Stock Photo

(*overleaf, bottom*) Public Safety Minister Ralph Goodale attends a news conference on 7 May 2018. Regarding our lawsuit against CSIS, he stated, "The matter is extremely serious, and the government will take the necessary steps to stop such abuses," adding that "there will be consequences when employees harass or bully colleagues." Credit: REUTERS/Alamy Stock Photo

(*top*) CSIS Director David Vigneault waits to testify before the Senate National Security and Defence Committee on 10 April 2019. Following the third-party investigation, initiated by the complaints of a group of colleagues and me, he publicly acknowledged that CSIS suffered from a climate of retribution, favouritism, bullying, and other problems. Credit: REUTERS/Alamy Stock Photo

(*bottom*) Prime Minister Justin Trudeau delivers a statement in the House of Commons on 30 January 2017 about the Quebec City mosque shooting, which he called a "terrorist attack." Responding to the civil lawsuit news release, he noted that "the alleged harassment within CSIS is being investigated and unacceptable." Credit: REUTERS/Alamy Stock Photo

Ali supported my run for the New Democratic Party in the federal election of 2021. I led a strong campaign with significant media attention, inspiring many women, youth, and people from unrepresented communities to participate in politics. Ali remains my greatest champion and loving partner.

AGENT
OF
CHANGE

1 EXILE

The smell of homemade ginger tea, Mom's speciality, infused my parents' kitchen table in their modest, orderly Ottawa home. My retired parents had just finished afternoon prayer, and I was relaxing in their warm care. I asked Mom, in Arabic, "Why did you and Baba move to Canada? Tell me about how you escaped the Civil War, in detail this time." Mom began recounting her time in Dire Dawa, Ethiopia, where I was born. My mother, Zeinab, became one of the first few women in Dire Dawa and probably all of Africa to drive a car, an ability that would later save many lives. She is an introvert, fiercely loyal, brave, and resilient: traits that served her well against the looming civil and regional war in East Africa. Mom is from the eastern city of Harar, known as the fourth holiest site in Islam, after Mecca, Medina, and Jerusalem. Harar is nicknamed *Madeenat-ul-Awliya* (the City of Saints) because Prophet Mohammed's followers found refuge there from the Quraish clan wanting to kill them. Harar was also the first place in Africa to embrace Islam, well before any Arab lands. Later on, under the protection of the Ottoman Empire, Harar became a hub for Islamic learning and commerce between Africa, India, and Yemen. I believe that this rich Islamic cultural heritage is partly why Dad, a Yemeni Ethiopian, came to love and embrace everything about Harari culture.

Almost immediately after Mom began telling the story, Dad interjected and took over. He put his hands gently on my knee and looked at me. His eyes by then were a watery blue grey from old age. In a near whisper, he spoke until he could say no more. The house fell silent. I wondered whether he was trying to remember or whether he was processing it all over again. I felt selfish for asking him to reopen his wounds so I could cope with mine.

Dad hardly ever refused my adult requests – I am beloved to him, my mother always says. I'm a lot like my mother, but I occupy my dad's heart, and his history haunts mine. To protect the feelings of my siblings, he's never dared show favouritism. He always tried to love and treat us all as equals – the three girls and two older boys.

My Ethiopian family includes Yemenite Arabs, Hararis, Oromos, and Somalis. Most of my family, including my parents, speak all five languages: Amharic, Arabic, Oromo, Harari, and Somali. I have family members who are Christian and Muslim, and Black and Arab. Because of my family's heritage, I recognize and respect ethnic and religious pluralism.

My dad, Abdulsalam, is a Yemeni national born and raised in Dire Dawa, Ethiopia, where his grandfather Mukbil migrated. Dad began working at seven. He sold razor blades on the Dire Dawa streets and sometimes in nearby cities. By his teens, he had saved enough money to buy kitchen products, kitchen accessories, stationery goods, and other household products. He secured a store at Kafira Market in the traditionally Muslim quarter of the city. Kafira Market is known for its Moorish arches and for the organized chaos of its narrow lanes. It attracted people from miles around: Afar and Somali herders, Oromo farmers, and Amhara merchants. Dad was following in the footsteps of his role model merchant mother who, early on, had taught him how to make and keep money. Slowly but surely, he accumulated a tremendous wealth for that time and place. He began importing and exporting household products to and from China and India via the Port of Djibouti. By the 1970s, Dad was a successful entrepreneur. He'd built a home with a large front yard and an adjacent suite for his mother. His wealth allowed his entire extended family, including his brothers and their families, to live comfortably.

At twenty, Dad had limited facial hair, a gap between his two front teeth, and a soft reasoning voice. He spoke little and smiled much. He was humble, confident, diplomatic, and respected by business associates and family alike. Having accomplished much, he wanted to start a family. Soon, a beautiful, tall, slim, and modest young woman returning from school caught his eye. That woman was Zeinab, my mother. She was only sixteen and from an observant Muslim family. Dad says that he fell in love with Mom's breathtaking beauty and calm demeanour. Mom recounts Dad asking her father for her hand in marriage. Her father, Ali, knew Dad and agreed to the wedding, not because Dad was a successful businessman but because he was a God-fearing Muslim who prayed at the local mosque and gave to the less fortunate – it's character that counts, Zeinab was taught. My parents, who were and are traditional, never spent time alone before their wedding. On their wedding day, Mom, shy as she was, couldn't distinguish between Dad and his best man wearing the fancy suit.

My parents lived in a large home with housekeepers, seventies-style imported furniture, and a private driver. Dad was an enabling feminist for his time and place and insisted Mom learn how to drive. She was reluctant at first – a famous saying then was "cars are machines that kill their makers" – but Dad had a way of empowering everyone around him. He didn't see women as unable. After all, he was raised by a strong woman, Mariam.

Mom and Dad eventually had five children: my brothers, Zyad and Salim; my sisters, Farah and Eman; and me. Neither Mom nor Dad completed their schooling, but they planned to give us, their children, the best education in America that money could buy. They hoped to work in Ethiopia while the kids, after high school, one by one, travelled to America for university and then returned home to live among their extended family. They, especially Mom, provided a nurturing, loving, and peaceful home – her life's purpose had become her children. My parents didn't argue much. Mom would only have to say "the kids" and Dad would save any discussion for later.

My family's struggle with political violence began the fall of 1974, during the height of the Ethiopian Civil War. The 225th and last emperor, Haile Selassie, was overthrown by a military coup d'état. A drought that lasted from 1972 to 1974 had swept the entire country into famine, and people were discontent. The government's response contributed to the deaths of more than 200,000 people. The Provincial Military Administration Council, known as the Dreg, assumed full power in September 1974. Unrest followed. In 1977, the Dreg, led by Mengistu Haile Mariam, declared Ethiopia a socialist state, strengthened relations with the Soviet Union, and carried out measures to nationalize all rural and urban lands. An "unprecedented era of indiscriminate detentions, assassinations, extrajudicial killings, and summary executions of all categories of

Ethiopians" followed.[1] Under Mengistu, the Dreg used terror as a state tool and killed hundreds of thousands of people. Only families who paid the required bullet fees for those gunned down were permitted to retrieve their loved ones' bodies from the streets to bury them without ceremony.[2]

My family's circumstances turned ugly fast in 1975, when Dreg soldiers barged into and looted Dad's shop. The Dreg were harassing and intimidating businesspeople and minorities they thought to be associated with armed opposition groups. During this unrest, many wealthy Ethiopians left for nearby countries, Europe, and North America. Some, who thought Dreg soldiers would arrest them at airports or who couldn't afford to fly, risked their lives by crossing the desert on foot to get to Djibouti – they feared the Dreg more than the hot, unforgiving desert sun. Dad didn't know that by staying he was risking his freedom, humanity, life, and family.

The conflict intensified in 1977, a year after I was born. A second war broke out, this time between Ethiopia and Somalia; the Somali government had taken advantage of the internal Ethiopian conflict and was funnelling support to Somali rebel groups in the Ogaden region in eastern Ethiopia. Somali troops descended on Dire Dawa, and from then on, armed military personnel, armoured cars, and nightly violence by Somali forces became common in the streets.

In 1978, the military dragged Dad and his staff, including his younger brother Mustafa, in for questioning. They claimed that Dad was financially supporting Oromo and Somali insurgency groups. He was arbitrarily arrested twice. The local police, who were more ethnically diverse than the Dreg and loyal to local businessmen, informed Dad that he was on a Dreg list to be arrested once more. Dad had already witnessed prisoner torture and executions and knew there was no guarantee that he'd survive a third arrest. He drove home in a panic, parked his car, spoke with Mom, looked at his children one last time, changed clothes, and went straight to the police station. Minutes later, Dreg officers showed up, felt the car's heat, and questioned my mother, while we, the kids, stood in the front yard. She told them he was at the police station, but they barged in anyway, destroying our property and lives for years to come.

When the Dreg arrived at the police station, the police refused to hand Dad over, pledging that he was apolitical and a respectable member of the community. Weeks later, the Dreg returned and unlawfully arrested him and his employees, including his brother Ziad. This last arrest, without charge, proved different. He wasn't released, and he was told, under threat of torture, to sign a confession avowing that he'd assisted and funded Oromo and Somali separatist groups. His business partners, including Ziad, had already signed confessions saying so – false confessions made under torture. Dad bravely stood his ground, denying the false claim.

Every day for more than three months, Dad was beaten, thrown around, hung by his wrists from the ceiling, and tortured with electric shock. He has since borne half-inch handcuff scars around each wrist, evidence of the physical pain that he endured. As a child, I'd look at his wrists and be reminded of the terrible things done to him in Ethiopia under communist rule. I'd then kiss his hands in respect. My children now do the same – they ask about Grandpa's marks, and we quickly change the topic to protect their innocence. If anyone speaks to Dad about communism, he frowns. Dad is a fierce defender of democracy and capitalism. The mere mention of communism and dictatorship will provoke feelings of misery and horror for him. I inherited those same feelings.

Had Dad confessed, his torture probably would've stopped, his confession would've been taken as evidence, and he would've been executed like many other men. Dad understood this, since he'd seen it happen to other political prisoners. In prison, through his business contacts, Dad managed to arrange a meeting with a top Dreg security official at his cell. Reminding the man of his Yemeni origin, Dad argued that he had no political stake in the conflict and that he only cared about his business interests, peace, and security. He described the insurgents as impressionable lost youth and a threat to stability. He proved that he'd made substantial donations and tax payments to the city and showed future tax payments on goods held in Djibouti for import. The officials verified what he said and later released him without charge. The experience left him bitter, and he decided to leave Ethiopia as soon as possible.

Those were terrifying times for Mom. In her seven years with Dad, she'd grown accustomed to a comfortable life as a homemaker. But during the time of his arrests and imprisonment, the violent civil war, and the city's Somali invasion, Mom changed from a shy, sheltered young woman to a dependable business partner. With Dad and his partners in jail, she'd become the decision maker for Dad's properties and businesses, and she lobbied politicians and security officials for Dad's release. When Mom saw Dad's torture marks during visits, she said nothing – she didn't want to jeopardize his chances of release. With me in arm, she visited him every day and brought meals, though Dad had to ask her not to bring meat since the soldiers would take anything that was worth eating. Good food was a double-edged sword – it could keep him alive, but it might prevent his release.

During his incarceration and with the Dire Dawa streets a battleground, Mom used her driving skills to drive me, my siblings, and other family members, mostly women and children, out of Dire Dawa to Addis Ababa, where it was less violent. Military checkpoints for finding and executing opposition were common on the dangerous hills and the dusty road to the capital. The Dreg once stopped us, forcing us to exit our vehicle while they searched it. They demanded identification and checked the adults at gunpoint for weapons, also demanding their political leanings.

I was too young to understand what was happening, but my mother recounts her terror. She knew that many families had vanished on that road, their bodies left for hyenas. Mom says that it was by the grace of God that they let us proceed, though she dreaded her return to Dire Dawa with me. Even though these missions were incredibly dangerous, Mom says she had to bring me with her because I wailed and wouldn't let her leave without me. My younger sister couldn't speak yet and the older three could be reasoned with, so they remained at home. Mom needed to drive back to secure my father's release and to safeguard our home and their business. She also had a secret mission to transfer funds abroad to a British bank in Djibouti.

Released from prison, my father was a changed man. He avoided speaking about those days. When forced to, he became emotional and tearful. He used his experience to teach his children important lessons, especially when we wanted to give up on school or when we acted like the privileged children that we were. His lectures, always private and in my parent's bedroom, would start, "My child, I sacrificed everything to bring you to Canada and to give you a bright future." Then he'd be silent, and we'd know why. What he'd endured was horrific. He reminded us we were God-fearing Muslims with values and must always speak and act with honour and self-respect. He encouraged us to be truthful. "A Muslim can be sinful but not a liar," he'd say. Fear was reserved for

Allah, not humanity. He gave us strong morals, educational expectations, and career goals. He qualified our successes as his and assured us that our failures were our own. He reminded us of the opportunities that he provided and of the Almighty's miracles – we had no excuse for failure. During his lectures, Mom would wait in the living room until we came back while Dad stayed behind. She'd shower us with compassion and love to compensate for Dad's seriousness and what we called "unnecessary torture talks," which were hard to endure.

The 1974 Ethiopian Civil War and the 1977 Somali invasion of eastern Ethiopia challenged my family. We almost lost Dad. Had he falsely confessed, he'd have been executed and his property and businesses would have been seized. Mom would've become a widow, and we kids would've grown up on the streets of Dire Dawa, hopeless and uneducated. Dad's refusal to confess was exceptional. He used his connections and communication skills to escape death.

We fled, leaving behind family and loved ones, diverse and vibrant communities, and businesses and livelihoods. We became refugees and immigrants. The torture and dehumanization Dad experienced in prison and the possibility of recurrence left my parents disillusioned and determined to leave Ethiopia for good. They continued transferring funds abroad so we could relocate to Yemen. Under the pretext of business, Dad took off by air on his own, leaving his wife and kids behind for the fear of being arrested in the airport in front of us. Then it was Mom's turn. She left two weeks after Dad, also alone. She was worried that they wouldn't let her, an Ethiopian citizen and one of their own, out of the country. My parents figured that once she was securely out, the government wouldn't keep us, their children, all Yemeni nationals, in the country. A week later, we five kids and my uncle Mahdi boarded a plane to Djibouti and reunited with my parents, all of us survivors of the Ethiopian Civil War. All I remember of that day is that we went to the beach, where the sand was white and the Red Sea blue. My siblings and I didn't understand why we'd left everything and everyone behind, but we were grateful to be together once more as a family.

Upon learning of our escape, the Dreg seized our home and Dad's businesses. The house was returned to us in the 1990s when we were living in Canada, but Dad gave it to his family. He didn't want to revisit that chapter of his life, even after Mengistu was found guilty of genocide in Ethiopia. Uncle Mahdi escaped and made his way to Sanaa, Yemen, where he lives with his family. Uncle Ziad and my dad's business partners were all released, and many left Ethiopia for good. In exile, Dad planned to relocate to Yemen but had a change of heart while in Djibouti. He wanted his children to receive the best education possible. He'd taught himself to read and write, but he envied those he relied on and trusted to do his business writing – that wasn't going to happen to his children. He'd use his money to educate us. Yemen wasn't the place for that, and he didn't think highly of the Saudi Arabian education system. But Egypt's education system had an excellent reputation. Even the royalty of Saudi Arabia, Iraq, and other Arab countries sent their children to school in Cairo. My dad, a visionary, determined that we were going to Egypt. Within a week, he'd booked a flight, and we made our way to Cairo, the heart and soul of the Arab and Muslim world. The city of a thousand minarets.

2 | A THOUSAND MINARETS

In the busy shopping district of Ahmed Urabi, in Giza, Egypt, a crowd watched Mom try to parallel park her light blue French Peugeot. She was afraid of damaging her shiny new car. After a few attempts, young men guided her by gesturing with their hands – a little left, a little right, back more, slowly, a little farther – and then zoom, she was in. The crowd cheered.

In late 1979, when we moved to Cairo, few women were driving there. Cairo was a bustling, male-dominated city. To the delight of spectators, Mom drove us kids to school and back every day except Fridays, which is the official religious holiday in Egypt and all Muslim majority countries. The car's back window was like a television set for me. The horrendous traffic, drivers cutting each other off, and honking and yelling made it feel like there was always an accident waiting to happen. If a large bus or truck passed too close, Mom would pray for our lives by screaming "BismAllah" – in the name of God. The densely packed streets were noisy and smelled of seasonal produce: mangoes, guavas, and watermelons in the summer, oranges and tangerines in the winter. There were no road signs or streetlights, but somehow things always worked out.

The Cairo streets belonged to men, but many women, old and young, pushed through. Cab drivers played loud Arabic music from car stereos and mosque minarets called the faithful to prayer five times a day, every day. More Egyptians were openly practising Islam then since the religion had been undergoing a quiet revival for years. Under President Anwar Sadat, Islam had become central to political, economic, and social life as the country moved away from Arab nationalism.

Muslim scholars like Mohammed Metwali Al Sharawi had become household names via their television appearances. Egyptian men and women were often attending Islamic study circles and religious gatherings called *nadwa* in Arabic. I saw men with beards and some women rush with prayer beads to pray at mosques. If an accident or fight broke out on the street, the crowds would disperse promptly, as if nothing had occurred: "Salee ala al Nabi" (Praise the Prophet), I'd hear men say while breaking up the disputing parties. Those arguing or fighting and those in the crowd would then praise the Prophet: "Salim Alu Alayee Wa Salam" (God's mercy and peace upon him).

Living in Cairo and gaining the Egyptian dialect would later serve me well as an intelligence officer. Cairo is the most populous city in the Arab world and the heart of the Muslim world. It's also the most cultural, especially in terms of art, cinema, theatre, poetry, Islamic knowledge, literature, and education. An Arabic saying goes, "Books are written in Cairo, published in Beirut, and read in Baghdad." Egyptian is the most widely spoken Arabic dialect, and artists from across the Arab world move to Cairo in hopes of making it big. Cairo's Al-Azhar University is the centre of learning in the Muslim world and the most influential Sunni Islamic learning establishment. Its diverse students come from around the globe to study and propagate at home the university's interpretation of Islamic holy scripture, or the *Quran,* and the *hadith*, the codified tradition. The Al-Azhar interpretation is seen as moderate, reformist, and balanced compared to interpretations in Saudi Arabia or other Muslim countries.

In 1978, my family and I arrived in Egypt from Djibouti on a six-month tourist visa, but we never became citizens. We couldn't. In the Arab world, at the time, citizenship transfers from fathers. Dad, my siblings, and I were all on one Yemeni passport, while Mom held an Ethiopian passport. We were Yemenis and Ethiopians temporarily residing on visas and each time we renewed our visas, we risked rejection. The process went like this: my parents would register us kids, pay the full tuition at our elementary school, and obtain a letter of approval from the school, valid for one year, with recommendations for student visas. Dad would then take these documents to the Egyptian foreign ministry to obtain both student visas for us kids and caregiver visas for him and Mom. Once the ministry approved the permits, Mom would present the permits first to the Ethiopian embassy and then to the Egyptian foreign ministry, while Dad presented our passport to the Yemeni embassy. This annual process took months in the slow Egyptian bureaucracy. My parents never applied for work permits because, officially, they were in Egypt for their children's education – they more or less trusted that we would all be able to stay as long as they were able to pay for our expensive private school, but they often wondered what would happen if the foreign ministry rejected our school's recommendations. Where would we go?

When we first arrived in Egypt, my family rented a spacious furnished apartment on Iran Street in the Doqi district of greater Cairo. During his first meeting with the landlord, Dad spoke with a Yemeni Arab accent, and she could hardly understand what he was saying. When Dad showed up with our payment a few days later, he used more Egyptian words. The landlord was surprised that Dad had learned Arabic "so quickly," since, unlike other Arabs, Egyptians have a low tolerance for non-Egyptian Arabic dialects.

Our neighbourhood was quiet. Rows of apartment buildings faced each other, and there were supermarkets right below. From our tenth-floor balcony, we watched children in the street play soccer between parked cars. Schools and large shopping districts were close. Most afternoons, Dad, a chain smoker then, would send me to buy cigarettes across the street. The shopkeeper, always curious about "the new foreigners," would ask me all sorts of questions. I'd smile, show him Dad's finished cigarette pack, pay for a new one, and walk away. Our curious neighbours visited us. They were welcoming – some women even promised to teach Mom how to make *mulukhia*, a popular Egyptian soup. My mother wasn't fluent in the Egyptian dialect and didn't know Egyptian culture. She was in a new environment for the first time, away from her family network and all that was familiar to her, and still recovering from our ordeal in Ethiopia. It was all too much and too soon for her, which is why she never let us out of her sight, allowing us to play in the street only if she could see us from above. Mom says we complained about the noise of honking cars and people yelling, but I only remember being utterly curious about everything.

Dad chose Egypt over Yemen partly because he was fascinated with Egypt's president, Anwar Sadat. Dad admired him for being a man of war and peace, as Sadat was known after his peace treaty with Israel. Dad saw himself in Sadat – a balding man with a pious Muslim rural background who endured imprisonment and political obstacles and opposed communism. Dad lit up at each of Sadat's presidential speeches and spoke of the president with great respect. Though I didn't understand Dad's feelings then, I now know my father admired Sadat's hate for the Soviet Union and his open-door domestic policies for privatization and capitalism.

On 6 October 1981, an Egyptian national holiday and a couple years after we moved to Egypt, Sadat was assassinated. My little sister Eman, who was watching a military parade on TV, shouted that Sadat had been shot. We rushed to the television to hear news about the assassination. Sadat and other ministers, all dressed in their uniforms, had been watching the parade from their reviewing stand. The parade was a display of Egyptian state and military power and included jets and armoured vehicles. Dissident soldiers from a passing truck had opened fire on the reviewing stand. Grenades and Kalashnikov fire raked the benches, killing two of Sadat's aides, mortally wounding Sadat, and injuring many others. The sixty-three-year-old president was rushed by helicopter to hospital but died on the operating table.

Like most Egyptians, we were saddened and shocked. For weeks, our parents were the only ones to leave our apartment, and that was just to buy groceries. We remained at home – no school and no playing on the street. Many Egyptians didn't have telephones because they couldn't afford them, but we had one. In the next weeks, our neighbours came over to call families and loved ones to assure them that they were safe. Schools, shops, and businesses were closed for weeks. Egyptians of all walks of life, eager to learn who would come to power, were glued to their televisions and radios. We soon learned that Vice President Hosni Mubarak would be sworn in as the new president. Mubarak's transition to power was smooth, given that Egypt was a police state. Still, Mubarak immediately instituted emergency laws, suspended constitutional rights, legalized censorship, and abolished habeas corpus. These emergency laws lasted three decades under his rule. Their removal would be one of the critical demands of the January 2011 Arab Spring uprising.

We eventually returned to school. My parents had placed us in Oroman for Foreign Languages, a prestigious private English-language school with a British curriculum. Oroman's morning assembly included light stretching exercises and standing at attention for the Egyptian national anthem. My Egyptian schoolmates and I didn't question loyalty, citizenship, or identity. The school principal, whose brother was our family's private tutor, was always welcoming of students. Though Oroman was a private school for students of paying parents, the school maintained a semblance of equality within its walls. Teachers and staff treated all students, mostly, the same. On the first day, all students were new to each other, so the bonds between my friends and me formed naturally. School was normalizing. Still, I knew that I wasn't Egyptian. I was different – a foreigner, Black, and with a different language, culture, and home life. Almost all the other kids were olive skinned. I cared a lot about fitting in and being liked, even if I didn't know how to. I only learned how to fit in once I discovered Egyptian television.

Like other Egyptian households, my family always gathered to watch Egyptian shows at eight o'clock. As we watched, I'd read the actors' and actresses' names aloud, impressing my parents with my ability to read in classical Arabic – the Arabic dialect is different than written Arabic, and I was a kid just learning how to read. As I watched intently, I'd transform into the character of each show's leading actress. The flight attendant, the young girl in love with her neighbour, the serious university student, the poor country girl forced into marriage, the rich and spoiled, the belly dancer, they were all me. I'd speak like my character and act and feel as she did. Egyptian cinema and music were my windows into the lives of others.

From these, I learned about Egyptian history, politics, and culture, including the patriotic struggles for Arab independence against the Ottoman Empire and the British and French colonizers. I also learned about Egypt's leadership role in the Arab nationalism movement, which shaped the Middle East and North Africa's political landscape. My favourites to watch were the romantic black-and-white movies starring Fateen Hamam and Omar Al Sherrif. In them, something tragic always happened to Fateen's character, but Omar's character would save the day. Omar was best known for his role in Western movies like *Lawrence of Arabia* (1962). He had olive skin, big brown eyes, dark hair, a soothing whisper of a voice, and a smile that showed how desperate he was to be accepted. Omar had converted from Christianity to Islam to marry Fateen, his co-star, and the love of his life. His kind face and beautiful smile contrasted with his muscular body. This gave him presence and made him a symbol of romance in Egypt and beyond. In his movies, he was always silent before speaking, and in this way, he melted the hearts of his viewers with long moments of intrigue. It's no wonder that I'd fall in love with and marry an Egyptian Canadian years later in Toronto.

In late 1979, less than a year after we settled in Cairo, Dad decided to go to Jeddah, Saudi Arabia, where well-paying jobs were plentiful. He knew he'd have difficulty obtaining a work permit in Egypt and that even if he was granted one, well-paying jobs weren't open to foreigners. So off he went across the Red Sea to Jeddah, returning every two months or so by plane or boat, with new household products and gifts and clothes for each of us.

Mom took on all parenting duties, but while she was running errands, my three older siblings ruled the house. To be noticed amid so many siblings, I had to speak up. I learned to be assertive, dramatic, and loud. I looked up to my older brothers, who always fought or played soccer and Atari video games. They seemed to know everything about cars, life, television, and politics. Farah, my older sister and life-long role model, was a straight-A student who always beat the boys in her class and my brothers. Strong, stubborn, and independent, she knew who she was, what she wanted, and how to get it. She and her friends hung out in sports clubs and wore makeup and fancy jewellery. I played with young Eman, mostly, and Samar and Kulud, a couple of girls in my neighbourhood. I was bossy, imaginative, and energetic. Eman was the most charming of us kids and would sleep with Mom when Dad was away. She danced and sang and was a great entertainer. Sandwiched between my sisters, I developed negotiation skills, diplomacy, deceptiveness, and selective hearing. As the fourth child, there were no victories for me, only compromises. I calculated, lobbied, and mediated situations to get what I wanted. Mom says I excelled at this. She liked how I'd skilfully bring everyone together.

Dad worked odd jobs in Jeddah, including a sales job at the Nissan car company. In 1983, we stopped renting in Cairo and bought a place in Giza – a large, new apartment closer to the Lebanon roundabout. We furnished it with the latest appliances. To our excitement, the building had a working elevator. When bored, we'd take it all the way up and down again. We never meant to annoy our neighbours or Uncle Ramadan, the building's security guard. Uncle Ramadan was from rural Egypt and had an accent that I'd only heard before on television. He always dressed in a *jalabia*, a traditional Arab garment for men. He secured the building, helped maintain it, and washed cars upon request. He kept many secrets for us kids, like when my brother Ziad, who didn't have a licence, stole the family car and drove it around the block. I joined him a few times, always telling Mom that I was getting her the newspaper.

Whenever my father was away, I'd eagerly await his bimonthly return, except when he'd bring business partners or relatives from Saudi. Those visits were all about the guests. Mom would organize their meals while Dad planned entertaining outings. Sometimes, he took us with them, and we'd tour Cairo, stopping at the pyramids, museums, and shopping districts. When Dad returned home, I'd sit close to him, hug him, and feel as secure as ever. He'd bring us presents and want us to recount, in detail, everything that he'd missed – we must be good at school, he'd emphasize. I'd babble about how mischievous the boys had been or how Farah always did what she wanted. Eman would watch curiously, envious of my gift to control the conversation and tell stories with passion. I'd tell Dad that Salim had been naughty in school. I'd report how Farah was kinder to Eman than to me, that she ignored me and never wanted to take me out with her, that Mom loved Eman more than she loved me, and that my friends wanted me to visit them. I liked Dad's trips back home because I craved his attention. He'd listen, smile, and promise to speak to the "offenders." I never followed up, but I always felt that he understood my little life struggles. Dad acknowledged my concerns. By doing that, he made me feel accepted.

Mom didn't say anything, but I could tell she also felt relieved and secure when Dad was home. They never got intimate around us – there was no kissing or holding hands around the kids – but Mom took special care with her appearance when Dad was there and cooked the most delicious meals. Every time Dad came home, it felt like a celebration.

Mostly, I learned to live in my own bubble, and everyone left me to that. I was comfortable and happy being alone. I usually feel alone, even with others. I was often the odd one out among my sisters, since I wanted to embrace Egyptian culture more than they did. When I was nine, I revealed to Mom that I often purchased *aish*, a traditional Egyptian pita bread, from a nearby bakery. My family and I lived in a privileged area.

Our building was on the same street as the Western clothing store Club Monaco. My siblings and I would dress in Western clothing, at least by Egyptian standards. We certainly never dressed in *jalabias*, long dresses local women wore. When I bought aish, I always wore a hijab. I'd wear my pink prayer hijab outdoors without telling Mom – it let me blend in and feel like a local, far different from how I felt in my privileged home and at school. My early experience wearing a hijab was positive, and I always looked forward to it.

I had a couple good friends at school with whom I'd spend entire days exchanging gossip notes. In grades 3 and 4, my teacher Adel taught me Arabic and Islamic studies. Adel was funny, always poking fun at himself and others. He trained the class to greet him by standing up to sing silly songs that praised his "good looks." He was a kid at heart and always had a comedic smirk, but he also had a long wooden stick for corporal punishment. He called it Aziza Al Labiba (Aziza That Stings). He hardly used Aziza Al Labiba, and never on girls. He knew that if he used it on girls, parents would complain and maybe have him removed as a teacher. He once punished me for passing notes by having me sit between two boys. I was mortified but, of course, that didn't stop me from continuing my note-passing operation. My mother complained about having to purchase notebooks so often.

Our student body population was roughly parallel to Egypt's: 90 per cent Muslim and 10 per cent Christian. I often played with Nermin, who was Christian, during recess. In our Islamic studies classes, Nermin and two other Christian students would leave the classroom to attend a separate class that catered to their beliefs. Nermin didn't like leaving. She said that she would eventually stop being different and convert to Islam. I felt terrible that she seemed so sad, but I was too young to really appreciate her feelings about being a minority in her own country. As a minority in Canada, I think I have a better understanding now.

I was at school on 29 February 1987 when violent protests broke out. Students were told to go home quickly. I felt others' panic, but I didn't understand it. Our neighbour with whom we carpooled asked us to get in the car with him. We didn't know where Mom was nor whether she was on her way. From the car, I watched Cairo's usual traffic jam turn into full-blown madness. Buses and trucks were driving on the grass and pavement, shops had closed, and people were running wildly on the road. At home, Uncle Ramadan told us that Mom had just left to pick us up. Worried, we prayed for her safety. Eman was in tears, and Ziad, the man of the house when Dad was away, didn't know what to do, so he just paced.

The violent protests were instigated by 25,000 Egyptian conscripts of the Central Security Forces, an Egyptian military force, reacting to news that Egypt was going to extend its three-year compulsory military service by an additional year without benefits or rank promotions for conscripts. Military service was mandatory for Egyptian men aged nineteen to thirty-four. The angry conscripts targeted tourist areas and destroyed two hotels. Mubarak deployed the military to restore order, using army tanks, armoured personnel carriers, and commando snipers to hunt down rebelling conscripts armed with shields, batons, and assault rifles. The riots lasted three days, and 107 people, mostly conscripts, were killed.

Those events shattered my family's security and peace. We lived in panic, which I was old enough to understand this time. Dad was in Saudi and Mom was fearful. For two weeks, she said she'd never send us to school again. We were, once more, confined to home, Mom using what was in the house for meals. I was upset and shocked to learn that the military had gunned down people in the street. I worried about walking on the street alone, and I missed my friends terribly.

Life returned to normal a few weeks later, and we went back to school. But my parents worried about riots, police and state culture, and emergency laws; that our student visas wouldn't be granted; and that our education wouldn't translate into good jobs in Egypt or Saudi Arabia, where we were at the mercy of bureaucracy. For years, my parents had spoken of and planned on settling in the United States, where they had family. Egypt was never meant to be more than a temporary escape for us, a strategy for our exile from Ethiopia.

Dad began speaking to families in Jeddah and Cairo about how to relocate to the West. Many counselled him to move to the US. Some suggested England or Canada. In 1985, Dad, after completing necessary visa requirements, travelled to England, America, and Canada. Relocating to the West was a huge decision, and he wanted to speak to families who'd already done it. In each of the three countries, Dad met with lawyers and immigration consultants to discuss his wish to relocate and obtain citizenship. He also managed to do some touristy things too, including visit Hollywood, much to the fascination of my American-movie-addict brothers. Finally, he decided to apply to the Canadian Quebec Investor Program, which required foreign applicants to invest in a Quebec-based business during their first three years in Canada.

In 1987, Dad was in Egypt more than before. He was often at the Canadian embassy fulfilling visa requirements and providing educational certificates or proof of medical examinations and vaccinations. Finally, he announced that we'd be going to Canada in a few months. We were all excited, especially my brothers. They loved what they knew about the West through shows like *Dallas*, *Miami Vice*, and *Knight Rider*. Looking back, we didn't differentiate much between the US and Canada. We understood little about where we were going. I was afraid of the unknown. I liked my school, friends, teachers, and neighbourhood. I felt at home. When everyone at school found out about our move, they were happy for us, which helped me to see the positives. Some of my friends told me that their fathers wanted Dad's phone number so they could enquire about immigrating to Canada themselves.

Abla Abeer, my home economics teacher, was the only one who didn't think I was lucky. She sat me down and told me my family was making a mistake. "What about?" I asked.

She said, "You're Muslims. You belong here in Egypt, a Muslim country. You should stay here." I was puzzled – I'd thought that I wasn't Egyptian. She said she'd read many books about North America and that racism was a real problem there, especially against Blacks. I told her that it was my parents' decision. I liked Abla Abeer's gesture. It made me feel like I belonged in Egypt. But when I told Mom, she said: "Egypt isn't our country. Being Arab or Muslim isn't enough."

In my bedroom, I played Dalida, the Cairo-born French Italian singer and actress, especially her song "Helwa Ya Baladi" (Oh, My Beautiful Country). I cried at the thought of leaving. Everything made me emotional. I'd go to the nearby convenience store to buy music tapes. I bought almost every single one they had, hoping they'd ease my transition. To date, nothing cheers me up like a classic Arabic tune. Though I'd been young when we left Ethiopia, I was old enough to know that I'd miss Egypt. Still, I trusted my family and hoped Canada would prove a great new home for us.

3 | REMEMBRANCE DAY

We landed on Canadian soil in Montreal on 11 November 1987 – Remembrance Day. We thought that we'd prepared for the cold but quickly learned that Canada was far colder than we could've imagined! We checked into a motel in Ville LaSalle and called one of Dad's friends, Uncle Sado, a Montrealer from Ethiopia. We shivered for a week until Uncle Sado took us winter clothes shopping. He spoke Oromo, not Arabic. In our family, only my parents spoke Oromo. Uncle Sado translated to the store clerk in a mix of French and English that we wanted the warmest jackets and boots. After an hour of sign language and many translations between Arabic, Oromo, English, and French, I finally got what I wanted: huge, light pink winter boots, fuchsia snow pants, and a matching fuchsia and blue jacket. I wore this outfit every time I went out. It was only mid-November, and young men would laugh and shout, "It's not even winter yet!" To my surprise, it would get even colder in Montreal.

Eman and I attended the French elementary school Terre-Des-Jeune in Ville LaSalle. Our older siblings went to a nearby high school. For the first year, like all immigrants to Quebec, we were in a *class d'accueil*, an introductory, all-day French language and culture class. The other students were from Finland, Jamaica, Poland, and Chile. There were no other Arabic-speaking children in the school that I knew about.

Our teacher Madame Collette, a short, stocky woman with a kind face, was our guide to Canadian culture and norms, which were vastly different from those in Ethiopia and Egypt. We learned how to fit into Canada and discovered that people in Canada changed their clothes every day. People in Egypt could only afford several outfits a year. We also learned that Canadians are much more formal in their interactions. For example, Canadians don't speak with strangers much, and they shake hands and hug, rather than kiss and hold hands like they do in the Middle East. Madame Collette taught us French words through visuals and by bringing items from her home. She'd organize field trips to supermarkets, museums, the library, ski hills in winter, and sugar bush farms in spring. She even arranged for us to go to a gym with other Canadians and for us new immigrants to have a dance party.

Madame Collette's swimming trips were my favourite. To this day, swimming is still the only sport that doesn't feel like exercise to me. In Egypt, I loved taking swimming classes at the prestigious sports club we went to. But in Montreal, I was eleven years old, a preteen who was becoming a young woman while adapting to a new culture. I was emotionally and socially in flux and unsure how to interpret my new environment and my new body, which was then changing into a woman's. With my rise in estrogen levels came a gush of emotions – sad, upset, happy, and peaceful, one moment to the next. I cared about what others thought of me and of my appearance. The idea of being in a swimsuit in front of family, schoolmates, and teachers petrified me. I tried to tell Madame Collette that I didn't own a suit, so she brought one in just my size. Intuiting my discomfort, though, she also told me it was my choice to swim and that I could sit and watch instead. Though I was reluctant, the moment that I smelled the chlorine and saw the sun on the water, I jumped right in.

Madame Collette was kind, insightful, and great fun. I'd often sit next to her to listen to her speak, though I didn't fully understand what she was saying. I sensed that she liked me too, but we didn't always get along. In class, I'd stand abruptly every time I addressed her. She didn't have Aziza, teacher Adel's punishment stick in Egypt, but I was well trained. Each day, she'd tell me that I didn't need to stand up, but I kept at it, until one day, in front of the whole class, she pushed me down by my shoulders, forcing me to sit. Convinced I'd done nothing wrong and feeling attacked, I looked down in shame. At home, I complained to my parents: "Why did you bring us to Canada? I don't like it here. I want to go back to Egypt!" To escape, I played my Arabic tapes in my room, but they reminded me of the friends I'd left behind and put me in tears.

I don't think I clearly understood that I wasn't Egyptian. It wasn't Canadian culture I had a hard time with. I loved it. But I hated being new. Not speaking French, having to guess what was expected of me, not understanding the culture, and having only one friend in class my age meant that I felt like an outsider, like I'd gone to a party and didn't know anyone though everyone else had known each other for years. I had difficulty learning thirty new French words every day and having my pronunciation corrected. Puberty exacerbated my anxiety about fitting in. My parents ignored my complaints, which, in retrospect, was helpful, because I only needed to express the awkwardness I felt out loud – it didn't matter who heard it. Later, my parents insisted that we hold weekly family meetings to talk about how we were doing. Those talks helped. I discovered that my siblings were also adjusting, and their stories put my struggles into perspective. But my older brothers and sister were in a regular school, and their need to belong wasn't as crucial. They spoke of holidays that I didn't understand, like Valentine's Day or Halloween, and about how kids at school wore ripped jeans. I wondered when I'd be sent to a regular class, not just a class for immigrants. I wanted to be with students my age. I desperately wanted to feel normal.

My parents never told us how uneasy they felt. They were having difficulty picking up French and were under enormous pressure to purchase and operate a business in Montreal, a core condition of the immigrant Investor Program that secured our family's visas. Given their lack of experience, French, and North American business sense, my parents sought out a local partner who could help my father start a business. My father eventually found a Pakistani Muslim man in Montreal that he thought he could relate to. Together, they bought a convenience store and a catering business. My parents also bought the apartment on top of the convenience store, and every morning, seven days a week, they'd go downstairs to work. They worked hard, but we still struggled financially. Unlike in Dire Dawa and Cairo, my parents didn't have defined breadwinner and housewife roles. They had to work together on all fronts. It wasn't easy. The catering business ultimately failed. To make matters worse, the investor took advantage of Dad's trusting nature. He and Dad argued constantly, and they eventually dissolved the partnership. Within a year, my parents had lost more than $100,000 of their savings, which made Dad feel insecure. He attributed his failure to his lack of experience in Canada and his minimal knowledge of French. So, in the fall of 1990, three years after arriving in Canada, he decided we'd move to Ottawa, Canada's capital city where English is widely spoken and where his children could continue their education in French.

That summer, since my parents had already fulfilled their Canadian citizenship requirements by investing in a Quebec-based business, we received a notice to appear to take our oaths of citizenship at a local Citizenship and Immigration office in downtown Ottawa – the final step to becoming Canadian citizens. It was an important day for us, one I'll never forget. The night before, we prepared what we'd wear so that we wouldn't rush the next day. My parents were just as excited as us kids and urged us to be extra vigilant in our morning grooming. We wore our best clothes, and my parents wore suits. At breakfast, I tried not to spill on my crisp white shirt. My parents' joy was evident and contagious as we drove to the Citizenship and Immigration office. Soon we were all giggling and laughing, and we teased one of my brothers that he wouldn't receive his citizenship as his nose was too crooked. He took the joke in stride and laughed as hard as the rest of us.

The Citizenship and Immigration office felt ceremonial. Against a backdrop of Canadian flags, other families going through the same process also huddled together. Like my parents, they were dressed in nice attire, some in their cultural ceremonial outfits, everyone snapping pictures of the momentous event. You could feel their jubilation and relief. They'd probably gone through similar trials and tribulations as my family had in their last three years. A woman at a table examined our document and directed us to the official ceremony room. Once the soon-to-be citizens had gathered, the ceremony clerk entered and explained the proceedings.

We all stood when the judge entered. He welcomed us and asked us to sit while he marked the significant occasion. I don't remember what he said, but soon we were holding up our right hands to take the Oath of Citizenship. We repeated it in English and French. My siblings and I were more comfortable in French since we had three years of practice, but my parents were better with English. One by one, my family and I approached the stage to receive our citizenship certificates, shake the judge's hand, and affirm our oaths. Then, we all stood to sing the national anthem. This is what I remember best – my first time singing the national song as a Canadian. The judge said, "Congratulations! As a new citizen, you share the same rights and responsibilities as all Canadians. Take advantage of all Canada has to offer. Welcome to the Canadian family." All I could think was that I was Canadian. *I belong to this country.* Until then, I had been upset about leaving Egypt, but this feeling changed after I saw how happy my parents were. I felt that we belonged here; we were citizens and had finally found home.

4 | REBEL GIRL

My first Ottawa school was Fielding Drive Public School. I was in grade 8 French immersion and the only English-as-an-additional-language student who could do most of their courses in French. Because of my three years in Montreal, I spoke better French than kids who'd taken French immersion since kindergarten. I made many friends at Fielding and happily adjusted to life in Ottawa. My friends and I often took the bus at lunch to McDonald's and sometimes got in trouble if we returned late.

Dayna, a girl at school whom I loved, took an interest in me, and often called me "the Egyptian girl" or "Egyptian eyes." Everyone at school thought I was Egyptian because when asked where I was from, I always talked about Egypt. I couldn't reference Ethiopia since I had been too young when we left. I thought my Egyptian background was why Dayna was so interested and kind to me. Dayna introduced me to everyone, shared her lunch with me, and never held back comments about how she liked my style, including my clothes. She encouraged me to wear my curly hair down and often touched me as sisters do. I liked that she didn't make me feel stupid for not being an Anglophone. She quickly noticed when others used words or expressions I didn't know and would explain them to me, making me feel included in conversations.

That year, 1991, many people were worried that Iraqi president Saddam Hussein would destroy the world with nuclear bombs. The fear that his bombs could reach North America was in the news every day. I was just as scared as the other kids. People were talking about the United States going to war with Hussein. Dayna, tearful, one day told me that she was terrified – she had extended family in Israel, and Saddam had launched scud ballistic missiles at where her family lived. I felt terrible for her and wondered whether she felt comfortable telling anyone else. I told my parents about Dayna and my concern about a possible war. Not understanding why they weren't as fearful as me, I asked my brothers to explain the conflict. After Saddam invaded Kuwait, my overly fearful teachers tried to keep the school's only Kuwaiti student in the principal's office as a security measure. I don't know what they were thinking. The hysteria and fear drummed up by politicians and the media had worked.

When we first arrived in Ottawa, my family rented a two-bedroom apartment on Springfield Street near Mooney's Bay. Then, in 1992, my parents bought a four-bedroom townhome for $60,000 on Caron Street in the St Laurent neighbourhood. Dad considered investing in a local business but feared losing more money and relying on others, due to his lack of experience in Canada. He liked the idea of being self-employed better and decided to work as a Blue Line taxi driver. He eventually owned his own plate, which required another investment of $100,000. After the failed Montreal businesses, buying the house, and then the taxi plate, he didn't have much money. He'd work long shifts, leaving before I woke and coming home as I went to bed. At night, he'd lease his taxi to other drivers and take a percentage of their fares. He continued as a taxi driver until retiring in 2015. My mother completed her high school and then a computer-programming course at Algonquin College. She'd make breakfast and lunch for everyone then ride the bus with my sisters and me. We lived frugally – no vacations, sports, or extracurricular activities like in Cairo. Life was school, work, and television, which is how I learned English.

For grade 9, I attended Ridgemont High School, whose student body was largely made up of a surge of immigrants who'd arrived in Ottawa that year. There were a few Canadian Caribbeans who were like best friends to me: Grismery, whose family came from Haiti; Carla from the Dominican Republic; and Salam from Lebanon, as well as many other Lebanese and Somali students impacted by the civil wars in their countries. The exposure that I gained by interacting with diverse communities at Ridgemont was like no other. I didn't entirely fit in with any particular group, but I interacted with all of them fluidly. I related to Arabs as a Yemeni and an Egyptian, to Somalis as a co-East African, and to Black

Canadians as one myself. I did this well and enjoyed feeling that I both belonged and didn't belong to any of these groups. This was my first experience moving between the different parts of my identity.

My best friends Grismery and Salam were on the school's basketball team. We attended dance parties and hung out at McDonald's in the Billings Bridge plaza, where I'd later work part-time. I didn't get into much trouble at Ridgemont since the older boys all played soccer with my brother and would tease my friends and me when they saw us. They were like family, and I feared they'd tell my brother if I was up to anything ill-behaved, like skipping class.

After moving to Caron Street in 1992, I entered a new school district and could no longer attend Ridgemont High School. I was disheartened to leave my friendships and start all over again. When I complained to my family, Ziad, who spoke English and French, went with me to the district school board to persuade them to let me to stay where I was. They refused. I didn't know anyone in my new school. I tried to be positive. I'd adapt, my family tried to convince me, and so I attended my fourth school in Canada. The constant readjustments took their toll. My positive attitude to change and resilience had reached its limit. I was increasingly confused and isolated because of language and other cultural barriers. It didn't help that my reception at Gloucester was less than welcoming.

In the first few weeks, Rebecca, one of the most popular girls, started making fun of me. Rebecca was taller than me, and one day in the hall, she and her friends mocked me. She walked right behind me and pushed her butt out to make it look bigger. Her friends laughed. When I realized what she was doing, I walked away silently and felt humiliated. Farah was a couple years above me at Gloucester and also had incidents with Rebecca and her friends. Too angry to make friends, I became isolated and often walked around alone. Eventually, other students, always minorities – Africans, Caribbeans, and Arabs – began approaching me. I had a few white friends but only in the classroom. We never met outside of school.

I always looked up to Farah. She was more confident than me. She was beautiful, short, and slim and had a great sense of style. She only wore designer clothes, and everything looked good on her. She was a straight-A student who skipped classes and didn't have to spend hours studying. She had a photographic memory, intimidating intelligence, and sound judgment, and she never bothered with petty things. She spoke her mind and questioned everything. I struggled academically, was more accepting of our parents' commands, and was increasingly shy. Farah taught me about womanhood, periods, and all the challenges and power that come from femininity. More importantly, she instilled in me a sense that we, girls, were superior to boys but needed to navigate our way through the system to reach our goals in a way they didn't have to. She learned early on that the world isn't fair. She always tried to outsmart my brothers and other boys in school. Surprising no one, she later pursued a career in the male-dominated field of chemical engineering. When she received her MBA, she rubbed everyone's face in her superior intellect and shared with me that one of her professors at Michigan University had told her not to be so forceful with her ideas, given how influential she could be. "I very much doubt a man would ever be given this piece of advice," she concluded.

Eman was just as fierce but more studious and subtle than Farah. She studied hard, was a straight-A student, completed her computer engineering degree, and many years later, received her MBA from the University of California, Berkeley. She was most attractive, stylish, and confident. The boys all had crushes on Eman, but she didn't return their attention. She kept to herself in her room, reading novel after novel until we began to worry. Ziad, in his concern, used his part-time security work to pay for Eman to take Tae Kwon Do lessons. Eman was later thrilled to join Farah and me at Gloucester – it was her first English school, as she'd only gone to French schools. My two outstanding sisters showed me that I had to prove my worth, stand out, dress well, and keep up with my studies. My sisters and I pushed each other to achieve our dreams. We supported and encouraged each other. Even today, when facing a serious decision, I hear their voices: *Huda, you can do this. Lean in, stand your ground, take care of yourself! That's the only way to be happy and give others love.*

Rebecca and her friends teased Farah because of our race, Farah and I concluded. Farah, loud and proud, teased them right back. One day, I saw Farah walk past my class window, followed by Rebecca and her crew, one holding a hammer behind her back. Without excusing myself, I ran into the hall just as one girl was pushing Farah into a locker. Farah fought back, but by the time I arrived, teachers had separated everyone. The teachers never saw the hammer. Since there was only some pushing and no one was hurt, the situation was never reported to the school office. Consequently, nobody genuinely dealt with the incident.

Although Farah and I were upset and our friends concerned, we knew it would be worse if we told the principal what had happened. So, the problem continued. I felt anxious walking to school. Eman was well-adjusted and had many friends, so she didn't give identity or race issues a second thought. She advised me to ignore them. But I was increasingly angry and believed that I'd never fit in – so I became a rebel. My grades dropped. I submitted assignments late and skipped class. Teachers gave up on me. They couldn't understand what I was going through. I started smoking and hanging out with kids who smoked, usually marginalized kids who were seen as bad.

My identity was rapidly shifting. My childhood memories of Egypt were fading. I began seeing myself as a minority and, specifically, a Black Canadian. At lunch, in the cafeteria, I sat at a table practically reserved for Black and other minority students. I shared my lunch and laughter with these friends. Though we had similar experiences, we never spoke about them. North American Black culture and its struggle with racism spoke to me. I abandoned my Arabic cassette tapes and started listening to North American music – hip hop, pop, and jazz. I idolized Mary J. Blige and Salt-N-Pepa. I braided my hair with long extensions like Janet Jackson and put on hazel contact lenses. I spoke English mostly, except when Dad was home. He expected us to speak Arabic or Harari in the house and was adamant that we did not abandon our roots. No matter how hard I resisted, he still compelled us to take Arabic classes on Saturdays. Ironically, in Egypt, Dad had made us focus on English and French, but in Canada, we had to maintain Arabic.

One day, Rebecca approached me by my locker. We'd both skipped our morning classes, and the hall was empty. She told me that she was going to fight me at lunch, and then she walked away. I panicked. Despite my new identity, I'd never been in a real fight. If I fought her, I'd be suspended, maybe expelled. I desperately wanted to tell my sisters, but I couldn't find them. Then, suddenly, I felt relief and calm. Rebecca and her friends had caused me to hate everything about school. As the lunch bell rang, I found Rebecca and her friends by her locker. This was my moment of truth. I wasn't going to wait for them to come to me. I needed to take control of the situation. I couldn't live in constant fear of running into her or her friends. Our fight was going to be on my terms. I looked at Rebecca and said, "Right now, we're fighting. Right now." I slapped her in the face with all my strength. The hallway, which had been bustling, silenced as everyone turned to us. Rebecca paused and took a swing, punching me below my nose and making it bleed. She was much stronger than I'd thought, but my past year flashed before my eyes and my adrenaline pulsed. I let my anger and fear of humiliation take me over. In seconds, I was on top of Rebecca, on the ground, and in complete control. I looked up. The entire school seemed to be in the hall yelling. Suddenly, I heard Farah. She was shouting at me to stop and was pulling me off Rebecca. "You don't want to hurt her, Huda! Get off!" At that moment, four teachers arrived. I pushed them off me and asked that no one touch me as I walked to the washroom to wash the blood off my face.

My fight with Rebecca was my first and only violent fight. I was suspended for a week. One of my eyes swelled entirely and painfully shut. I felt terrible that things had resulted in a fight but didn't think I'd had much of a choice. It seemed inevitable. Still, I questioned myself. Had I gone too far? Should I have waited for her to make the first move? Should I have just gone home and avoided the fight altogether? At home, my parents were surprised. I let Farah explain. My parents knew it wasn't in my nature to fight. I'd always been mild mannered. When they heard that Farah and I were being harassed and that we'd been intimidated because of our background and identity, they were concerned. We told them that we would be going through mediation with Rebecca and her friends the following week to resolve our dispute and tensions.

The mediation sessions included Rebecca and two of her friends. We never became friendly, but the harassment and teasing stopped completely. Had the fight not occurred, I think that I would've continued to live in fear. It would've impacted my development and confidence. I learned that conflict and misunderstanding happen and produce violence and that mediation and resolution are possible. In time, I felt better about school, and the fight solidified my reputation as a rebel. I didn't feel like a rebel, but I liked my new status, and I wanted other people to think that I was a tough girl. No one dared mess with me, and I realized that I could handle conflict and not shy away if confronted. I used my new popularity to defend others. For instance, some girls were teasing a friend of mine about her large breasts, calling her a cow. I approached one and told her that if she continued to harass my friend, she'd have to deal with me. It stopped.

I began to read and pay more attention to Black culture and its relation to social justice. Farah was the main organizer of Black History Month at Gloucester. She'd drag me to Black fashion shows and have me participate. I felt beautiful and supported around my Black friends, a positive mental break from the constant anxiety that comes with living racialized. I was outraged in 1991, when Rodney King was beaten on camera. Riots followed the acquittals of the police officers who'd beaten him. I identified strongly with the demonstrators and couldn't believe how Blacks were being treated in America.

Back in Montreal, when I was twelve, Eman and I had ridden the city bus with Mom. The first time, we sat at the front, next to an old Black man with grey hair. He smiled at me and said, "Allo," a French way of saying hello. He was leaning forward and waiting for my reply. I'll never forget how he looked at my sister and me. His gentle face was full of love and compassion. His smile comforted me. There was something different about his reception of us. At the time, and for many years, I didn't think about racial divides. I now wonder whether he was looking at us because we were Black like him. Did he smile because we were also Black? Was that enough to merit his unspoken care? Was it because he knew that the world isn't always kind to people of colour? Maybe he wanted to show me that he loved me for being Black like him. Maybe he wanted me to love myself and to be myself. Perhaps he understood the difficulties that I'd later face in a way that Mom and Dad, new immigrants and new to this type of racism, didn't.

In high school, after the racially instigated conflict with Rebecca, I began noticing civil rights and social justice issues related to Black North American communities. Icons like Malcolm X, Martin Luther King Jr, and Rosa Parks were new to me. I learned how Parks, in 1955, had refused to give up her seat on a city bus in Montgomery, Alabama, thereby triggering the United States civil rights movement. As a Black Muslim, I connected to Malcolm X most. I began wearing clothes with an X on them. Though I was moved by these iconic figures who'd fought for equality and justice, as a new African immigrant whose family hadn't experienced that degree of racism, I didn't understand the depth of their struggles.

By 1996, my last year of high school, I'd replaced my rebellious side with a desire to do something with my life. But I didn't know what that something was. Farah was at the University of Ottawa, and Eman had advanced a year by taking courses during the summer – though a year younger, she was going to graduate the same year as me. I needed to get my act together if I didn't want to feel like a loser next to my sisters. At first, I thought I'd go to Seneca College in Toronto and become a pilot. I loved the idea of travelling. I passed my qualifying physics exams to Seneca College and gained acceptance to the program. But my high school guidance counsellor suggested that I take an aptitude test. The test suggested that I pursue a law career. This was accurate and revealing – I'd often pictured myself going into law or law enforcement.

I spoke to my sisters about what I should do, and they recommended that I stay at home in Ottawa and enroll in Carleton University's law program. A friend of mine knew an engineering professor of Egyptian origin and contacted him. He gave me a tour of the campus, which ended at Oliver's Pub in the University Centre. I sat with my Pepsi and absorbed the music and energy. The students were freely drinking, laughing, and acting obnoxiously. I couldn't wait to start university. It felt like life was about to get so much sweeter.

5 | THE PITCH

From 1996 to 2000, I enjoyed morning bus rides past Carleton's beautiful grounds. Highlights included large centuries-old trees, the flowing Rideau River, and rolling hills. As a new student, I hoped that I'd fit in and thrive. I liked the extensive underground tunnel complex, rarely walking outside between buildings during the brutally cold months – a relief. One student from Toronto told me that he hadn't stepped outside once during an entire winter semester!

Dad couldn't afford university tuition for us. Luckily, I received student loans. My sisters were both at the University of Ottawa, Farah taking chemistry and Eman computer engineering, and my brothers were studying at Algonquin College. Mom had already completed her studies at Algonquin. Given how hard everyone in my family was working, I felt pressure to get good grades and graduate. We all had part-time jobs. My brothers were security guards and my sisters and I worked retail. I was in the shoe department at the Bay in Saint Laurent Mall, where I gained an appreciation for the diversity of workplace challenges. My job also prevented me from partying and wasting time on weekends. Dad was still working long twelve-hour shifts, six days a week. I think he secretly envied our postsecondary educations. He'd say, "Education is the key to success, and the opportunity is yours," "If you fail, you fail only yourself," and "If you succeed, you'll reap the benefits. It's on you. It's your future," which Mom also emphasized. Dad went on and on about how difficult life had been for him and about how he'd sacrificed wealth and comfort to bring us to Canada, so we'd have an education and a home.

To balance my heavily academic life, I maintained memberships at the Athletics Club, where I exercised, and at the International House. One day at the University Centre, I discovered a table for the Muslim Student Association. I approached out of curiosity. A man named Abdallah greeted me. He told me that they organized many activities like the Friday prayer and that they had a prayer room and Ramadan Iftar programs. "We're always looking for volunteers," he said. Thinking that I'd never volunteer given how busy I was, I smiled. Then the other man, Khalid, said, "Volunteering is optional." I don't know why, but his response offended me. I wondered whether he was judging me because of my immodest fashion or because I approached the table with a male student friend, a shunning act for a pious Muslim girl. I smiled at Khalid and, to prove him wrong, said, "Don't be surprised to see me at your functions." I'd soon join the group, meet many Muslim Canadians, and become friends with both Abdallah and Khalid.

Through the Muslim Student Association at Carleton, I gained regular access to communal Friday prayers and a sense of what it meant to be a Canadian Muslim. We had Fridays off in Egypt, but in Canada, everyone was expected to go to school and work, and there hadn't been prayer rooms at Gloucester High School. I'd only occasionally attended the main mosque in Ottawa. Attending Friday prayers at Carleton made me realize how diverse Muslim Canadians are. I'd sit and socialize with Muslim students from Afghanistan, Pakistan, Somalia, Palestine, Oman, and other countries. After getting to know many of them well, I was sometimes nervous to see them on campus later. Many were more observant of Islam than I was. I wondered whether they judged me for talking with male students or for wearing immodest clothes. Still, many would greet me with "Alsalamu Alaykum," an Islamic greeting meaning "peace be upon you." I began attending Muslim Student Association lectures and Ramadan dinner parties. I was attracted to theological and historical discussions on Islam and Middle East politics. I enjoyed the Arab club parties most. Twice a year, Wally, a Palestinian student, rented party halls, and there, among friends, I learned the traditional Palestinian and Lebanese dance *debka*. Wally held my hand, led the dance, and exaggerated every movement until I got them right. The music was loud, and the young, mixed crowd was full of energy, many trying to attract the right person.

I began praying regularly, both at Carleton and at home. Praying five times a day, dawn, noon, late afternoon, sunset, and evening, meant that my spiritual heart was awake and connected to my Creator. This is what I love most about Islam – the feeling that one can aspire to more than the material world. God is great and something bigger than this world awaited me. When I prostrated, *sujood*, with my forehead on the floor in humility to the Creator, I felt a sense of awareness of my humanity, my inabilities, his might. I felt at peace. To this day, when facing difficulty, I rely on prayer.

With my newly tranquil spirit, I performed much better academically and brought my GPA to an A– in my last two years of studies. I was relieved. In my first year, no matter how hard I studied, I'd receive only Cs or Bs on assignments. My Bachelor of Law program included much theory. I learned about Canadian public law, such as the roles of and interaction between the three government branches: executive, legislative, and judiciary. I learned about the nature and structure of Canadian legal decision making, including the constitutional and legislative frameworks that form our federal government. I explored how law structures and limits public power and learned how to research and analyze case studies, think critically, synthesize complex ideas, and make presentations. I took courses on public, private, criminal, and family law; international human rights; sentencing and policing theories; and legal research methods. One thing I didn't learn about was colonization and its continued impact on marginalized communities in the context of law and security.

These courses examined political, legal, and social issues in a Canadian context and compared them to other Western countries. Some courses spoke to me more than others, especially a fourth-year seminar on feminism and another on gender bias in Canada. I learned that Canadian law was derived from English common law, which can be traced back to when women weren't considered equal in the eyes of lawmakers and enforcers. Women were then defined as men's property, and they continue to be defined like this in many parts of the world. Sexism and patriarchal bias disempower women legally, politically, and socially, thus causing great injustice. Although I'm from a patriarchal society, I fully supported the progressive ideas I was learning. I wrote a paper on sexual assault and the significance of consent, including between married partners. I learned and appreciated how complex such cases in the justice system are and how the integrity of women's minds and bodies is fundamental.

At Carleton, I learned that social change is possible. My professors were mostly liberal, critical, and strong advocates of social justice and values. I arrived early for lectures, sat front and centre, and stayed after class to ask professors questions that showed how much I cared about the subject matter. Professors discussed theories and challenged their students on philosophical and moral issues, asking what the right thing to do is in different contexts and if an application of law had been fair, transparent, or just. I learned about democracy, freedom of speech and expression, and my role and responsibility to uphold both.

I focused on political science electives. I wanted to bring my GPA up with "easy" courses that I already intimately understood. One was on Middle East government and politics. For the term paper, Professor John Sigler asked us to examine thorny issues – the status of Jerusalem, borders, security, water, and Palestinian refugees – which, if resolved, could lead to a comprehensive peace settlement between Israel and Palestine. I was beginning to take an interest in Middle Eastern politics. While preparing my research paper, I stumbled upon Salman Rushdie's *The Satanic Verses*, which was considered blasphemous in many Muslim-majority countries because, in it, Rushdie indirectly relegates Prophet Mohammed, his wives, and the apostles as devils and prostitutes. When the book was first published, and for many years after, the Iranian government issued a fatwa ordering Muslims to kill Rushdie. I was astonished to learn this. Hearing the debate in public and in the media, it was simultaneously fascinating and novel for me that freedom of expression was such a fundamental right in the West. I was also intrigued by the charged emotions and serious repercussions of the debate on all fronts.

A political science course on Canadian national security changed the direction of my career aspirations. In it, I learned about espionage, subversion, treason, scandals, and commissions. I learned that Canada's national security framework is comprised of the RCMP, CSIS, the Department of National Defence, and the Privy Council. Historically, the Canadian security and intelligence community evolved out of the British system as Canada matured from a colony into an independent state. However, after World War II, Canada strengthened its security relationship with the United States. My classmates debated passionately about the roles of the RCMP's Security Service in the 1970s and the implications of a sovereign Quebec. As a new Canadian, I didn't have a position on these topics, so I listened carefully, noting how critical national security was and how it invoked passion and controversy from all who discussed it.

One morning, while buying my daily coffee, I was brought in closer proximity to the world of national security. I ran into my Canadian national security professor at the campus cafe. He asked whether I was enjoying his class. I replied that I was, thinking he didn't like that I was so quiet and that he was about to ask me to participate more. Instead, he asked whether I spoke other languages. I explained my origins and that I spoke Arabic, French, and Harari. He said that I should consider a career as a linguist with CSIS.

CSIS interested me, as did national security in general, but I didn't see myself as an Arabic linguist. I thought Arabic grammar was too complicated, much more so than French and English, and that translating would be laborious. Still, I thanked him for the suggestion. I looked up CSIS online, but there wasn't much information, so the idea fell off my radar. I never thought I'd one day work for CSIS as an intelligence officer nor that one of CSIS's main focuses would be investigating Islamic extremists.

My close friends were in other programs, but we hung out on campus. Our group included two Syrian Canadian sisters, Abeer and Manal, who were from Hama and studying statistics and biology. Their parents fled to Saudi Arabia after the 1982 massacre in Syria, which killed more than 20,000 people in one week. They spent their childhood in Saudi Arabia, just as I did mine in Egypt. The three of us had grown up in countries that didn't accept us as full citizens. They were among the most stunning, sophisticated, and traditional Arab young women on campus. They lived with their widowed mother, a strong woman like Mom. Then there was also Nermin, a Somali Canadian studying linguistics whose infectious smile put everyone at ease. She was born in Cairo and had grown up there like me. Her father was the Somali representative to the Arab League and had contact with Egyptian politicians, diplomats, and cinema stars. At the onset of the Somali Civil War, her family relocated, permanently, to Canada. The group was rounded out by Jennifer, a Canadian Palestinian Christian studying biology. Jennifer's family had fled Palestine to

Lebanon during the 1967 Arab–Israeli conflict, then to Muscat, Oman, and Canada.

The five of us were a pack. We each had complex backgrounds and were smart, driven, and outgoing. Our bond was strong and reinforced by our similar family histories and childhood experiences in other lands. We often spoke of how proud we were to be Canadian, since our parents made sure to remind us how fortunate we were to be in Canada. We didn't go clubbing and didn't drink. Instead, we'd go to restaurants, shop in Montreal, and hang out at Abeer and Manal's home, where her mother fed us Syrian food and showered us with affection.

Early in my third year at Carleton, I was approached at a bus stop by a University of Ottawa law student. Riad Saloojee was taking an elective course at Carleton and introduced himself as a Muslim South African Canadian. He said he'd seen me at Muslim Student Association events and asked about my origin. He was friendly and easy to speak with, and I quickly felt comfortable. I thought he was intrigued by my African and Muslim roots, which were like his. We didn't stay in touch, but in my fourth year, we coincidentally enrolled in the same international human rights course. He was, by far, the sharpest and most articulate in class. His answers to the professor's questions were often followed by silence, which provided the rest of us time to reflect on his assertions. Riad could've made a lot of money, sharp as he is, but he was born to be a social justice leader. In 2000, he founded the Canadian chapter of the Council on American Islamic Relations, today the National Council of Canadian Muslims, an Ottawa-based national non-profit funded by grassroots membership. Its mandate includes community education, media relations, antidiscrimination, and public advocacy for the Canadian Muslim community. Immediately following its inception, I began supporting the chapter with a modest monthly donation. I was a struggling student, but I wanted to give to causes that spoke to me. The organization had a strong presence in the Muslim community, especially among educated Muslim Canadians. I believed in its leadership and staff and knew many of them well.

I graduated in 2000 with a Bachelor of Arts Honours degree from Carleton. My family was especially proud. They dressed up for the ceremony and smiled and laughed as I crossed the stage to get my certificate. Dad and Mom hugged and kissed me tight. I was happy to show them that their support and sacrifices had led to my success at school. At the time, only 23 per cent of Canadian high school students graduated from postsecondary education. I had come a long way since arriving in Canada, learning two new languages, improving upon my high school grades, and graduating with an honours law degree. After the ceremony, my parents announced that they were purchasing a new home in Ottawa's south end – a detached house with four large bedrooms, a fireplace, and a big back yard.

Having quit my job at Hudson's Bay, I began part-time work at the Royal Bank of Canada while searching for a meaningful career related to my law degree. I was disappointed to learn that the Government of Canada's starting salary was only $35,000 per year for most junior positions. Given the wild growth of Ottawa's technology sector and the unreal wages my sisters were being offered in their fields, I decided to register for the University of Ottawa's Management Information Systems program; however, I lacked the required high school–level calculus. So, for the summer, I moved into Farah's Corning, New York, apartment. Farah had relocated after completing her chemical engineering degree at the University of Toronto, landing a job in her field with Corning Inc. She tutored me until I completed the course a month later. I was proud to have finished a course that I'd found difficult in high school, proving to myself that I'd grown a lot since then. Farah had a very diverse group of friends, including many white and Black Americans. She talked about how, unlike in Canada, the two groups are segregated in America. I often envied how Farah's Black American friends were able to openly discuss their experiences with racism.

In the fall of 2000, I began studying Management Information Systems at the University of Ottawa, which added to my student debt. I felt at ease with my workload and campus culture. Early in the semester, the Second Palestinian Intifada broke out, and I'd often sit in the school's computer lab to follow the news. One day, I watched a video of Mohammad Al Durrah, a twelve-year-old boy, and his father. They'd sought cover from Israeli gunfire behind a concrete pillar. The footage was just over a minute long, the pair holding onto each other in terror, the boy curled behind his father, the father covering the boy's head. Then, a burst of gunfire and an eruption of dust. After the dust subsides, Mohammed is slumped motionless across his father's legs, his hands covering his face.

His father is also motionless, his eyes and mouth open and his head suspended to the right. I was deeply disturbed. All I could do was watch. My chest tightened, and the air seemed to thin. A girl beside me peeked at my screen and commented. She said she was Jordanian and of Palestinian origin. She'd moved to Canada to continue her education and become a model. Sarah was her name and we immediately connected, forming a long-standing relationship that I cherish and am proud of. Later on, she would abandon her aspiration to become a model, and, on the contrary, chose to be modest and beat me to wearing a hijab.

Later, Sarah and I attended a protest at Parliament Hill that was calling for Canada and the international community to stop the violence in the Middle East. We marched with our arms across each other. We each enjoyed exercising our rights in a free and democratic country. I was interested in social justice and felt powerful to have such a voice. At home, I wrote a comment on the BBC website, my preferred source for international news: "The promise that was given to the Palestinians 52 years ago by the League of Nations, now the United Nations, needs to be implemented. International peacekeeping troops are required to stand between the Israelis and the Palestinians in the occupied territories." I never supported violence. I supported an international effort to establish a peaceful resolution in the Middle East. To my surprise, the BBC called me for comments, but I didn't return their call. I didn't want to be on the news.

After a while in my new school courses, I realized that I enjoyed business classes but wasn't apt at computer programming. One night, frustrated by a Java programming algorithm, I thought about what I wanted to do with my life. I recalled my high school career aptitude test, my interest in law enforcement, and how I'd enjoyed studying law at Carleton. I realized that I was looking for more than just a career. I wanted to do something that helped others. I wanted to make a difference and travel. I applied to the Canadian Border Security Agency (CBSA) and the RCMP. Then, I remembered my conversation with my national security professor about working for CSIS. I looked up CSIS on my computer once more and read the CSIS Act and CSIS's requirements for becoming an intelligence officer. The sense of purpose, safeguarding Canada, protecting people, working in a legal setting, international concerns – it all sounded exciting and like a perfect fit for me. I had a real interest in politics and all things international, I had a legal background, and I spoke Canada's two official languages. I printed the application form on the website. I didn't sleep one wink that night. All I could think about was how great it would be to work for CSIS.

The next morning, I skipped all my classes; gathered my Canadian citizenship card, driver's licence, and transcripts from Carleton; filled out the forms; and submitted my application. CSIS was all I thought about from then on. I was going to get in, and I was going to become a force to be reckoned with.

6 | RECRUITMENT

The bustling coffee shop was full of people. I hurried in, stood in line, scanned the room, and waited. I spotted a woman in black pants, a casual blouse, and no makeup. I don't know how I knew it was Laura, the spy I was scheduled to meet, but I did.

"Hi, Huda, I'm Laura." She smiled. I smiled back and followed her to a small table. After receiving my application, CSIS had requested that I meet with an intelligence officer – standard protocol for CSIS hopefuls. Laura was my first contact with CSIS. Upbeat and friendly, she asked what I already knew about the service. I told her that I'd taken a course on national security and had read the CSIS Act but that, in truth, I didn't know much. She nodded.

"I once knocked on someone's door and introduced myself as an employee of the Canadian Security Intelligence Service," she recalled, leaning towards me, her voice low. "The man said he wasn't interested in buying home security and slammed the door in my face. I had to ring the doorbell again and explain. Once he understood I was with CSIS, he let me in." She allowed herself a wry smile. I imagined my parents reacting the same way and relaxed, but I also wondered whether Laura had used this story with other recruits to sound friendly, especially given her employment in such a powerful organization. Laura spoke for around twenty minutes about the agency's mandate and national security in general. She provided a brief overview of counterintelligence threats from Russia and China and spoke about international terrorism. She focused on groups like Al-Jihad and the Afghan Mujahideen, Islamist resistance fighters who battled the Soviets during the Soviet Afghan War from 1979–89. "A career with CSIS would be like no other," she said to me, taking a sip from her coffee. She explained that I could work in a specific area, like counterintelligence, or move around every few years between different departments.

I could tell she found the job exciting, and I felt my own excitement rise. *What an incredible place to face new challenges and learn new things,* I thought. As a twenty-five-year-old, university-educated, multilingual woman, I felt confident that I had what it took to work for CSIS. I was young and full of hope and energy. I was also naïve about CSIS and the workforce in general. I thought that the work world was merit based; work hard and reap the rewards, as I'd been told all my life. I'd eventually learn the bitter truth.

A month after I met Laura, CSIS invited me to an information session at headquarters in Ottawa. I was anxious and curious as I walked up the front steps to the massive grey building with rows of turquoise windows. A security guard asked me to present my identification. I showed my driver's license and was inside in short order. Emblazoned on the grey granite floor was a large CSIS crest, which I recognized from my invitation letter. The CSIS crest includes a red maple leaf in the centre, a gold and red crown at the top, and an enclosure of large blue palisades. The crown and gold and blue colours represent the links between the RCMP and CSIS. I watched employees walk up to the revolving doors, punch in their pin numbers, and enter the space. *Will I ever be one of them?* After presenting myself at the security desk, I received a visitor's pass and took a seat until a Human Resources officer arrived to escort me in. The others also waiting seemed just as nervous as I.

The officer introduced herself as Amy and led the group past a sliding door into a tiny room with entirely glass walls. We huddled close as the door shut behind us. We were trapped together until it opened, and then we were released into a large foyer on the first floor. Looking up, I could see that each floor was built around the foyer and that all six levels of the building had a direct view of the ground floor. We walked past a big, open cafeteria and a library, known as the Information Centre, into a large boardroom. I saw world maps on the walls of almost every office and professionals in suits walking around with folders. Everyone seemed to be on a mission of international scope. The scene filled me with purpose. I took a deep breath. I strongly desired to be among these national security experts. I felt a keen sense of duty and of belonging to Canada. Working at CSIS would be my way of fulfilling my civic duty – what an honour it would be to help safeguard fellow Canadians.

Amy approached the front of the boardroom and faced the recruits. "Welcome, everyone. Please be seated," she said. She walked us through the competitive selection process. Then she stopped, looked around to ensure that she had our attention, and proceeded to explain how paramount secrecy was and how it would become a central theme in our lives. She then provided an overview of the organization. CSIS receives direction on Government of Canada priorities then collects information, investigates, and reports back to its partners in national security, including Global Affairs Canada and national law enforcement agencies, such as the RCMP. Amy explained that the ideal intelligence officer is knowledgeable about national and international events and understands how these events relate to the CSIS mandate. The officer is bilingual, mature, self-confident, and quickly able to assess situations and take appropriate action. Amy outlined CSIS's main branches: Counter Terrorism, Counter Intelligence, Counter Proliferation, and Research Analysis Production. She also provided an overview of CSIS Security Screening – it presents the Government of Canada with security clearances and advises on the admissibility of foreign nationals to CBSA and Immigration, Refugees and Citizenship Canada (IRCC).

"You need to be discreet about the application process," Amy advised. "And if your application is successful, you'll need to be discreet about your work at CSIS. Intelligence officers participate in deep-cover operations. The fewer people who know you're a spy, the better you'll be able to perform. Only your immediate family members should know of your interest in working for CSIS."

Working on covert operations sounded exciting. She also mentioned that intelligence officers must sign a mobility clause agreeing to be transferred anywhere in Canada at any time and at the service's discretion. As a young, unattached woman who'd adapted to living in three countries and two distinct Canadian provinces, I was thrilled by the prospect of discovering more of what Canada had to offer. I imagined being posted to Vancouver, surrounded by mountains, forests, and the ocean. Pay started at $35,000 per year, and there was a five-year probation period.

That didn't sound great. An intelligence officer's salary at CSIS was less than a tax collector at Revenue Canada. *Is this to ensure people don't join the spy service just to make money?* I still had $24,000 in student loans. I'd also accumulated $1,000 of credit card debt. I figured I could live with my parents for a couple of years and work at CSIS headquarters in Ottawa to make do. Adventure and purpose would trump salary.

The session ended with a video that illustrated international events through images – Russian spies; flags of states, like Iran, that sponsor terrorism; and terrorist groups, such as Hezbollah. These images were action-oriented, fast-paced, and fascinating, and they required analysis from each applicant. My engagement and excitement increased with each image as I recognized the foreign languages and cultures on the screen. I was intrigued, curious, and hooked.

Looking around the room, I realized that I was one of only two visible minorities. Most candidates were young white women. I figured that my view of national security as a male-dominated field was stereotyped and out of touch. *Great, but do I stand a chance against all these bright-looking women?* I smiled uneasily at everyone. In a full suit, I was undoubtedly dressed right. Surprisingly, some candidates were dressed casually, probably because it was just an orientation session without managers. Still, I wasn't going to risk it. As a minority, I felt I had to make the best impression I could with every CSIS representative. Each interaction counted. I recalled my university days when I didn't feel as eloquent as Anglophones in my classes. I could come across awkward in English, a product of regularly switching between four languages. Surely, the other applicants would express themselves more precisely and in a more sophisticated manner than I could.

The job didn't just require a university degree; it also required drive, ambition, and motivation as well as life experience. I had plenty of all of these. In my customer service work, I was told I was likeable and had a gift with people. I credited that to my humility, self-worth, and respect for others. I also possessed a profound level of maturity, which undoubtedly stemmed from the many challenges I faced throughout my life up until that point. What we went through as a family and the trials I experienced throughout my youth added a great deal of depth to my character and shaped my overall outlook on life.

Amy held a short question-and-answer session after orientation. I was one of the first to raise my hand. "How long would it take to specialize in a particular field?" I asked eagerly. I wanted to work in Counter Terrorism. I figured I'd be a great fit, given my background, experience living in the Middle East, and linguistic profile. Amy smiled. "I get this question a lot from prospective candidates," she told me. "At the moment, IOs need to be well-versed in all the service's operational programs. Although specialization might be beneficial, as a small organization, CSIS needs people to have a breadth of knowledge and the ability to adapt to different threats." She paused and looked around the room before shifting her gaze back to me.

"IOs also need to be able to work as analysts and investigators – two functions that require very different skill sets." As she was explaining this, I nodded agreeably, hoping she was taking note of my keen interest.

Within a few weeks, I received a call requesting me for an interview that would determine my suitability for work at CSIS. The interview was conducted by another Human Resources official and an intelligence officer. I relied on my orientation notes and repeated much of what Amy had said. Without hesitation, I listed our international allies in the Five Eyes community: the Americans, British, Australians, and New Zealanders, including their respective foreign and domestic security services. I spoke about several international events and how they related to Canadian security interests. I was prepared and motivated and built rapport with each of my interviewers. When they asked about mobility, I stated that I'd be willing to relocate anywhere in Canada, according to the needs of the organization. I was young and adventure-seeking. They asked whether I'd been involved in criminal activities or substance use or abuse. My answer was exactly what they wanted to hear: "Never. Not once."

"Why not?" asked the intelligence officer, his brow furrowed.

"I'm Muslim," I explained calmly. "My religion forbids drugs, alcohol, and obviously any criminality."

The next step was to take a psychological assessment exam, including psychometric testing through a series of multiple-choice questions, most of which were bizarre and repetitive. "Do you usually have the same breakfast?" "Which do you prefer, cats or dogs?" "Does it often rain?" The same questions were asked several times in different ways. It was hard to determine what my results should be and what they were looking for. This part of the recruitment process unnerved me because I felt like I couldn't control the outcome. Luckily, I passed.

A week after the exam, I completed a psychological assessment. The psychologist asked about my life as a student and as a customer service rep at the Royal Bank. She then surprised me with results from my multiple-choice exam the week before. "You have strong leadership qualities, but you're not the type of person to seek out leadership," she said. "You're not competitive enough. If someone else is leading, you're the type to sit back, even though you possess what it takes to lead or might be more knowledgeable than the person in charge. You're confident but also reserved."

The service seeks classic Type A personalities – competitive, ambitious, aggressive, and control-seeking. I exhibited some of these traits but also showed Type B personality traits, like patience, flexibility, and a more relaxed approach, probably because of my role as the middle child among so many siblings. I knew how to go after what I wanted, but I also often relinquished control to others. For example, as the fourth child, I accepted that someone else always knew more, and I sat at the back of the car, no questions asked. So, I got nervous during the interview and tried to recall and report every instance that I'd been the primary decision maker or had helped friends make decisions. When I saw the psychologist taking notes, I kept talking, hoping I was saying what she was looking for.

I was relieved weeks later when I learned that my file was progressing – one step closer to working for the Canadian spy service! I thought about it daily, but as instructed, I refrained from talking about it with anyone. I knew the application process took months, so I continued my classes at the University of Ottawa. Acceptance to the service was my sole motivation. I registered for an introductory course in Russian language and culture to give me a leg up at my potential future job. My Russian was terrible, and I was, by far, the worst student in the class but I desperately wanted to pass the course and include it on my resume. After all, what good spy doesn't know at least some Russian?

At home, I continued to learn as much as I could to prepare for being an intelligence officer. I kept track of national and international events by following news from the CBC, the *Ottawa Citizen*, and the *Globe and*

Mail. This wasn't new to me – I had a longstanding interest in politics, especially Middle East politics. But I now followed developments closer than before. Before bed, I reread the CSIS mandate, the intelligence cycle, and the entire CSIS Act several times, often practising aloud in front of a mirror. My national assessment panel interview, the determining step, was on 5 July 2001. I was sick to my stomach as my anxiety got the best of me. I wanted the job so badly! I'd invested much time and effort into getting as far as I had. I'd been to CSIS headquarters at least five times.

The morning of the interview, I dressed in a blue blouse and a stylish black suit. I spent thirty minutes straightening my hair – I always wore my hair straight, including to university, work, and evening events. Although I still cherished the hijab, I wasn't wearing one at this time in my life, likely because Farah's views often superseded my own. Farah and Eman loved dressing modern, and Farah had flat-out refused to wear a hijab in Egypt when Dad thought she should. I was following her lead. My hair is shoulder length with medium-sized curls, like those of Karyn Parsons, who played Hilary Banks in *The Fresh Prince of Bel-Air*. But you'd only know this if you lived with me. My sisters and friends often commented on how much more beautiful I looked with curls, but I felt I looked better and was more socially acceptable with straight hair. I think this unconscious feeling of inferiority about my hair and race was fuelled by the lack of Black women's representation in magazines and entertainment.

My parents and my brother, the only ones who knew about my CSIS application besides my three character references, wished me well the morning of my interview. My brother hugged me and said he was proud of me for aiming high. "El Mukhabarat Heta Wahda, ya Hudhud" (the security service, all at once for a first career!) he said, smiling. My nickname in Arabic is Hudhud. The *hudhud* is a type of bird often said to be inquisitive and was mentioned in the Quran as belonging to King Solomon. In that story, and according to the Islamic tradition, the hudhud ventures off his assigned duties in Palestine to bring the Queen of Sheeba's peoples, in the modern-day Yemen, into monotheism, uniting the two nations.

The interview was in a large boardroom. When I entered, I was greeted by Peter, a former RCMP officer and a chief in CSIS's Research Analysis and Production branch; Tom, a midlevel manager; and Amy, the HR representative. Like me, they were all dressed in suits. Peter shook my hand firmly and locked his curious eyes on mine. His welcoming manner put me at ease. He had a dossier on his desk, which I guessed was my entire life story. When asked, I reiterated my suitability and motivation to work for the service and my knowledge of the CSIS Act. I'd answered these questions so many times by now that it was almost second nature. But these characteristics wouldn't be the determining factors. There was also a role-playing exercise. A man – I assume another Human Resources representative or an intelligence officer – entered the room. I was to approach him and leverage information from him as my three interviewers looked on. I panicked about being scrutinized. They watched and took notes. Instead of leveraging information, I spent the ten allocated minutes asking about his background and role. I never got to any security information or details about national threats. The ten minutes felt like an eternity as my audience carefully took notes on everything I said. I kept questioning whether I should've taken a direct approach instead.

At the end, Peter asked what my biggest strength was and how it would benefit CSIS. This was my opportunity to highlight why I was a good fit and what made me unique. I began explaining my background, travel experience, linguistic skills, and personality. I stressed that I was adventurous, educated, respectful, work-driven, and willing to embrace new technology. Despite my accomplishments and characteristics, I maintained a humble demeanour, indicating I was willing to take direction and learn from mistakes. I noticed that Peter was taking notes, but his facial expression gave nothing away as I explained my history.

Finally, I gave him the answer he was looking for:

> My biggest asset is my ability to communicate across cultural lines. This is part of my DNA. It's my source of strength. I excel at cross-cultural communication. I won first place month after month at the Royal Bank for enlisting the most customers. My communication skills and ability to build rapport with people allowed me to foster positive thinking with diverse customers. I won first so often because I connected with clients, many of whom were foreigners and visible minorities who'd be reserved with white staff members. These people sought me out for help because they felt at ease with me and could reveal their lack of comfort with Internet

banking technology without embarrassment. I was thus able to enroll many of them into the system.

This response was a game changer for Peter, who was clearly the decision maker in the room. He shifted in his seat and leaned forward, paying attention to every detail I noted. He understood how valuable I could be for CSIS, which requires intelligence officers to conduct interviews, gather information, and recruit sources who are sometimes visible minorities. His eyes sparkled, and I could see him playing out the possibilities in his mind. "We need different perspectives at CSIS," he said, closing his notebook. With those words, I knew I had the job.

Neither Peter nor I realized that within a couple of months, CSIS's focus and the focus of every other security agency in the world would be on Muslims, a community I'd represent as the sole female Arab Muslim intelligence officer at CSIS for years to come. At the time, no one at CSIS asked me about my religious background nor commented on my values as a Muslim. Such questions and comments weren't appropriate; 9/11 changed that. Years later, after requesting my Human Resources file, I was able to see what the panel thought of me. Here are some quotes:

Ms. Mukbil demonstrated above-average interpersonal skills, communication skills, maturity, inquisitive[ness], adaptability, and culture sensitivity to suggest that she has the potential to become a good Intelligence Officer, we recommend Ms. Mukbil proceed further in the recruitment process. Ms. Mukbil did not display signs of nervousness, she was confident, yet not aggressive or arrogant. She appeared passionate about her feelings and made persuasive arguments.

Because of her background Ms. Mukbil had interacted with people of various social strata and ethnic backgrounds. In her job as a Customer Service representative at the Royal Bank, she deals with people of all backgrounds, especially the underprivileged.

Note: I never said "underprivileged." I said Arab and African diplomats, who are generally wealthy in their countries. I find their interpretation of Arabs and Africans as underprivileged interesting, to say the least.

I spent my summer waiting to hear back from CSIS. At the bank, I was promoted to the VIP section on the second floor where I assisted wealthy customers who paid hundreds for faster and more efficient banking. Given the bank's downtown location and proximity to Parliament Hill, many of my clients were politicians and foreign embassy staff.

By mid-July 2001, CSIS Internal Security, the branch responsible for vetting new recruits and service employees for reliability and loyalty, as pertaining to national security, had completed its field investigation of me, having interviewed my manager at the Royal Bank. I'd provided the names and contact information of three friends from university – Abeer, Nermin, and Jennifer – and they were all also interviewed. By the end of July, CSIS had completed my personal reference check and called me in for an Internal Security interview, a critical step in the selection process that gives Internal Security a chance to meet candidates, ask follow-up questions in preparation for a polygraph exam, and give applicants an opportunity to discuss any concerns they have about joining the service, such as potential conflicts of interest or excessive debts they need to pay.

The Internal Security check is costly and time consuming, so it usually only takes place once a CSIS manager refers a candidate as suitable. Internal Security is the gatekeeper. If it finds that a candidate doesn't meet the service's threshold for reliability and loyalty, the application is dropped. Because each service employee has access to official national secrets, Internal Security's number one priority is to ensure applicants are not affiliated with or directed by a foreign power that could infiltrate CSIS. Once this is established, Internal Security must determine whether anything in an applicant's background precludes them from being loyal to Canada. They screen for ideological and political associations, such as white supremacy, communism, a proclivity to conspiracy theories, and whether the candidate has any weaknesses or character traits that could make them vulnerable to blackmail. These include alcoholism, gambling, indebtedness, overspending, and extramarital romances.

The interviewer, an older white man with grey hair and glasses, escorted me to his office. He seemed fatherly and was pleasant enough but also a little intimidating. After my last interview, I relaxed and looked forward to another positive CSIS interaction. He asked me personal questions about my country of origin, nationality, and political views, including clubs, associations, or protests I attended. I told him that I was a member of the Muslim Student Association at Carleton University and the University of Ottawa and that I volunteered with students to organize Islamic Awareness Month, Ramadan Iftar parties, and student prayer gatherings on Fridays. I also said that I made small regular donations to a Muslim advocacy group. He expressed no support for or objection to any of these statements, saying only that one could freely donate to any Canadian charitable organization and that the university clubs I was a member of were not a security concern. I told the interviewer that I'd participated in two pro-Palestinian demonstrations. When he asked why, I said that in 2000, after Oslo, the Middle East peace process had been declared dead. I felt that the international community should implement a new resolution via the United Nations. When he asked for my opinion on the use of violence for political ends, I told him I was fundamentally against it.

If I shifted in my seat, it was because I felt nervous about my student loan debts. Everyone I met at CSIS looked rich. They drove nice cars, were well dressed, and spoke perfect English or French. When I told the interviewer, he expressed no surprise. He knew my parents had less-than-average income. He commended me for pursuing postsecondary education while working part-time. I began to feel more at ease. He was kind enough to sense my anxiety, so I talked about the skills I'd gained from working, at which point he stopped me. This information wasn't useful for him, since he was assessing my loyalty and reliability, not my skills. I'd become nervous and embarrassed talking about my debt and had lost focus.

Not once did my Internal Security interviewer ask about my religion. He knew I was Muslim but didn't ask whether I prayed or attended a mosque or what my opinion was of the Taliban, Al Qaeda, or any other international terrorist groups. Before 9/11, it wasn't necessary for every Muslim on the planet to publicly condemn the ideology and violent actions of other Muslims in faraway lands. Neither he nor I could've imagined that being Muslim would soon become politicized nor that I'd one day face such contempt and backlash at CSIS both for expressing my religious beliefs and for my eventual decision to wear the *hijab*.

Shortly after the Internal Security interview, I was invited back to take my polygraph. Funny as it sounds, I was excited to take a lie detector test. A slim, friendly-looking, middle-aged blond woman in jeans met with me and guided me into a small, windowless room. I was a little surprised. I'd been expecting a man. Thus far, every decision maker on my file had been a man, and I'd seen far more men representing the organization than women. I was also partly expecting a stereotypical "tough guy" interrogator. Let's say this was quite a distorted image.

"Hi, Ms. Mukbil! I'm Paige. Please come in and have a seat," my interrogator said happily, gesturing to a larger-than-average chair. The room had a desk, a second rotating chair for the polygraph, and a bookshelf with a 1960s-looking radio, which may as well have had a flashing neon sign saying CAMERA INSIDE! I suddenly realized this was the real deal. Not knowing what to expect, I felt uneasy.

Paige began by building rapport, including by telling me about the time she'd visited Egypt. We chatted for a couple minutes then she abruptly changed her tone and asked whether I'd ever lied and, if so, when and why? I was taken aback. I tried to control my reaction and admitted that of course I'd lied, but they were little lies of no relevance. She asked me to recall and report them all. I was puzzled, but I obliged. "Okay, well, last week, my mom gave me a cheque to deposit in her bank account. I didn't deposit it on the same day because I forgot. When I got home, she asked if I'd made the deposit, and I said yes. I deposited the cheque the next morning, and that was that." I told her about a second lie I'd told to one of my university friends who felt a guy she liked didn't like her back. I told her that I thought he liked her, even though I didn't believe it, so I wouldn't hurt her feelings. I explained that sometimes I lied to get myself out of annoying conversations. Paige took notes furiously. It seemed that she was taking these white lies very seriously. I was getting a bit irritated. I have a low tolerance for such ridiculousness, and my faith in what she was doing diminished.

"Are those all the lies you can remember?" she asked. "Yes," I said, thinking there was no way she could believe those were my only lies. Yet, really, I had nothing to hide and fully expected to pass. Paige stopped taking notes and explained how the polygraph test worked; it measured my physiological reactions to each question and the responses I'd give. If I lied, the machine would detect the associated physiological changes. Paige began fastening pieces of equipment onto me: a blood pressure cuff around the upper arm to record my heart rate and blood pressure, two rubber tubes fastened around my chest and abdomen to measure my respiratory patterns, and, finally, two protruding electrodes attached to my fingers to record my sweat gland activity. I was completely strapped in. I wondered whether they'd selected a woman in case I was uncomfortable with a man touching me.

Paige went back to her seat and asked me questions that we'd already reviewed together. I can't reveal what these questions were due to national security considerations and my ethical and legal obligations to protect that information. She didn't give any feedback after my answers and always moved briskly to the next question. After thirty minutes, she told me to stay where I was. She walked out of the room to confer with her supervisor. She'd left with a stern look on her face, which I felt was probably due to the complicated nature of the task. After a few minutes, she returned. "The results are inconclusive. You didn't pass your polygraph test."

"I didn't lie about anything!" I said. I was surprised, concerned, and confused about what this meant. She began taking the polygraph components off me and left the room again. The thought that I might not work for CSIS creeped into my mind, and I started pacing around the room. Paige walked back in. "What are you doing standing? You were to remain seated!" she snapped at me. Her yelling upset me. I told her I was disappointed by the results because I had my heart set on working for CSIS. She threw her hands in the air. "How do you think I feel?"

I was devastated. I'd been hopeful about this job for over eight months. I had no idea what went wrong during the examination. It seemed that I wasn't going to land my dream job after all, and *she* was disappointed? I wanted to tell her off and storm out of the room, but I didn't. I walked out of the building with my hopes, dreams, and aspirations shattered. I was totally confused. I'd never felt worse or so let down. I had no loyalties to any country except Canada. Not once did it cross my mind that I might be considered a counterterrorism risk. I'd never in my life demonstrated support for political violence. *Is it because I interact with embassy staff at the Royal Bank? Is it because I have friends in university from all over the world?* I couldn't figure out why the polygraph was inconclusive.

I went home upset and angry. From the look on my face, Mom knew something was up. I told her that I'd failed the polygraph and that it was unfair because I'd done nothing wrong. I explained that they'd asked questions about foreign national embassies that I'd visited and about my international travels. Of course I'd encountered foreign nationals at work and at the university international clubs. It made no sense.

I tried to convince myself that I didn't want to work for an organization that didn't believe in me. "They don't get it. They don't get me," I repeated to myself, knowing I required time to get over what had happened. I couldn't stop thinking about it. I felt that I'd been unfairly treated. I couldn't get CSIS out of my mind. I felt violated, misunderstood, and sadly hopeless.

Days later, I received a call from CSIS's chief of polygraph services. "Huda, I'm sorry to hear about the results of your first polygraph test. I'm calling to invite you to come in for a second interview," he said.

"I'm really sorry too. But I'm no longer interested," I responded. "I never thought I'd say this, but I felt humiliated, and I'm not sure I want to work for the service anymore," I added.

"Huda, we understand your position. But given how far you've come in the process, I think you owe it to yourself to come in one more time. I'll be conducting the examination myself." He reassured me the questions would be changed to suit my file. I felt better that my feelings and concerns had been acknowledged. I agreed to return for a second test a week later, which I passed without effort. I later learned that the first polygraph examiner was a new trainee, which, to me, explains why she seemed so upset. She likely didn't yet have the skills to detect either a positive result or deceptive outcome which would give her reason to deny the issuance of a security clearance. "Inconclusive" was neither here nor there. But it wasn't just about the new polygraphist, it was more about systemic barriers. My profile was different and the questions and responses I provided were different from other recruits given my racialized background and life experiences. The CSIS chief polygraph examiner recognized this and changed the questions to make them more relevant to my own context.

A month after that polygraph test, in early August 2001, I met with an executive manager at CSIS. This was the last step in the selection process and more of a "welcome aboard" type of meeting. The executive asked me how I felt about the Security Intelligence Review Committee (SIRC) and the Inspector General, CSIS's review bodies. I explained that I found it reassuring that CSIS was subject to oversight and held accountable for its actions by a system of checks and balances. Mistakes happen in every field, and these can help an organization better align with its mandate.

While I waited to hear back, the terrorist attacks of 11 September 2001 were carried out. The tragic murder of innocent New Yorkers shocked and united the world in its condemnation of Al Qaeda and the Taliban-led government in Afghanistan. It was clear that the world had entered a new phase in international relations, intelligence, and security.

After the horrific events of 9/11, I received an official letter from CSIS. I thought I knew what it was, so I was nervous opening it. Inside, I found an employment offer for the intelligence officer position to be signed and mailed back. After eight months of dreaming of joining CSIS as an intelligence officer, I was overcome with joy. I ran and told my parents and my brother, who was still living at home. "I got in!" I screamed at them. Then I called my other siblings who lived on their own. "I got in! I got in! You know, that place I told you about." I didn't forget what Amy had told me at orientation. I had to speak about my work in secrecy and live the part. They congratulated me and acted like they had no doubt that I was going to be selected. They also thought that I was silly trying to hide where I'd be working.

"When do you get your badge?" my brother asked.

"Soon," I told him. "You'll have to help me become an aggressive driver now. I'll be getting a car to go out and investigate."

My brother laughed. "Dream job," he replied.

I considered myself lucky to have been selected. I was honoured and filled with joy and pride. Nothing else in the world seemed to matter on that day. Nothing.

In February 2002, before officially starting, I was asked to come in, sign some documents, and take the Oath of Allegiance. This was a special moment, unlike anything else I'd experienced. I'd found my purpose in life and was committing to it – to the law, to upholding democracy, and to keeping Canada safe. Not only did this moment symbolize my life's purpose, but it also gave me an identity as a Canadian patriot. In front of witnesses on 11 February 2002, I stood tall and proud and repeated after the CSIS officer:

I, Huda Mukbil, do affirm that I will be faithful and bear true allegiance to Her Majesty Queen Elizabeth the Second, Queen of Canada, Her Heirs, and Successors.

I, Huda Mukbil, swear that I will faithfully and impartially to the best of my abilities perform the duties required of me as an employee of the Canadian Security Intelligence Service, so help me God.

I, Huda Mukbil, swear that I will not, without due authority, disclose or make known to any person any information required by me by reason of the duties performed by me on behalf of or under the direction of the Canadian Security Intelligence Service or by reason of any office or employment held by me pursuant to the Canadian Security Intelligence Service Act, so help me God.

As I signed the Oath and the Security of Information Act, I became a designated peace officer and an official representative of the Government of Canada. This was very special.

7 | RAISON D'ÊTRE

To say that my whole life changed on 11 September 2001 would be an understatement. Revisiting that time, as I am now, is always difficult for me. The morning of 9/11, I was in class at 8:30 a.m. and was scheduled to work at the bank at 11 a.m. Eman, at home, had left me voice mails while I was in class. I called her back. She told me that planes had deliberately flown into the World Trade Center buildings and that it was chaos in New York. Possibly all American flights had been cancelled. Training myself to think like a counterterrorism expert in preparation for work with CSIS, I immediately questioned this. *How could commercial flights have been diverted into New York without military planes taking them down?* At the bus stop, I kept looking around, wanting to talk to anyone. When my bus arrived, it would just be a short three stops to the bank, where I could turn on the news.

My mother's friend Reem happened to be on the bus. Reem, an Eritrean Canadian in her late fifties, was wearing a black *abaya*, a long traditional dress from the Middle East, and a black hijab. I didn't notice her at first, but she was calling my name loudly and pulling on my pants. "Huda, Huda, Huda!" In Arabic, she said, "Taalee eglesse gambi" (Come sit beside me). Reem had lived in Saudi Arabia before coming to Canada, and she spoke that Arabic dialect. She held my thighs firmly and made me sit beside her. Her body was rigid, and her serious face commanded that I obey her. I sat. Reem, fearful, scanned the bus. "Did you hear the terrible news?" she asked in Arabic. "Yes, Khala" – the greeting for a maternal aunty in Arabic. Even though we weren't speaking in English, she lowered her voice more and crouched to talk to me. "Many have been killed," she said. Reem was clearly in shock and disbelief. "They're saying that Muslims are responsible for doing this." Her eyes were wide and her pupils dilated. I could tell she felt that other people on the bus were looking at us. I understood neither her concerns nor why she was so emotional. I judged that she was probably oversensitive, like my mom. I gently rubbed her shoulders as I stood. I said "khair, khala, la tkhafi" (It'll be okay, aunty – don't be afraid) and "hakhali mama tetesel feeki" (I'll make sure Mom calls you).

I wasn't thinking of the potential repercussions of the attackers being Muslim. I wanted facts. Maybe because I didn't wear a hijab, no one assumed that I was Muslim or an Arab. As a university student, I must've been sheltered. People at university weren't openly racist or bigoted. I expected Americans and Canadians to be outraged about the attacks and at Al Qaeda but not against North American Muslims, Arabs, or fellow citizens. There'd be backlash, of course – people were angry, and it's easy to become irrational then – but it would be measured and short lived. My old aunty was being paranoid, I thought.

When I got to the bank, which faces Parliament Hill, my colleagues were walking out. One told me that the bank had closed because thousands of clients were calling to move their investments. My colleagues and I walked until we joined a silent crowd that was watching a large television in the food court. The first plane collided with the World Trade Center and then there was smoke, debris, and people running for their lives. Then, minutes later, the second plane crashed into the second tower and people were leaping from windows. There were tears and screams and the shock and sadness on many faces. We listened to the announcement that more attacks had occurred in Pennsylvania and Washington, DC. Many of us held our mouths with both hands. "Oh my God!" people murmured. It all felt sad, shocking, and surreal.

I was trying to analyze what this meant. *What country or group of people would dare invite the wrath of the US military, not to mention the international community? What Muslim Mujahedeen groups* – as the media and CSIS, in my interviews, called them – *could be so evil and suicidal?* Over the next weeks, I watched American and Canadian news and collected national newspapers, carefully considering why the attacks had occurred and what would happen next. I also read and watched the heartbreaking interviews with firefighters, survivors, and relatives of victims.

I wondered how these events would impact CSIS and its counterterrorism investigations. What would my role be? I wondered whether CSIS would call me in to start earlier. *Could I bring value given that I speak Arabic? Should I call?* But I didn't know who to call.

The day after the attacks, I walked into a lecture at the University of Ottawa. The young professor stood patiently at the front of the hall until everyone had settled in. "We are at war," he said sombrely. "Canada is now at war. Our values and our way of life are being threatened by Muslim extremists." His words pierced my heart strangely. *Who's at war with Canada? What and whose values are being threatened?* Did he mean Al Qaeda had attacked the United States in protest of American or Western values or policies, including US military presence and support for authoritarian regimes in the Middle East? Over the next weeks and months, similar statements about values and a clash of civilizations popped up in conversation in the media, on campus, and in private discussions. These comments were divisive and oversimplistic.

President George W. Bush, on 20 September 2001, said, "They hate our freedom of religion, freedom of speech, freedom to vote, and assemble and disagree with each other."[1] Bush had constructed a binary between moderate and terrorist Muslims and another between those siding with "us" and those with "our" enemies. He'd left little room to reject terrorism yet still disagree with United States foreign policy relating to the Middle East.

Ideas about conflicting values were being offered by anti-Islam theorists, like Samuel Huntington, Bernard Lewis, and Daniel Pipes, who blamed Islam for the violent Iranian hostage situation, the Gulf War, Saddam Hussein's acts of madness, and the 1996 terrorist attacks on US embassies in Kenya and Tanzania. They were ideologues who lacked a comprehensive, fair, and accurate analysis of history and politics. But while their views were dangerous, they hadn't had a platform until 9/11. After 9/11, Islam, Muslim practices, Sharia, and the role of Muslim women were all up for debate. I was shocked to hear so-called experts reduce the religion of over a billion people, of Africans, Chinese, Arabs, Turks, Persians, and Chechens, to a singular theology and code of beliefs.

Later that September, as I was walking to class with a few Arab Canadian girlfriends, some wearing hijabs, one of my non-Muslim friends called me over: "Hey, what are you doing with those terrorists?" I smiled uncomfortably. I was puzzled by the accusation, but my anger was boiling. It was the first time that I'd heard anyone refer to people I knew as terrorists.

"Don't say that!" I said. "They aren't terrorists. They're my friends." I tried to remain composed. I didn't want my emotions to get the best of me. "Why would you think they're terrorists?" I asked, trying to understand why she'd generalize. I wanted her to realize that she was being unfair.

"You know Arabs were celebrating when people were dying in New York. That's just not right," she replied.

"My friends were right here in Canada, and they definitely weren't celebrating," I assured her. I was annoyed and defensive. I also needed to get to class on time. My friends were patiently waiting a few metres away, unaware the conversation was about them. They smiled at my friend and signalled that we had to get to class. They began walking slowly so I'd have a chance to catch up. Once they were at a distance, I turned to face the girl. I thought she'd have known better than to accuse my friends. "By the way, I'm Arab and Muslim too, and I don't support terrorists." She looked surprised, and we just nodded and went our separate ways.

I didn't hear a word the professor said. I couldn't stop thinking about what that person had said. *Why would she think that my Arab friends were terrorists?* I also asked myself why I'd felt the need to tell her I was Arab and Muslim. I was bewildered by it all. Later that day, two Muslims were run over by a motorcycle on campus. I didn't believe this until I read about it in the campus newsletter. The same week, there were reports of backlash in the US. The worst was that an American Sikh man, Balbir Singh Sodhi, had been shot dead on 15 September at his gas station in Mesa, Arizona. I was always taught not to take my security for granted. Though I didn't think anyone would identify me as Muslim, I was concerned for my parents, especially my mom, her hijab-wearing friends, and the identifiably Muslim people in my life.

Being Muslim implies having to dress modestly, pray five times a day, and not gossip or attend dance parties. It was a lifestyle that I wasn't good at maintaining. I was a young, adventurous university girl who cared more about looking fashionable, being popular, and attending parties with friends in downtown Ottawa – the clubs, not the alcohol. I enjoyed fancy restaurants for young and energetic crowds. My religiosity only sprung up during Ramadan, when I fasted and was more mindful of my daily prayers. My parents often reminded me that fasting during Ramadan means more than just depriving oneself of food – it's a spiritual journey towards reconnection with God. For me, being Muslim was private and began when I entered my parents' house, where I'd say, "Al Salamu Alaykum," an Islamic greeting, and be reminded of my need to pray. As far back as Egypt, I've never known my father to miss a prayer. He'd annoy my siblings and me by turning the television off and reminding us it was prayer time. I'd be furious, but I knew not to say anything. I'd walk to my room in silence or join him in prayer.

The events of 9/11 racialized being Muslim. Muslims and Muslim-looking people were experiencing racism with the surge of Islamophobia. For the first time, I was being forced to defend my religious identity and to categorize myself as a moderate Muslim opposed to political violence. I learned to publicly articulate my views and defend them: *I'm a Muslim, and I stand against violence, as most Muslims do. I stand against Al Qaeda and other extremist groups.*

I was also an aspiring intelligence officer and had to do more – be informed and fight extremism. It was my career mandate and life mission. For me, fighting terrorism was my moral responsibility and religious duty, as commanded by the Quran. "If anyone saved a life, it would be as if he saved the life of all mankind."[2] I recognized that I felt the need to save lives by fighting terrorism, but what went unrecognized was my deep desire to defend my religious beliefs, ones that were inherently peaceful and that have shaped who I am as a person.

8 | OFFICER IN TRAINING

The police carry guns and badges as symbols of authority and power. Similarly, CSIS officers have their badges, and while we do have firearm training, our most powerful weapon is secrecy in the name of national security. A layer of that secrecy was unveiled to me in the CSIS training program on the first floor of headquarters in the Training and Development branch. It comes baked into an authoritative culture of command and control, white masculine entitlement, and race-coloured glasses, worldviews that were entirely new for a fresh-out-of-school immigrant girl like me. It was unbearable, but CSIS needed me for my unique skills, and I had bought into the fact that, in a post 9/11 world, Muslims had to stand up against terrorism for societal membership. With slight turbulence, we made it work.

The CSIS intelligence officer training program is divided into two parts. The first is the Intelligence Officer Entry Training (IOET), preparing recruits to work as analysts at CSIS headquarters for a couple of years. IOET was seen by us recruits as the time you must put in before passing the Intelligence Officer Investigator Course (IOIC) program to work as an investigator, hitting the streets and searching for terrorists. That was what we all signed up for, and I was particularly interested in becoming a CSIS liaison officer in a foreign country. All recruits are on a five-year probationary period in which they must complete the two courses and work as both an analyst at headquarters and an investigator at a regional office. Traditionally an officer completes the IOET and is immediately enrolled in IOIC with the same group of trainees, but at times, the two courses are taught together. I took the courses separately, the latter in 2005, before my deployment to Toronto Region. The IOET is heavy on the technical skills required to conduct research on service databases, use classified information for analysis, and send messages to CSIS regional offices and partners in government and international security and law enforcement organizations. In contrast, the IOIC is heavy on CSIS investigative tools and methodology. I was to wait another three years to obtain my training in source recruitment, investigative interviewing techniques, cover operations, and basic firearm manoeuvring. Both programs are designed to instill institutional loyalty, secrecy, and excellence.

We were praised time and again for having been chosen and enduring the long, dreadful selection process. We fit the criteria that the department wanted: young enough to mould, highly ambitious, competitive, driven, and reliable, and we had sound judgment and strong leadership skills. But we were warned that if we made poor judgments or demonstrated character faults, we'd be stripped of our titles and out the door.

In September 2002, assigned to an IOET class with twenty others, I was excited to start my career at the spy agency. New recruits in an IOET class continue training with the same class members throughout their time at the organization, so many of the faces I saw on my first day would remain in my orbit throughout my entire CSIS career. The fourteen weeks of in-house, pass-or-fail training were run by four experienced intelligence officer supervisors. Each supervisor reports to the training and development chief, who reports to the director general of the branch, who reports to the assistant director of Human Resources, who reports to the deputy director of operations Jack Hooper, who reports to director Ward Elcock.

I walked into an uncluttered classroom with plain white paint and light brown desks placed in a horseshoe arrangement, an ideal setting to generate discussion and allow centre stage–like space for four supervisors. I scanned the room for the desk with my name tag, and heard a colleague exclaim, "Oh! They're using our middle names." She let out a nervous laugh and sat at her desk. Everyone nodded in realization, found their middle names, and sat down. I didn't know what they'd have used for me – middle names are rare in Muslim countries. My excitement turned to unease. I didn't want to make a bad impression on my first day. Only a couple empty seats remained. I looked at the two names. Claire-Michelle and Abdul Salam. Then the light bulb went off – Abdul Salam is my father's name. *But why would they use my father's name?* "Excuse me," I said, grabbing my name tag on my way to the front. One of the four supervisors looked up. "I think there's been a mistake," I said.

His eyes darted to the name tag, up to my face, and back to the placard. "I'm not sure what you mean," he said slowly. "Did we misspell your middle name?"

"Umm, not exactly." I didn't know whether to point out that Muslims don't have middle names or that *Abdul* Salam is a man's name. I demonstrated a flat smile. "Abdul Salam is my father's name. I don't have a middle name." With these words, I suddenly felt hot and began to sweat beneath my black suit jacket. "May I have a new name tag that says Huda?"

"Sure, Huda, I'll have one prepared at the next break." I distributed another nervous smile across the room.

Human Resources had made a concerted effort to represent different Canadian provinces, genders, and minorities in my specific class. We were twenty intelligence officers – ten men and ten women, including four visible minorities. We were from Ontario, British Columbia, Quebec, Newfoundland, and Alberta. This was the most diverse CSIS class since the service's formation in 1984. The other visible minorities in our class were Kurt, who was Jewish; Jennifer, who was from the Philippines; Suzanne, who was East Asian; and Michael, who was part Jamaican.

Our diverse backgrounds didn't go unnoticed by service managers. They'd often stop, pre-presentation, to comment on our diversity and ask each visible minority whether they spoke a foreign language. "And you – do you speak anything aside from English and French?"

"I speak English, French, Harari, and Arabic," I'd reply. The reaction was always the same – they'd lean forward, raise their eyebrows, and look at me more closely, as if seeing me for the first time. I was worried one manager's eyes would pop out of his skull.

"You speak Arabic? Well, that's a useful language in this new era. I can't think of a branch that wouldn't love you on their desk."

None of the minorities in my class realized that we were making history by diversifying CSIS.

Gender, bilingualism, sexual orientation, and racial diversity at CSIS were reforms pushed by the Security Intelligence Review Committee (SIRC). They called it an attempt at the "civilization" of CSIS, and they were clear on the fact that it was met with resistance internally.[1] When

CSIS was split from the RCMP and created through an act of parliament in 1984, 95 per cent of the members of the RCMP Security Service chose to transfer to CSIS.[2] These officers took part in "para-military training and the parade square discipline of the RCMP, and emphasis on police investigation."[3] In 1988, four years after the SIRC review of CSIS, a lack of commitment to change that is noted as symbolic was CSIS's continued recruitment of former police officers.[4] While the United Kingdom's intelligence community is known to recruit from elite British universities, CSIS history and makeup meant a heavily omnipresent police culture that demands absolute obedience. Even during my training program, former RCMP officers were contractually hired to train new recruits.

As the 1990s rolled on, SIRC credited the organization for its commitment to increase the number of women and francophones within its ranks. It was slow, but progress was being made. In early 1990, women at CSIS represented only 20 per cent of the intelligence officer category, with very few in senior positions.[5] The organization and its predecessor, the RCMP, had a long history of excluding Canadians for their race and sexual orientation. For example, the first Black woman at the RCMP joined in 1982.[6] Canadian LGBTQIA+ community members were denied employment and those who were employed were purged from service in the federal government, including the armed forces and the RCMP, until the 1990s.[7] At CSIS, little if any progress was being made on hiring, promotion, and retention of Indigenous peoples and racialized Canadians: a trend that continued. As late as 1993, the representation of designated groups in the senior management level category was as follows: one member of a visible minority group, and one Indigenous person.[8] When I entered CSIS in 2001, I couldn't spot the one racialized CSIS manager. Leaping forward, a 2014 Canadian Human Rights Commission Employment Audit report found that CSIS had 0 per cent visible minorities in managerial positions. Throughout my career, I was constantly made to feel that my presence was proof of progress, a sign that the organization had come a long way making space for racialized Canadians. I became the evidence by which the organization could conceal institutional racism and, later, Islamophobia.

CSIS has three operational branches: Counter Terrorism, Counter Intelligence, and Counter Proliferation. The Counter Intelligence program seeks to identify and neutralize threats to Canada posed by countries around the world, including security- and intelligence-hostile activities, like spy recruiting from sensitive Canadian governmental departments. Counter Proliferation investigates chemical, biological, and nuclear warfare threats. It monitors threats of rogue countries, like North Korea, Iran, Iraq (at the time), and Syria, that develop and use these weapons and may transfer them to terrorist organizations. Finally, the Counter Terrorism program seeks to prevent acts of terrorism in Canada and against Canada-allied countries. My IOET class, which was conducted during the NATO-led war in Afghanistan a year after 9/11 but still before the looming Iraq War, focused on counterterrorism. Our class case studies highlighted Ramzi Youssef, a man serving a life sentence for his role in the 1993 World Trade Center bombing, and Ahmed Ressam, a man that lived in Montreal, Quebec, who was convicted and charged with planning to bomb the Los Angeles Airport in 2000. In our CSIS data search exercises, analysis, and findings, it was a racialized Muslim that we were trained to investigate. When given examples of how to conduct searches on the bulky computers of the nineties, names used during exercises were, more often than not, Middle Eastern names like Mohammed and Ahmed.

Service presenters also referred to "John Doe" subjects of interest as "Mohammed or Ahmed," radicalized terrorists who were radicalizing others, ready to kill Westerners due to hate. This was deeply offensive, but the militant culture that loomed over made it extremely difficult for me as the only Muslim person in an entire department of training and development to stand up to this racialized logic ingrained, in not-so-subtle ways, within training for IOs. One day, as I was conducting research in CSIS databases, I stumbled on the N-word. I found my voice to speak against anti-Black racism in a way that I was not prepared to speak about anti-Muslim and anti-Arab prejudice. I privately summoned my trainer to request that this be changed. He agreed and said he would look into it.

Many of the presenters would say how useful it was to have an Arabic-speaking intelligence officer on the team. For me, there was nothing to be proud of in this context. I soon hated raising my hand. I felt shame for not speaking up about how ignorant some of the comments were. By raising my hand, I felt complicit and defeated at the same time. I couldn't express these feelings to anyone, not even outside work. No one at my job knew how deeply I loved my religion and culture. At the time, I felt it was important to fit in. I understood that CSIS and other security and intelligence agencies were new at properly articulating these threats. This was the era in which the "war on terrorism" was front and centre in the media and public consciousness. I thought the presenters were well-intentioned for the most part, so I ignored their ignorance. I bore their casually insidious comments as I felt they weren't directed at me or most Muslims who had nothing do with violence. Then, a colleague noticed.

"It must feel great to be so sought after and in demand, Huda," Kurt said over lunch. "Every senior manager in the service is salivating at the thought of having you on their team." Kurt was one of my classmates. We were eating with the other officers in training at the designated recruits' table in the CSIS cafeteria on the first floor. I looked away, not knowing how to feel, and wondering how and why I was the first Arab Muslim intelligence officer in the service. I figured that Kurt could relate – he was Jewish and spoke Russian, a useful language in our line of work. I was used to feeling different, but I was uncomfortable receiving attention for being Muslim. I smiled, trying to own it. "It's great," I fibbed. "I just hope I end up working in Counter Terrorism, where I can really contribute." Kurt was also hoping to work in CT. He was probably the only one in my class who could interpret my feelings and was always attuned and sensitive to how I might perceive comments about being Muslim or Arab.

In IOET, my colleagues and I were told that secrecy would now be an integral part of our lives – we were to be discreet with whom we discussed our employment. We could inform our families but no one else. No one could know what we did, what files we read, where we went, or anything else about our jobs. This protects sources, covert operations, and, thus, people's lives. CSIS and its intelligence officers ask sources to put their lives on the line and to betray dangerous rogue states, nonstate actors, and terrorist groups. Thus, the organization and its officers have a duty to keep sources safe by guarding CSIS methods and operations. If sources and methods are compromised, potential informants won't be confident in CSIS, and CSIS could lose its edge in eliminating threats to national security. This was rightly drilled into us.

Service investigative methods include open-source research, physical surveillance, interviews, human source operations, sensitive signal communications information, and use of reports and analysis from allied foreign intelligence agencies. Sometimes, intrusive methods are used, including residence searches, financial-record analysis, and communications intercepts, all of which require Section 21 warrant powers granted by the federal court of Canada.

Representatives from other security and intelligence branches like the Privy Council, the Communication Security Establishment, Global Affairs Canada, the RCMP, CBSA, and IRCC presented to our class on the relationship between their own organizations and CSIS. We also received self-defence training, including verbal and physical techniques, to be able to successfully confront aggressors. After our self-defence lessons, my classmates and I would grapple with each other on mats. Luckily for me, it was always with another female officer.

Team building is an essential component of the IOET. Class time focused on phasing out individualist thinking. We were repeatedly told that we'd need to rely on one another throughout our service careers and that our classmates would become our most trusted network for questions and problems. My classmates and I spent a lot of time together. Every day for our fourteen weeks of training, we sat at our designated cafeteria lunch table. We swapped personal stories about how we came to join the service and what our aspirations were. Though we each joined for our own reasons, we shared a civic duty and a calling to make a difference. Some were seeking a lifetime of meaningful adventure, like me. One or two thought that the service was a step towards a career in national security policy or politics. Overall, we were a cohesive group, and, true to our supervisors' words, my classmates were the first people I called when applying to competitions or supervisory positions and lateral transfers. I reached out to them when I needed inspiration or to talk to someone from the organization who really knew me.

The IOET, like CSIS as a whole, was counterterrorism-centric. In October 2001, Canada's Anti-Terrorism Act had amended the Criminal Code, the Official Secrets Act, the Canada Evidence Act, and the Proceeds of Crime (Money Laundering) Act, among others, to implement measures for combatting terrorism. The amendments meant several agencies would have roles in counterterrorism, including the RCMP's newly created Integrated National Security Enforcement Teams (INSET), the Financial Transactions and Reports Analysis Centre of Canada (FINTRAC), and Communications Security Establishment (CSE). The threat of terrorism was central to many in-class IOET presentations. The service and its partners were quickly trying to grasp how and why groups like Al Qaeda were targeting America and, possibly, Canada. There was fear that Al Qaeda had sleeper cells in Canada that CSIS hadn't uncovered.

The presenters, mostly middle-aged white men, stressed that Muslim extremists from Saudi Arabia, Egypt, and Pakistan were taking advantage of our free and open society and were ideologically hell-bent on destroying Canadian and Western society. The presenters suggested that these extremist Muslim men could live among us for extended periods, sometimes years, until given instructions to attack. *Muslim* and *terrorist* were often used synonymously without apology, and I'd sink into my chair to be invisible every time. I was offended and upset, but I did my best to be charitable towards the white male speakers with no travel experience outside of North America. Even our so-called senior Middle East expert had never been to a Muslim-majority country. These people had little international exposure to Islam and Muslims and thus failed to understand the religion and its followers. I tried to convince myself that they meant well when not distinguishing between Muslims, fundamentalists, and extremists. I posited that their hearts were in the right place and so I kept my concerns to myself.

In the IOET, my classmates and I learned how to analyze terrorist groups' leadership, members, motivations, and capabilities. As an exercise, we analyzed the Ahmed Ressam case. Ressam, an Algerian, had received terrorist training in Al Qaeda Afghanistan camps and had been living in Montreal before driving to the US to bomb the Los Angeles International Airport on New Year's Eve, 1999. We wrote analytical reports and intelligence products to be disseminated to regional offices or Government of Canada clients and foreign intelligence partners as exercises to be evaluated by our trainers.

One major class assignment involved in-depth research into a terrorist group and a presentation on what impact the group could have in Canada. We were assigned countries randomly.

"Huda, you'll be working on Somalia," Michael told me, handing me a dossier.

"Yes, Michael. You know, Somalia is not far from Ethiopia," I said, smiling. "Would you like me to talk about the Civil War and the failed Western military, including Canadian intervention?"

Michael paused. I could tell that he didn't know what I was talking about. Then he picked up the dossier. "I think we're going to reassign you," he said. Later that day, I was informed that I'd be switching countries with my classmate Keith. He'd be working on the Somali Civil War presentation, and I'd be presenting on the Irish Republic Army. Keith approached me after class. "I don't know the first thing about Somalia," he confessed with a slight smile. "Can you help me?" He wasn't the only one – a handful of intelligence officers, also assigned Middle Eastern countries, came to me for advice on how to approach their projects.

I was unfamiliar with the Irish Republic Army, so I hit the Research Centre and checked out several books on the conflict. I was just as uncomfortable with my subject matter as others were with Middle East conflicts. Following my thirty-minute presentation was a question-and-answer period. "What kind of role do you think religion played in the movement?" Michael asked.

"It definitely played a role," I replied, "but I view the whole movement together – political power struggles, economics, and religion. Just as power vacuums will impact the number of terror attacks in a country, so will religion. They're all equal factors in my eyes." As I answered, I realized that I wasn't exactly sure which conflict I was talking about. By that time, Islam and Muslims were being blamed, as both a religion and a race, in media and popular culture. Little weight was put on history, power, culture, and corruptions. I began to sweat. I wondered whether he was trying to put me on the spot.

My class of twenty recruits was broken into four groups, each overseen by a supervisor assigned to examine and evaluate us. Every recruit had to demonstrate interest and retain information from hours-long lectures on different branches within CSIS, their roles, and major cases. Our behaviour and interactions were closely scrutinized every day, as was our dress – semi-casual business. A few recruits were reprimanded for sneaking out non-classified documents to study at home. We were constantly reminded to be careful. There was an incident in 2000, when a briefcase with top-secret documents had been stolen from a service officer's car outside the Air Canada Centre in Toronto while she was at a hockey game. The briefcase and classified documents were found in a dumpster, and the employee was fired. The incident was reported in the media as one of the most serious internal security breaches in CSIS's fifteen-year history. It was best to stay late if we wanted to study, the trainers said.

I took the course seriously, presented myself at 8:30 a.m. every morning, and only went home once dismissed. I got along well with all my instructors and colleagues. My supervisor, Michael, was reserved and thoughtful and took time to explain service policies and procedures but didn't micromanage or try to find fault with us, which other instructors apparently did with their students. I was told that some instructors added undue pressure to trigger stress-related emotional reactions as a means of determining if students would still act with good judgment. I guess I lucked out. Regardless, all supervisors were professional and had a wealth of exciting stories to share that always kept us intrigued. For fourteen weeks, I didn't miss an hour of class and completed every task to the best of my ability.

The IOET course reinforced that intelligence officers are at the core of CSIS. We analyzed cases, ran investigations, and communicated with senior management who were mostly former RCMP or military. Our supervisors stressed that the chain of command was integral to the culture. All communication, recommendations, and ideas were to be shared only with direct supervisors, and it was up to them to move the information up the line. As newbies, we didn't know everything and didn't need to know everything. Supervisors knew larger concerns and weren't to be questioned. Information was provided on a need-to-know basis. Curiosity was one thing but questioning and being *too* curious were unacceptable. Nosy intelligence officers could find themselves under scrutiny by Internal Security. Worse, they could get fired for attempting to breach policy or protocol.

In our final training phase, my class was divided randomly into groups. Each group was assigned to a different regional office in Canada – Montreal, Toronto, Vancouver, the Prairies, etc. I was selected to go to Vancouver. *Great!* I'd heard many positive things about the West Coast but hadn't been there. My excitement didn't last long. Hours later, Michael told me that I'd be going elsewhere. "One of the IOs has a family emergency in Vancouver," he told me in private. "We've decided to accommodate her request to go to British Columbia, and we're going to swap the two of you. You're going to Montreal instead."

That's fine, I thought. *Montreal is a great city, and the regional headquarters is right downtown. It'll be fun.*

Some of my group's members drove. Others, like me, took the train. Lindsay was in my group. As soon as we arrived in Montreal, we were inseparable. Other members arrived with their partners, but we were both single and open to adventure. We shared many stories – her about Vancouver, her home city, and her travels in Japan teaching English and me about the Middle East. She was curious about Egypt. I was in awe that she'd travelled alone as a young adult, immersing herself in a different culture. I hadn't done anything like that. We talked about politics, especially about George W. Bush's controversial election in 2001 – she was a big fan of Al Gore and was disappointed when he lost. We compared trainers and talked about our experiences with CSIS. I really liked her. She had a positive, kind demeanour and was always laughing, showing off her slightly crooked teeth. Her laugh was mesmerizing.

We were in Montreal for a week to work one-on-one with real intelligence officers, helping them complete surveillance and investigative assignments. My intelligence officer, George, was a tall, good-looking man who didn't smile and seemed born to wear a suit. He had a list of people who he'd identified for interviews. Our suits seemed like a flashing neon sign announcing that we were government workers, but I wanted to make a good impression on George, so I wore mine. We spoke with an Arab man with possible information on Hezbollah threats. When we entered his business, his phone rang, and he answered in Arabic and a Lebanese dialect: "I don't need your help. I can handle these government people." Someone had seen us enter the shop and warned his friend that perhaps we were spies or tax collectors. I kept my poker face. Looking out the window, I determined that the caller was likely the owner of the grocery store facing the shop.

"We're with the Canadian Security Intelligence Service," George said formally when the shopkeeper hung up. "We're seeking your assistance." George stressed confidentiality and explained the CSIS mandate. I felt important as George flashed his badge. It was the first time that I felt the power of an intelligence officer and the response to it. I hadn't received my badge yet, since I still had to pass the course.

The shopkeeper, taken aback by the badge and our dark suits, was uncooperative with George's questions in English. It pained me to see

George, a Francophone, and the owner using English, a language neither spoke well. I jumped in with Arabic to see what would happen.

I first had to disarm the shopkeeper. Per my training, I understood that rapport-building is key to acquiring useful information. In perfect Arabic, I said "Marbaha, Ana Huda, Iza badak neehkii Araby, ana bahki Arabi. Ana wa zameli George, andeena bad al asela, wa natamana musa3detak," which translates as, "Hello, my name is Huda. If you prefer, we can speak in Arabic. My colleague and I have some routine questions and would like to speak with you today."

George and the shop owner looked at me with excitement. A ten-minute conversation ensued about where I was from and how the shopkeeper and I, as Arabs and Muslims, were both loyal and appreciative of Canada, the greatest country on Earth. "Taban, taban" (Of course, of course), we agreed. George waited for my translation. I told him, in English, that the shopkeeper was eager to help Canada and CSIS. Smiling, the shopkeeper appreciated my inclusive language, which had provoked his civic duty and, thus, his cooperation. He answered all our questions.

As soon as we exited the shop, I asked George whether we could enter the grocery store across the street. He and I walked in and bought olive oil for George, who now wanted to show me his appreciation for multiculturalism in Canada. The owner, who I suspected had called the shopkeeper, was attentive and excited as he spoke with us. "Come to Montreal and work here," George said, repeatedly. We'd both clearly enjoyed working together.

My four classmates and I were staying in a hotel in downtown Montreal. Each day after work, we met in the lobby to explore the city centre. I spent most of my free time with Lindsay. We were different. I was still a little shy and hated attracting attention from large groups. Lindsay didn't try to generate attention either but was confident enough that she didn't care if she did. We went shopping on Saint Catherine Street together and bought new clothes, excited about having this most amazing career before us.

On our last day in the Montreal office, all five of us met the director general of the Quebec region, Luc Portelance. He sat at the head of a table, with me on his left leaning in. He asked us about our experiences in the region – everyone told fascinating stories – and what we thought were the challenges in our line of work. I questioned Mr Portelance about the value of using intercepts when subjects of investigations already suspect it and the cost associated. "Music to my ears," he said. "Our line of work is contingent on the number and quality of the human sources we recruit. They're our bread and butter."

That night, my group and I agreed to get drinks and a late dinner and take a walk downtown. It was Ramadan, the holy month of the Islamic lunar calendar when observing Muslims fast from dawn to dusk. Muslims fast by abstaining from food, drinks, sex, and vulgar thoughts and language. During this month, Muslims are also encouraged to give more to charity, have family gatherings, pray at mosques, and perform kind deeds for all. These acts redirect one from ego-feeding, worldly activities. A hungry stomach cleanses the body and soul, enabling empathy for those in poverty. I was starving. Lindsay asked to join me for dinner in the Marriott restaurant before our outing. I couldn't wait. We laughed and talked about the week and our first experiences in the field. As I recounted my outing with George while digging into my dinner, I realized something didn't taste right – the meat had a texture I wasn't used to. I spat it into a napkin and looked at the sandwich. The meat was white and grey. I called the waiter. "Excuse me," I said to him. "Something doesn't taste right with the chicken. Is there any other kind of meat in the sandwich?"

"Well, yes, madame. The meat patty is made of chicken and pork. Is something wrong?"

"There's pork in here?" I asked incredulously, mostly angry at myself for not realizing. I was so hungry that I hadn't even bothered to carefully read the ingredients.

"Why, yes, madame. It's in the fine print on the menu."

I looked at the menu. He was right.

"I'm sorry I got upset," I said. "I can't eat pork. Could you please just bring me the bill?"

As the waiter went to print my bill, Lindsay looked at me sternly. "You can't let them get away with this. You need to eat. I'm not going to let you go hungry. You haven't eaten all day."

I shrugged. "There's nothing I can do. I should've paid attention. It was written on the menu. I thought I was safe with chicken, but I didn't keep reading."

"It doesn't matter," Lindsay said in a low voice. She shifted to face the waiter as he came back with our bills. "I'm sorry," she said in a louder tone, staring defiantly up at him, "but my friend isn't going to pay for this meal unless you can get her a real chicken sandwich."

"Madame, I'd, of course, like to oblige your friend, but the patties are made with pork. It is listed on the menu right there. There's nothing I can do."

"You mean to tell me that in this fancy hotel, you don't have *any* chicken unmixed with pork? My friend hasn't eaten all day, and you're going to turn her away hungry without a replacement meal? She can't eat unless she breaks with her religion?" The waiter paused. Lindsay sensed his weakness and went for the kill. "Perhaps you should go back to your chef and see what he can do." It wasn't a question.

"Yes, madame. Of course."

Within a few minutes, I had a fresh chicken sandwich in front of me and a new plate of fries that Lindsay and I triumphantly shared. I then took Lindsay to a shisha bar. We giggled and blew smoke rings on the patio. We talked nonsense for hours before meeting the other intelligence officers. Then we went to a club and danced until the venue shut down.

By the end of training, I was beginning to see myself as a service employee. I started using *we* in reference to intelligence officers. This new exhilarating world was mine to conquer. In class, we learned that threats were everywhere – some real and others perceived. We were now privy to information that the public would never know, including threats that might have materialized had they not been disrupted or passed on to the RCMP for potential prosecution. We couldn't discuss details, interesting twists, achievements, or failures with anyone outside our core group, even with other service employees. We could request warrants to violate a person's privacy, if needed, for the sake of national security. There was a special unit that did breaking-and-enterings, and we could be included in those operations, if approved. *How cool is this?* The privilege and sexiness of it all was overwhelming. It was hard to believe that it was real.

There was a departmental tug of war for where I'd end up. Research Analysis and Production, CSIS's strategic analysis branch, wanted to understand global terrorism threats against Canada. Counter Terrorism and Counter Proliferation were ramping up on a possible Iraq war, looking for weapons of mass destruction and at the possibility of Canadians travelling to Iraq to fight alongside US forces. Every department wanted an Arabic speaker. Peter, chief of Research Assessment and the person who'd interviewed and hired me, felt entitled to me – he told me so. I felt powerful knowing that I'd end up there. I teased my trainer by telling him that, unlike my colleagues, I knew exactly which branch I'd be joining.

"Don't be so sure," he replied with a smile.

At the end of training, each intelligence officer received an envelope indicating the department that they'd join. Even though I thought I knew my result, I was nervous when my supervisor handed me mine. Instead of reading Research Assessment and Reports, I found *Counter Terrorism, Sunni Islamic Extremism, Middle East, supervisor Richard Laskey.*

This was amazing. I was excited, happy, and relieved to have not ended up in Research Assessment doing analysis, despite Peter's confidence in me. I was going to work in the service's most active investigations unit where stakes were high. I could make a difference there. Counter Terrorism was what I understood best and where I could contribute most effectively. I could make a name for myself there as a counterterrorism specialist. I convinced myself that I could endure occasional comments about Muslims and Islam so long as I could advance investigations, disrupt terrorist plans, and make an impact. Maybe I could even educate my colleagues on Islam along the way.

It was late Friday afternoon, so I sent Richard an email letting him know that I'd been assigned to work under his supervision and that I'd be in the office on Monday at 8:30 a.m. Richard, who didn't know me, replied in seconds, informing me how excited he was to have me on his team. Finally, after more than a year and a half trying to make it, I'd be working as an intelligence officer on the Counter Terrorism Middle East desk.

9 | SUNNI ISLAMIC EXTREMISM

In December 2002, I began my career on the Counter Terrorism Sunni Islamic Extremism Middle East desk, which directed the core national and international Al Qaeda–linked investigations. It was the service's central nerve, garnishing the attention of deputy director of operations Jack Hooper and director Ward Elcock as well as senior national security officials in the government of Canada and international partners like the CIA and FBI. Being on this desk gave me rich exposure to key service personalities, culture, and direct and intimate knowledge about CSIS investigations.

On my first day, Marshall, the chief of Counter Terrorism, walked into the large, windowless office that I shared with two male intelligence officers. Richard, my new supervisor, was also there. Marshall was a tall grandfatherly figure with a timeworn face and the commanding voice that you'd expect from a former RCMP officer. He was the service's only Arabist, meaning he specialized in Arab history, culture, and language. He greeted my colleagues by mixing up their names while locking eyes on me. As if he'd waited all weekend to do so, he walked up to my desk and said, "*Marabah*, Huda." His Arabic pronunciation of my name and the Arabic word for *hello* were perfect and impressive.

"*Marabah*," I replied with a smile. "You speak Arabic?"

"Some. I picked up a bit while posted to the Middle East a few years back. You've arrived at a great time, Huda."

I sensed that he enjoyed saying my name and I enjoyed hearing it pronounced correctly by someone at work. I didn't show it, but the fact that I was a Sunni Muslim working against Sunni Islamic extremism wasn't lost on me. The desk name could've been less generalizing and offensive, but I was new and wanted to be accepted, so I didn't complain. Marshall's reception quickly dissolved my anxiety for being both the new girl and the youngest officer on the desk.

"There's a meeting later today with the CT director general and the deputy director to update them on the development of our cases," he said. "The deputy chief is going to attend as well. I want you to be there. You'll get to meet everyone all at once." Marshall spoke with a reassuring smile. I didn't convey any emotion but inside I was jumping at the thought of participating and hopefully contributing to such a high-level meeting.

When I walked into the meeting, I was the only woman, minority, and Muslim in the room. Marshall said, "We have many exciting projects for you to work on. One involves the training camps in Afghanistan. I heard Jack is going to be your mentor. He's been on the desk for two years, very knowledgeable. So, you'll have him and Jeff to guide you through it all." I could sense his excitement at having me on board.

My officemates' excitement was palpable. They'd heard much about me via "Ruminet," a term for in-house rumours – part of office culture and a product of a hierarchical, military-like workplace where managerial decision making lacked transparency. No success or mistake went unnoticed in CSIS's highly competitive environment, where ambitious people competed for recognition. My colleagues, all men, asked me many questions about growing up in Cairo, partly because our desk covered Egypt, Saudi Arabia, Yemen, and Jordan, and Canadians linked to threats in these countries. I told them what it was like growing up under military rule and emergency laws following Sadat's assassination. I explained that I was born in Ethiopia but never spoke about why and how we left. I also didn't tell many at CSIS that I held Yemeni citizenship. I didn't want to be associated with Osama Bin Laden's country of origin – being the only Muslim was hard enough. Their questions about Arabic pronunciation, customs, and traditional values were easier to answer, but what motivates a suicide bomber, that I couldn't say without critically examining American foreign policy. That kind of reflection wasn't welcomed at CSIS; I knew that much before I got on the desk. So, I thought that given that my colleagues had been working the desk longer, I wanted to learn what they had to say from *them*.

I began reading the investigative files attentively. *Why would anyone want to kill themselves and others? Why would killing Westerners be a goal? How did Islam become a driving force for those people?* In my first months as an analyst intelligence officer, I learned much about our national counterterrorism investigations through incoming reports from the regional Toronto, Ottawa, Atlantic, British Columbia, and Prairie offices. My role was to assesses the reports from Toronto Region and prioritize which files required urgent attention and further action. Regional offices sometimes needed headquarters to seek information from international partners. In such cases, I'd draft requests to those partners, like the CIA or FBI, then report to my supervisor for approval. At times, I'd ask regional offices to follow up on these requests. In our exchanges, I learned about subjects of investigations, thresholds for becoming a counterterrorism investigation target, investigative tools, and how to determine appropriate usage of these tools.

To keep abreast of international counterterrorism trends, I read American and British classified intelligence reports on terrorist groups in Afghanistan, Pakistan, and the Middle East. Every security agency in the world, including CSIS, was focused on Al Qaeda, its history, its guest houses for foreign fighters, and its training camps in Algeria, Egypt, Yemen, etc. Al Qaeda fighters woke at dawn, prayed together, read the Quran, ate together, and trained together. They used Qur'anic interpretations and hadith to justify their violent acts. I read reports derived from US interrogation of detainees, including interrogations of Abu Zubayda, mistaken as a leading Al Qaeda operative. It was later determined that the CIA tortured Zubayda, including through waterboarding. I learned of the CIA's torture program, or "enhanced interrogation techniques," but not in clear terms at the time. I sensed that my managers knew more than they were telling me and that their conversations about the CIA were more guarded around me as time progressed, especially after 2004. I wholeheartedly believed that neither the American government nor the CIA would ever torture or be involved in forced renditions and proxy torture. I was wrong.

At my desk, I listened to recordings of Al Qaeda leaders – the tapes must have been found in the Arab guest house in Afghanistan. In the tapes, Al Qaeda encouraged followers to see soldiers and guards as collateral damage for having protected unjust rulers like Hosni Mubarak, who'd jailed many Egyptian Islamist violent extremists. I read extremist texts and learned how they differ from popular interpretations. To become a counterterrorism expert, I also felt that I needed to understand the nuances between fundamentalists, Salafi Jihadis, and takfiris. Viewing my religion through extremist lenses was painful. I endured sleepless nights, during which I analyzed how historical references could be interpreted to support political violence.

I wanted to understand the rage that drove both educated and uneducated young men to these movements. What deep political struggles in Muslim-dominant countries were being used to justify violence and to motivate followers to join extremist movements? War? Resource exploitation? Corruption? Historic grievances? For extremists, the world is black and white, wrong and right. You're either with them and will fight the evil colonial imperialist enemy (i.e., the West) alongside them, or you're against them, which I clearly was. If an extremist captured me, they'd slit my throat for being a Western woman working against them.

My confidence grew as I gained expertise in Muslim extremist theology and Al Qaeda. No other intelligence officer in Counter Terrorism could pronounce Arabic names or instantly recall the titles of cities, towns, and refugee camps. Most importantly, I didn't mix up the names of our subjects of investigation. Counter Terrorism intelligence officers and service managers were soon well aware that I spoke Arabic, but I could also precisely articulate extremist views with analysis and without exaggeration. With my interpersonal skills and team spirit, I was approachable, respected, and well-liked.

I was making real contributions to national and international security, and my skills were valued. My team included my immediate deskmate and mentor Jack, who always arrived at the office first. He'd greet me with a warm smile and wait until I was settled at my desk. We'd then discuss developments on our files. Jack was waiting to be posted to the Prairie Region. Married with young children, Jack had a calm demeanour and wasn't pretentious like others in the office. He was a man of faith – a Mormon Christian. By nine in the morning, Victor would come in with his girlfriend, who was also an intelligence officer. The two lovebirds had met in training and become inseparable. If Jack wasn't around, Victor would answer my questions. I sometimes rotated whom I distributed my problems to.

Another colleague, Tim, was Irish Catholic. He said that he could relate to the world views of some CSIS targets, especially their views of patriarchy and traditions. Tim didn't socialize much. He was focused and a great writer. I enjoyed reading his messages and analytical reports, and I imitated his writing style and even signed off with "Cheers," the way he often did. Jack and Victor made fun of me for doing so, but that's how I'd learned French and English during my youth – imitation is a form of learning for me. I speak many languages, but I never felt exceptional in any of them.

I adored Simon, a senior investigator and experienced analyst from Newfoundland who'd worked in Calgary for some time. Management respected him. He never dressed in suits, like junior intelligence officers did. He wore casual clothes and even jeans. He'd come in late, stay late, or leave early. No one seemed to care or time him. For lunch, he'd bring a half roast chicken from the grocery shop across the street. I believe that he swallowed it whole in his office. He was waiting for an international posting. Simon would walk into our bullpen, sit back on a chair, and give us his perspective on issues, revealing our ignorance in the process. "Who can name the president of Mexico? Why don't Canadians know that?" He'd name the president and then criticize US politics, unlike anyone else at the service. He had family in the US and therefore felt entitled to do so openly without anyone questioning his love for America or his loyalty to Canada. If I saw Simon in our bullpen, I'd rush in to hear whatever he had to say. He made everything enjoyable. His sarcasm and big-picture views put things in perspective for me. Whenever I was with Simon, I knew that I was about to be schooled, and I enjoyed it.

I socialized with everyone in the branch, including administrators and managers of other Sunni Islamic extremist desks divided geographically, for example Levant, Maghreb, East and South Asian countries. Counter Terrorism's chief administrator Lillian and I liked each other and often exchanged jokes. Alex, another new officer hired a few months after me, was one of the first openly gay men in the service. He often hung out in our office. He was always authentic, outspoken, and articulate. He seemed to fit into CSIS's old boys' club and was popular among young and new intelligence officers alike. He spoke of the generational divide between us and senior management, who seemed more conservative and traditional. I concurred with him but was never loud about it. Alex wasn't on my desk. He worked on the Sunni Islamic Extremism South-East Asia desk, along with two other new intelligence officers, Julia and Rebecca, who'd visit our bullpen often and chat about their challenging cases. I always looked forward to seeing them.

Rebecca's supervisor, Larry, had mentoring tendencies and wondered what we new intelligence officers talked about. One day, he walked in while we were sitting around. "Huda, I saw the message you sent to the CIA yesterday. Do you know the difference between information and intelligence? Because you got it wrong. Information is information. Intelligence is when you have information from sources that's been assessed and made into an assessment. I'm sharing this because we all make mistakes like this at the beginning, but now you all know. It irritates me when intelligence officers do this, and some senior ones still do it, too." He added the last part to make me, or us, feel better.

My supervisor, Richard, had an office across from ours. Richard was chatty and often told interesting stories. His lively, inviting laughter could be heard miles away. Richard was as dedicated and professional as a supervisor could be. He came in at six and left by six, without ever asking for overtime or taking a proper lunch. He was always on task, approving messages, allocating duties fairly, and communicating his ideas about expectations from senior management. Richard looked up to Marshall. He wanted to become an expert in counterterrorism. He and Marshall both kept me close. Richard was sometimes curious about what Marshall and I discussed.

Richard let other Counter Terrorism branches know about my expertise. Colleagues from Security Screening, Counter Proliferation, and Strategic Assessment and Production would knock on our door with questions about their files – investigation targets, sources, incoming delegations from Arab countries, Muslim practices, and translations of expressions used by subjects of interest. The list of questions directed my way was long and grew daily: "Do Sunnis and Shia pray at the same mosque?" "What are the distinguishing factors between the two denominations?" "What is the ideology and role of groups like the Muslim Brotherhood?" "What about Hizb Al Tahrir – how are they different from

Muhajiroon?" "What does it mean when a Muslim writes their will?" "If a target writes his will, does it mean he's about to martyr himself?" "When should the will be flagged?" "Can Muslims hunt animals as sport?" "Why do some Muslim men wear their pants short?" "What is *Sunnah*? "What is *hadith*?" "The *hawala* system?" "*Fitna* and *taqiyya*?" "Can someone conduct the *hajj* more than once, or do you think it could be a cover for meetings, as it was during the Afghan war against the Russians?" "Can you distinguish between Arabic and Farsi?" "Could you look at this information I received in Arabic via warrant powers and indicate what needs to be sent for translation?"

In our meetings with officials and representatives from other parts of the Canadian security apparatus – all relatively new to counterterrorism, having received their mandates after 9/11 – my manager would defer to me about the motivations of targets or subjects of interest. I provided unique insights about why someone might be attracted to extremist radical ideology. Over time, colleagues clearly saw me as an expert, and I began to fully inhabit the role.

My first time visiting the US embassy for a downtown meeting with the legendary FBI was exciting. The FBI officer was Black; my first interaction with a racialized security official. He was amicable and a little flirtatious with me, but I didn't mind getting such flattering attention. We also met with intelligence officials from a number of countries including a delegation from Russia at CSIS headquarters. Marshall and I were much more guarded about what we shared with the Russians. We spoke about Al Qaeda and that we were seeking Russian information on Afghanistan. At the end of the meeting, one of the Russian delegates said, "Canada is a great country and accepts people from all over, but you shouldn't accept immigrants from Muslim countries. They multiply like rabbits." Marshall winked at me. I smiled to show I wasn't bothered – it was the Russians, after all. Besides, Marshall looked horrified enough for the both of us. He quickly commented, "Yes, Canada is a great country. It has a rigorous screening process that allows the best and brightest to immigrate here."

Richard once sent me to represent the service at a weeklong conference hosted by the Department of National Defence. I was to take notes and participate in seminar discussions on international counterterrorism threats with Canadian security officials including the Privy Council and American intelligence agencies like the Defence Intelligence Agency (DIA). On the first day, a general, whom I recognized from headquarters, greeted me on the elevator. I wondered why he was looking at me. He seemed to like me and asked where I was from, telling me then of his travels in Muslim countries. During the conference, he barged into the room, interrupting a myriad of conversations, specifically to offer me his office in case I wanted to pray. I felt incredibly uncomfortable about the whole ordeal. Later, he asked that I accompany him to Starbucks. I did. He was a director and knew my chief and supervisor, so I felt obligated. I thought he might want to ask me questions related to counterterrorism. After an hour, he revealed that he wanted me to come to his place, nearby. He commented on my almond-shaped eyes. To be respectful, I told him that I was in a serious relationship. He surprised me and said, "I don't mind you being in another relationship." He continued his flirtation. For weeks, he'd call my office. Whenever he had a meeting with my chief, he'd come talk to me. He made my skin crawl, yet I accepted it as one of the things women just have to deal with at work. I reported his persistent interest in me to Internal Security and they advised that I should just continue to show lack of interest towards his advances. Eventually, he just stopped calling, but the whole situation still makes me shiver when I think about it, even two decades later.

Reading top-secret intelligence assessments and reports was fascinating. I enjoyed the human element – the chance to peek into human psychology. What makes people betray their countries, friends, and families to work as double agents or sources? What are their personal stories and history? Intelligence work is like a puzzle; once you start, you desperately want to complete it. I was addicted to the work and life of counterterrorism. No lunch date could pull me out of the office. With massive raw data pouring in from the Americans, there was always work to be done. Richard said that being an intelligence officer gets into your blood. It was in mine. I liked being in demand and relevant and having sought-after knowledge and expertise for the post-9/11 world. Everyone wanted answers and was consumed with preventing another terrorist attack. I had a mission: I was helping to save lives. At the time, not having been exposed to source operations, I had high trust in my managers and in the information I was reading on the service database.

When I visited my old classmates in Counter Intelligence or Security Screening, they told me that they felt sorry for us in Counter Terrorism. They'd heard that we faced a daily tsunami of emails and intelligence reports from foreign agencies, had to follow up on numerous threats, and had management breathing down our necks for updates on every file. Counter Terrorism was, then, the first and only branch I'd worked in, so I thought that my reality was the same as any other intelligence officer's. Clearly, this wasn't true. I was proud to learn this. It reaffirmed that I was at the forefront of CSIS operations, a great honour and privilege.

In response to requests from Alex, Julia, and Rebecca, I launched, in my second year, a lunchtime series of presentations on Islam to educate colleagues and dispel misinformation about my religion. I wanted to bring in expert speakers, so I wrote to management for permission. Management approved the course but instructed me to run it myself. They didn't want new intelligence officers "exposed" to anyone outside the service whom they'd have to screen for security reasons. I agreed and concluded that I should've thought of that. For ten weeks, I taught fifteen Counter Terrorism intelligence officers about Islam and Muslim culture. I used John Esposito's books and other highly regarded Islam scholars to build my presentations. I created slideshows of Islamic art, culture, diversity, and calligraphy. The presentations were well received, and question-and-answer sessions generated good discussion. People felt comfortable asking questions about all aspects of Islam, political expressions in the Middle East, family dynamics in Middle Eastern or Muslim households, and investigations subjects. Marshall walked in during one presentation. He was the chief, so everyone sat up straight. He sat to the side smiling and later thanked me privately: "Maybe one day, you'll run a Counter Terrorism desk." I appreciated that he saw leadership in me. I was still too shy and humble to view myself in that light. When the courses were done, my beautiful colleagues gave me gifts and cards to thank me for my efforts, which I hadn't expected. I was genuinely touched when intelligence officers, thereafter, continued to seek my perspective on things.

I was more than disappointed when, in 2003, the Bush administration, including Dick Cheney, Donald Rumsfeld, and Condoleezza Rice, ordered the invasion of Iraq. Bush asserted that Saddam Hussein supported terrorism and possessed weapons of mass destruction. His administration had also established its Guantanamo Bay prison camps in Cuba and was publicly defending torture and rendition, which is torture by proxy. They were eroding American and international human rights and the Geneva Convention and using the War on Terror as pretext to invade Iraq. On 15 February 2003, millions of people protested in marches and rallies in nearly 800 cities around the world – the largest protest in human history. London saw perhaps the largest demonstration, with up to one million protesters in Hyde Park.

I'll never forget the day – 20 March 2003 – that America bombarded Baghdad. While at work, I learned from Bush's announcement that the war was to commence that evening. I expressed disbelief to colleagues. At home, I felt anxious, angry, and helpless to control world politics. When I was little, I'd shout to my sisters, "I'm going to take over the world." In my work at the service, I tried to combat extremism, but suddenly I couldn't eat, drink, or do anything but wait for the televised mass murder. My parents and I gathered around our television, switching between Al Jazeera, CNN, the BBC, and the CBC. We listened as Bush announced the war's commencement. The screen filled with images of the airstrikes, the so-called Shock and Awe campaign, bombing Baghdad and its innocent citizens indiscriminately. I thought it madness that the world was watching these scenes unfold on television. Iraq, a once great country, had been a leader in the Arab world in terms of education, medical technology, and women's rights. All of that was being destroyed. Why did an entire nation and its people have to pay such a hefty price for such a flimsy pretext?

I cried. I sat on my parents' Persian carpets, which they'd imported from Saudi Arabia. I wept. Mom came close to tears. "I'm sorry," she repeated. "What are we to do?" Tears fell down my father's face. He was silent and in shock. We stopped switching channels. Only Al Jazeera broadcasters could express what we were feeling. I lost my innocence about the world that night and felt insignificant. The bombing was as horrific as 9/11, but unlike 9/11, when people all over the world mourned for the dead Americans, hundreds of millions of people weren't mourning Baghdad's dead innocents. I thought that every American and Brit should have to condemn their country's indiscriminate killing, just like every Muslim had to condemn Al Qaeda's murderous attacks.

I felt a little better when Canadian prime minister Jean Chrétien refused to join the American-led war. Dad also continuously praised the prime minister's decision. This was so important to me and if I'd seen the prime minister in person, I would've hugged him for his independent decision making and leadership. At least my government and country had a sound moral compass. I was proud Canada made its decisions independently of the US.

At CSIS, however, Canada's decision not to go to war set off alarm bells. There was real panic about the backlash the service could face in terms of cross-agency cooperation and information sharing. I quickly became uneasy about sharing my feelings openly with anyone. No one I interacted with at CSIS was as vehemently opposed to the war as I was. If they were, they were self-disciplined enough not to show it. We as officers were to remain politically neutral. I kept my thoughts and feelings to myself, masking my emotions. As an intelligence officer, I thought that I needed to be in command of myself. Although I'd been with CSIS for almost two years, I still didn't properly appreciate how the culture frowned upon open criticism of US policy. The US had one of the biggest, best funded, and, in many ways, most technologically sophisticated intelligence agencies in the world. CSIS worked closely with the CIA and had piggybacked on its many years of global intelligence. Openly opposing the invasion just wasn't done and would be seen as biting the hand that fed us. I couldn't come to terms with such silencing and indifference, but I couldn't do anything about it either.

Gradually, I began to see that the US was using the "war on terror" as a pretext for political objectives, a betrayal of its mission to eradicate terrorism. I felt that the US had occupied the moral high ground when it invaded Afghanistan and then ousted the Taliban regime, which had permitted Al Qaeda to train and operate within its borders. I was onside with the American struggle against communism. I supported its attempts to broker a peace deal in the Middle East. And of course, I stood with America after 9/11 in fighting terrorism. To me, all this was largely black and white. The flimsy justification for a war against Iraq changed my perspective. In my view, the US surrendered the moral high ground by invading Iraq. Slowly, I developed contempt for politicians and security officials who were using the fight against terrorism for political gain.

I sometimes wondered whether I was a hypocrite or even a fool. I questioned my values and morality. Disillusioned and angry at world politics, I retreated by speaking less with others. My colleagues wouldn't have understood. I loved my career but was hurt by the inhumane and immoral politics of the time. The only thing that gave me hope was that Canada had chosen to not go to war. Don't get me wrong: I'm not a pacifist. I believe that war is sometimes necessary. I would've volunteered to fight in both world wars – Canada's involvement, then, was required, justifiable, and moral. But I didn't see the Iraq War as the same. CSIS's obsequious relationship with the US fostered censorship within the service and limited its ability to make independent decisions from the highest level down. Open criticism of the US and its foreign policy wasn't tolerated. Guantanamo Bay, Abu Ghraib, waterboarding, abusive interrogation methods, torture – none of it was up for debate.

At work, I approached my files seriously. My biggest fear was that I'd somehow overlook or underestimate a threat and that something terrible would happen as a result – professional suicide and with potentially grave consequences. I checked my bias. Generally, at the time, at my level, I felt CSIS was targeting investigation subjects fairly and transparently. I read enough warrant power requests and I took part in meetings where the director approved targeting authorities.

During my time on the desk, Syrian-born engineer Maher Arar's case was a pressing concern for the service due to the significant media attention it was gaining. Maher had been arrested in 2002 at JFK International Airport in New York while travelling home to Canada from Zurich on his Canadian passport. He came to security attention following a meeting he had with Abduallah Almalki who was also falsely accused of being a member of Al Qaeda. American authorities held him for nearly two weeks before putting him on a plane to Jordan and, ultimately, to Syria. Maher was held for ten months by Syrian military intelligence and psychologically and physically tortured. CSIS visited with Syrian intelligence while Maher was incarcerated but did not seek his release.[1] The Syrians later, in 2003, released him, following substantial diplomatic efforts by his wife and civil liberty groups, like the Canadian chapter of the Council on American Islamic Relations and a letter from Prime Minister Jean Chrétien, which said, "I can assure you there is no Canadian government impediment to his return."[2] Yet Justice Dennis O'Connor's later inquiry into the actions of Canadian officials deemed that Canadian government officials had "leaked confidential and inaccurate information about the case to the media for the purpose of damaging Maher's reputation or [for] protecting their self-interest or government interests."[3] The commission also determined that there was no evidence that Maher had committed any offence or that his activities had ever constituted a threat to Canadian security.

Maher had been arrested and sent to Syria during my 2002 IOET training. My understanding, then, was that CSIS had not been involved in his arrest, rendition, detention, and torture. I was wrong. While the RCMP suffered much of the criticism of Canada's involvement in Maher's case, documents reviewed by the Commission of Inquiry showed that CSIS had consistently opposed efforts by Gar Pardy, from the Department of Foreign Affairs, to have Maher brought back to Canada.[4] Sending a Canadian citizen to his country of origin where there were no human rights set a dangerous precedent. What disappointed me most, once I'd read the commission's findings after they'd been made public, was how CSIS had rejected the Department of Foreign Affairs' proposed statement, which read that "the Government of Canada has no evidence that Maher was involved in terrorist activities," which would've been true. Instead, they proposed the following: "Mr. Arar is currently the subject of a National Security Investigation in Canada."[5] But he wasn't.

A year into my position on the Sunni Islamic extremist desk, I received an email from Riad Saloojee, director of the Canadian chapter of the Council on American Islamic Relations and my former classmate at Carleton University. He was encouraging the Muslim community to support Maher's wife, Monia Mazigh, and their two children. She was lobbying politicians to secure the release of her husband. The email stressed Maher's innocence and drew attention to his family relations, his career as an engineer, and, most importantly, his Canadian citizenship. The email emphasized that he'd been travelling on his Canadian passport and so should have been sent back to Canada. He wrote that only a handful of Muslims were standing with Monia and her children. His words pierced my heart. The email pointed out that this could happen to the reader's father, husband, or brother. My heart sank further as I imagined

Monia comforting her children. It reminded me so much of what my mother went through when desperately trying to have my father freed from imprisonment in Ethiopia.

In my parents' home office, in front of the same computer on which I wrote my CSIS application, I questioned myself: *Why did I decide to work for the service?* So much had changed. The war on terror had become an excuse for the suppression of human rights and for torture. I wanted to help Monia lobby the government. I wanted to stand with her at protests. I wanted to call all my friends from university and urge them and everyone they knew to support Monia and her kids. At university, I'd occasionally played the role of an activist. I wasn't the kind of person to take up every cause. Still, I attended protests. I cared about the plights of others. I took a stand on important issues, as one does in university. I learned that I had a voice and that I, thus, must take a stand against injustice.

However, I also recalled my early discussions with Internal Security. In no uncertain terms, the officer had discouraged me from attending protests; everything I did reflected on the service. I was its representative. I couldn't call anyone or push for Maher's release. My hands were tied. As a CSIS officer, I was outside my community and restricted in terms of where I could go. I had to keep a low profile. I couldn't do the right thing, not in this case. This frustrated me. I'd always sought to do what was right. But that was complicated. For the first time, I felt pulled in two directions. My education, role, and training at CSIS had taught me to always think about my country's broader safety and security concerns. Muslims were being publicly called upon to condemn terrorism, and they did. I had a unique opportunity to fight terrorism. I'd made a career and life mission of denouncing it and of acting against it. But I also felt compelled to fight for the civil and human rights of those wrongly caught up in the war on terror. Standing up against Maher's torture was deeply important to me.

The guilt welled up in me. I had to remind myself of the importance of CSIS's mission, despite the organization's focus on the Muslim community. I told myself that as the only Arab Muslim woman in the service, I had an important role to play in that mission, like educating my colleagues about Islam and Muslims. Truthfully, I'm still ashamed that I didn't do anything to help. I was somewhat comforted to know that much of the Canadian public shared my view of Maher and that Canada's official position was he should be returned to Canada. I also learned that some intelligence officers felt the same. A few of the newly hired and more progressive intelligence officers had commented that Maher's citizenship should have compelled the Americans to send him to Canada.

When Maher was freed and allowed to return to Canada in October 2003, his supporters organized a televised press conference. My colleagues, managers, and I crowded around Richard's office TV. There was only one other woman, from another Counter Terrorism desk, in that office packed with men. The room was full of chatter as the press conference began. We were all curious. I was emotional. I watched Riad Saloojee next to Maher and Monia. I didn't tell anyone that I knew him from my university days. The trio looked anxious, but I could see Monia's determination to support her husband. Maher's traumatic experiences clearly clung to him – he looked exhausted. I wondered what Monia was feeling. What was it like to see her husband like this? What had she said to him when she first saw him? How were their children handling this?

Right when Maher appeared in front of a microphone, the office chatter died down. I recall Richard mentioning the fact that he was a good-looking white man with an education, so the public would sympathize with him. After his remarks, a few intelligence officers snickered, and many nodded in agreement. *What!?* I thought. *What a horrible thing to say!* At that point in my time at CSIS, I really liked Richard. He was one of the best managers in the branch and we had a great working relationship. I was surprised and disappointed by his comments about Maher being white. Race was a thing no one spoke about at the time. I was overwhelmed by emotions and knew it would be a bad idea to remain in my supervisor's office. I excused myself and walked downstairs to the Information Centre, where there was a small room with another television. I turned it on but left the lights off. In the cramped room, I stood and watched the press conference alone. I wept because the family had done nothing to invite such a grave ordeal into their lives. I didn't know them, but they reminded me of my family and how Canada had become my home and place of refuge. No one should ever go through this pain, I thought. No person and no family should be subjected to this kind of insult upon their humanity. Never in a million years would I have guessed this could happen to a Canadian and be carried out by another democratic country, in this case the US, though I expected nothing else from the Syrian government, given its repeated human rights violations.

Ms Mazigh gained popularity for her activism during her husband's release from Syria. In 2004, she joined the New Democratic Party of Canada, running in my riding of South Ottawa. Many I spoke to outside of CSIS were excited about her; she was an educated woman who spoke both official languages, had lobbied to free her husband while taking care of their children, and had forced the government to hold a public inquiry on Maher's deportation to and detention in Syria. How could you not admire that? She was an icon in my eyes and my parents' who had always voted for the Liberal Party until that year. So, when one of my university friends invited my family and me to a barbeque fundraising event for her, I was thrilled that I'd get to meet her. I didn't care what CSIS thought. My thinking had changed. If my attendance at the barbeque became an issue at work, I'd tell them that I'd met a respectable aspiring Canadian politician. At the barbecue, as Ms Mazigh was finishing with supporters, I walked straight over and shook her hand with both of mine. "You have my family's support," I told her. I figured she must hear this a lot, so I tried to convey how genuine I was with my tone.

"Thank you," she said in her Francophone accent, smiling. She was small in stature with fair skin and kind eyes, and she wore a hijab. Others began gathering around us to speak with her, and she excused herself to greet her supporters. "Good luck!" I said and walked back to my friends.

Weeks later, at headquarters, I had a briefing with Marshall in his office. After we'd reviewed my file, I told him about the funding event for Ms Mazigh's campaign. "She was lovely," I added earnestly, not containing my excitement to have met her. Marshall's expression didn't change, and he switched topics to discuss my new assignment. I assumed that he didn't want to get into a political debate. During our conversation, he cocked his head, furrowed his brow, and launched into a story that made me uncomfortable to say the least. He spoke about an Italian officer he'd worked with during his time with the RCMP. The officer was working to infiltrate a drug gang in Montreal. It would later be revealed that one of his family members was involved in the drug scene. Though the officer always did great work, after other RCMP officers were informed of his connection to a gang member, they never trusted or treated him the same.

Once Marshall finished telling his story, I quickly gathered my files and left the room, confused about why he'd chosen that specific moment to recount this particular anecdote. I didn't know any terrorists. I didn't associate with anyone who supported terrorism. What did I have in common with this RCMP officer? He wasn't impressed that I'd attended the fundraising event. But I didn't understand why that would upset him. At the time, I didn't realize he was preparing me for what was to come.

Marshall was promoted within the branch to Counter Terrorism's deputy director general. I congratulated him. Richard was on his way out too, to a posting overseas. My deskmates had moved on to regional desks, and I'd somehow become the senior and most knowledgeable person on my desk. Only two years in, I was a mentor to new intelligence officers on the Middle East desk. I took my role seriously – maybe too seriously, some later told me. I thought they should live and breathe the files. The generous post-9/11 security budget meant that there were enough new recruits coming in for everyone to notice and they demanded a healthy dose of balance, questioning things like mobility, a major headache for all officers.

Months later, I received an upsetting email from Laura over at Counter Intelligence. Lindsay, my friend from IOET training who'd gone out with me in Montreal and defended me in the restaurant, had just been hospitalized after experiencing a seizure. Laura had attached a document to the email about how class members could support Lindsay's family who were visiting from Vancouver. I immediately responded that I'd cook Lindsay's parents supper on Saturday. I couldn't believe it. Lindsay was my age and had always been healthy. She exercised all the time. She'd just met a tall, handsome intelligence officer who'd recently joined CSIS, and she was smitten. The last time I saw her, she was with him by the service elevators. They were in love and both looked so happy. We'd started with CSIS at the same time, taken our oaths the same day, taken French-language training classes together, and ended up in the same class. We were on the same journey.

That week, Laura called to tell me that Lindsay had passed away. I was shocked and in disbelief. I kept hearing her asking to go for coffee, as she'd done the week before. I kept recalling her beautiful smile, red hair, and playful, mischievous eyes, and the way her body swayed left and right before she spoke. I remembered her travelling stories about

Japan and how she liked the deep voice of CBC News broadcaster Ian Hanomansing and how she brought people together and got me dancing in Montreal. I told my supervisor that if there was nothing pressing, I'd like to take the afternoon off. He immediately approved my request and was very supportive. I meant to go home, but somehow, I found myself driving to Ottawa's main mosque on Scott Street. I hadn't been there in a while. I sat quietly and alone on the carpet reflecting on life. I'd never known anyone my age to pass away. Why had this happened? I couldn't understand. That there was no warning scared me. *When will I go? Will it be unexpected? What will happen to me? Am I ready?* I felt guilty for being so focused on my career, for not taking time to do charitable community work, and for regularly missing my prayers. When I was at university we had a prayer room for Muslims, and my Muslim friends and I would often remind each other of our requirement to pray on time. At CSIS there was no place for prayer nor was there anyone to pray with. The foreign language translators were mostly Christian, and I didn't connect with anyone at CSIS who was Muslim. Missing my prayers regularly was disappointing and it made me feel spiritually empty. Prayer and knowing that there was a greater power made me feel less anxious. Surely I needed this more than ever as I was in an environment that looked for and anticipated threats in order to counter them. I realized that I must live a more balanced life. I also became convinced that I should not postpone wearing a hijab, getting married, and starting a life outside of work.

Now that Marshall had been promoted and other officers had moved on, I too wanted to embark on new challenges, so I asked for a transfer within the branch to the Counter Terrorism Signals Intelligence unit. In reality, I wanted some distance from operational files, to gain more technical skills, and acquire liaison experience. For several weeks, I was travelling to the Communications Security Establishment (CSE) and learning how to conduct research on their databases. I was embedded as a CSIS Counter Terrorism secondee in the CSE Counter Terrorism section. My role was to flag signals intelligence products – foreign communications intercepts that are transcribed, analyzed, and produced into intelligence reports – and determine their relevance to CSIS operations and the wider intelligence community. I was to produce daily signals intelligence reports that would be disseminated across all national security organizations in Canada. Additionally, I would be the go-to on any sharing of information between CSIS counterterrorism investigations and CSE information.

Before I left, my supervisor and chief completed my annual performance evaluation for 2003 and part of 2004. I was pleased that they recognized how hard and professionally I'd been working to build my career. Marshall echoed Richard's assessment and added, "Huda is a valuable ambassador for an Analyst for Counter Terrorism operations. She is now someone all Counter Terrorism analysts, supervisors, and managers can depend on to advise on Counter Terrorism operational practices, policy, and progress files." Marshall even approached me and said, "One day, young lady, you'll run a CT desk somewhere and direct operations. Keep at it." After hearing his words and reading his performance evaluation of me, I'd never have thought that a headscarf would get in the way of my professional aspirations. I was wrong yet again.

10 | FIRST THROUGH THE DOOR

My counterterrorism work influenced my need to wear the hijab. Looking back now, I think part of it was to resist the oppression I felt but could not face. Another part was in solidarity with those whom structural Islamophobia so adversely impacted, but whom I could not help. After the advent of the war in Iraq, I felt crystal clear that my religion was under attack by governments, extremists, the media, and even colleagues and rhetoric at CSIS. Politicians were treating extremism as a mainstream phenomenon in Muslim-majority countries, not just Iraq, and rendering their misrepresentation as pretext for short-sighted political gains. This frustrated me, as a counterterrorism expert and a Muslim.

In December 2004, I travelled to Toronto with my girlfriends for the Reviving the Islamic Spirit conference at the Metropolitan Convention Centre. I was excited to dine out, stay up late, and talk love and boys. The conference included a bazaar where we shopped for hijabs and wandered through the overwhelming crowds of thousands. We revelled in the belonging we felt. The crowds doubled in the evenings and the buzz increased. Over the loudspeaker was the Sami Yusuf song "Allahu Allah," a cheery tune sung in English, Arabic, Urdu, and Turkish that makes everyone feel included. The diversity and beauty around us – Blacks, Arabs, Indians, Turks, Asians, and whites – left us speechless. I loved seeing so many interracial couples. The community was vibrant, sophisticated, traditional, and modern. After reading about so much evil extremism in the office, I felt a great need to be among Muslims and to live and celebrate my faith every day.

Things were going well for me at CSIS – I'd received two excellent annual reviews, was respected, and had proven my worth. That I was an Arabic speaker and a Muslim were still seen as added value to my skillset. I faced Islamophobia, but I thought those people didn't understand *my* relationship to my religion. I wondered what colleagues would think of me if I wore the hijab – so, I asked them. I was nervous. They were young, open-minded, and well-educated and fully supported me. "Huda, of course it wouldn't be a concern for anyone. We all know you're Muslim." One, fasting for Lent, said that we should all be able to practise faith as we wish. My friends asked me many personal questions that I was happy to answer: "Why do you want to wear it?" "Why do some women choose to wear it and others don't?" "Will it make a difference once you're in the field conducting interviews?" I explained my decision and weighed in on other women's choices to wear the hijab. I assured my colleagues that any Muslim I talked to in the field would already know I was Muslim. It didn't matter whether I was wearing a hijab, just as I could tell in five minutes whether they were Arab, Persian, Turkish, or Afghan. It takes one to know one, as they say. There are always clues. When I worked at the bank, Syrian men would identify me as an Arab while still in line – they'd noticed when I looked up as they spoke Arabic. People would start speaking to me in Arabic over the phone based only on the way I said hello in English. I didn't feel the hijab would at all compromise my ability to do my job.

When I finally decided to wear the hijab, I was at Signals Intelligence and travelling between CSIS and the Communications Security Establishment (CSE), facilitating sensitive requests and prioritizing counterterrorism files requiring CSE attention and action. I produced daily assessment reports that CSIS disseminated to Canadian security and intelligence partners. Roger, my supervisor who was close to retirement, had minimal computer skills and was intimidated by CSE communications technology. Since Roger wasn't adequately trained, I basically ran the desk. I had a reputation for being competent and dependable and for having a strong work ethic. Knowing this, I was confident that I could wear a hijab without being questioned or being looked down upon, though I knew many still held negative stereotypes about the hijab and women from the Middle East.

I always began my day with a morning prayer, something I had started to do more regularly since Lindsay passed away. In the mirror, my face, framed by the hijab, seemed brighter than usual. It was glowing and beautiful. I often told friends that I felt more beautiful when wearing a hijab. They'd laugh and tell me I was silly. I wore it as I left but took it off in the CSIS parking lot, where I felt anxious and alone. I'd be the only one wearing one and the first to do so in a building where thousands worked. I'm somewhat shy and didn't want to draw attention to myself. I walked into work disappointed with myself – I'd thought I was self-assured and independent. I kept busy that day and didn't chat as usual. I called a friend, a CSIS Toronto Region communications analyst of Egyptian background. He respected my decision and told me not to be frightened when it drew looks and questions. "Yes, you are right." I felt *frightened*, I agreed, happy to have found the right word. "Huda, people will stare because they're not used to you wearing it. I'd stare too. Don't take it the wrong way."

The following day, I worked up the courage to do it. When I walked into CSIS, I eyed the security guard. He was friendly, but though we usually exchanged pleasantries, he stopped me. I told him I'd decided to wear a hijab and would amend my photo identification as soon as possible. He looked puzzled but remained friendly and let me in – one hurdle down, a few thousand to go. I received a few stares during my elevator ride and walk to my office, where I was relieved to finally be surrounded by friends and colleagues. A few colleagues dropped by to congratulate me. I felt supported. Some even said they liked my hijab, a silky, light blue grey. I assured everyone who asked, supervisors and colleagues alike, that nothing had changed. "Yes, I shake men's hands." "Yes, I speak to men in private places." "Yes, I'm still committed to being an intelligence officer." "No, I didn't get married last weekend without telling anyone." "Yes, if an operation requires it, I'd take off my hijab – saving lives is my priority."

By early afternoon, I needed a break. Many employees in the cafeteria stopped to look at me. I tried not let on that I was anxious about my new look. I smiled nervously and tried to seem confident. After grabbing a tea, I walked to the usually friendly cashiers, with whom I often chatted. Seeing my hijab, the cashier expressed surprise. I replied that I hoped she liked it. "Well, hon, as long as it was your choice and not your husband's or father's, it's all good." I smiled and nodded. *Argh! She thinks wearing a hijab means I'm not an independent woman. Is this what everyone's thinking? Hopeless. How did they think I could make decisions on national security files but not on what I wear?* I was upset, but I knew that one day of wearing a hijab wouldn't change stereotypes. I sighed. These were the first steps on a long, challenging road. On my way home, someone cut me off. I honked, gave the middle finger, and cursed: "Fuck you!" I felt terrible. What had come over me to act and swear like that? I was ashamed of myself. *I'm so bad*, I thought. *I should've never put on a hijab.* My anxiety had gotten the best of me.

My parents were surprised. I hadn't told them about my decision, and they hadn't known I'd worn the hijab to work that day. Mom seemed concerned. "How did your first day go?" I told her it was fine and that a lot of people had stared but, in time, they'd stop. Dad stood up, walked over, and kissed me on my forehead the way Prophet Mohammed would Fatima, his daughter, as she walked into the room – a sign of love and approval. He was in tears. I think he was surprised that I'd made the decision to wear it without talking to him and Mom. I was touched by his gesture.

Why was I so naïve? How did I not know that wearing a hijab would be so controversial? Why hadn't I considered that management would take offence? I didn't yet appreciate paramilitary intolerance of individualism or that as a woman and minority, I wouldn't find support in that culture and its systems. It hadn't been long since RCMP officer Baltej Singh Dhillon had fought his legal, emotional, and public battle in the 1990s to wear a Sikh turban on duty. I'd naïvely worn the hijab at CSIS. Most managers were former RCMP officers. The culture was deeply conformist and intolerant, and I was an unprepared fool.

11 | OPERATION CREVICE

That long and cold winter of 2004, Marshall was promoted to deputy director of Counter Terrorism. My supervisor, Richard, and deputy chief, Gary, were also transferred to other units. William and Charles became my chief and deputy chief, respectively. My direct Signals Intelligence supervisor remained Roger. Many of my colleagues had completed their two-year terms at headquarters and had been sent to regional offices to work as investigators. I'd become one of the most senior intelligence officers in Counter Terrorism.

The threats we were working on had changed, too. After 9/11, CSIS and other intelligence organizations had focused on Islamist extremists, including extremists in the West, with direct connections to and training with Al Qaeda and other terrorist groups abroad. The Iraq War changed that. War, greater securitization, and alienation had angered a generation of young Western Muslims and radicalized some, especially in Britain. Former MI5 director Eliza Manningham-Buller stated that "a year after the invasion, MI5 was 'swamped' by leads about terrorist threats to the UK."[1] Several CSIS files were linked to MI5 investigations, like the Momin Khawaja investigation, Canada's first Islamist extremist case. The British had reported to CSIS that Momin Khawaja, a Canadian Ottawa resident and contractor for the government entity Global Affairs Canada, was a member of an Islamist extremist network operating in England. The British Metropolitan police named both the ensuing international operation, which included the Americans, and the terrorist network Crevice. It was surprising that a Canadian government contractor with security clearance could be involved in international terrorism. That would indicate a failure in security screening process at CSIS and Global Affairs. Frankly, it was frightening that we hadn't discovered this before the Brits. CSIS now had to confront the idea that Khawaja and any associates of his might have been preparing other terror activities in Canada. Crevice members in Britain had obtained aluminum powder and 600 kilograms of ammonium nitrate to use in explosives. In its operations, the British police had confiscated this material and replaced it with a nonexplosive substance while maintaining surveillance to identify contacts, support networks, or potential attacks. They observed Crevice leader Omar Khyam with Khawaja in an Internet café, where the two examined a potential remote-detonation device. Khawaja's return to Canada triggered CSIS surveillance operations and a massive twenty-four-hour investigation by CSIS and the RCMP, the latter in the lead. The Counter Terrorism floor was overflowing with executive managers, supervisors, intelligence officers, and administration staff, all wearing stern faces and buzzing in and out of meeting rooms. I was astonished at how robust and efficient the service could be.

Larry was the supervisor of Counter Terrorism, Sunni Islamic Extremism, South Asia desk's team, which consisted of Julia, Rebecca, and Alex, and he took the lead, though most of the desk participated. I wrote the first message to the British and Americans, and Charles commended me for a "job well done." I nodded and thanked him. Over the next few weeks, my colleagues and I worked on link charts, incoming domestic and international communications, and briefing notes to management that were sent off to decision makers like deputy director of operations Jack Hooper and director Ward Elcock.

William was the lead manager on the case. He was well-respected, energetic, and eager. He instructed us all to keep track of our work hours and to submit overtime for compensation, but we didn't mind working extra hours. We wanted to contribute and be in-the-know on the case's developments. Our colleagues in Counter Proliferation, Counter Intelligence, and Security Screening had some idea of our case but didn't know who, what, when, and why – the need-to-know policy still applied. Our team understood that the case would test how we did our jobs, our working relationship with the RCMP, and our interplay with foreign allies with whom we shared intelligence and evidence. Importantly, it would be the first terrorism case prosecuted under the new and controversial

Anti-Terrorism Act, enacted after 9/11. The case was a test of the act that gave our threat-countering role purpose and clarity. This was why I'd joined CSIS – to do meaningful work that saved lives.

On 29 March 2004, police and tactical bomb squad teams arrested Khawaja while he was at work at Global Affairs Canada. A police search of his home led to the discovery of a homemade transmitter, receiver circuit boards, and a mobile phone-jamming device that would ensure only the bombers' signal would set off the explosive. Khawaja became the first Canadian arrested, charged, and convicted under Canada's Anti-Terrorism Act. A day later, the British captured and charged other members of the Crevice network.

Crevice demonstrated to CSIS that individuals can quickly radicalize, train, and prepare operations logistics online using sophisticated and covert communication. It shifted CSIS's focus from middle-aged men to young Muslim males and long-time Western citizens, with or without international travel to hot zones. Khawaja was a computer programmer with postsecondary education and a promising career. He resided in the middle-class Ottawa suburb of Orleans. Khawaja had been working at Global Affairs Canada, giving him access to sensitive information about Canada and Canadian embassies abroad. He lived a privileged life and enjoyed democracy's freedoms but betrayed them for what he considered a higher religious calling. Homegrown extremism was a new threat involving enemies from within. The phenomenon, rightly, garnered much attention throughout the intelligence community.

Hoping to gather information and recruit sources, intelligence officers in Ottawa began conducting interviews with anyone who knew Khawaja. Muslims in Ottawa became frustrated with how CSIS and the RCMP were interacting with them. The Khawajas were well known in the Ottawa Muslim community. People who knew him were shocked that he'd been involved in the plot. Nevertheless, they were anxious about being engaged by the RCMP and CSIS.

In July that year, CBC published an article titled "Canadian Muslims Complain of CSIS Harassment," in which Omar, a Canadian Muslim wanting to remain anonymous, spoke with the CBC.[2] He said he'd been rushing to an early evening prayer when two CSIS officers met him at the door. Still upset, Omar told CBC Radio, "The first thing [one of the agents] said was that they were from CSIS and that they would like to speak to us about Momin Khawaja, who is currently detained. When I said I didn't know the individual, he said, 'We know that you know him and he is in a lot of trouble, and all you are worried about is your prayer.'"[3] Riad Saloojee said to the media that "the encounters with CSIS were most frightening for people who came to Canada from police states." He also said, "It tends to be in most cases a fishing expedition, sometimes perhaps sort of a witch hunt type of interrogation or type of questioning. And this really makes people very, very confused, and very traumatized."[4]

I was still a desk analyst, not an investigator in a regional office, so I didn't accompany CSIS officers to interviews. I often wondered why this friction was happening. I knew the Ottawa Muslim community. I was certain they were as surprised and disturbed by the revelations as anyone. But many RCMP and CSIS colleagues weren't great cross-cultural communicators, and all were white – though, in fairness to my colleagues and Muslim community members, talking about a terrorist case, radicalization, and politics isn't everyday conversation.

That summer, while my parents were in Toronto, my friend Faridah and I watched movies at my house one night until late. Suddenly, she asked what it was like to wear a hijab and work for CSIS. I was surprised. I hadn't told her that I worked for CSIS, but I connected the dots. I figured she must have heard from a mutual friend, the husband of my friend who provided a reference to CSIS when I was going through the hiring process. Faridah was born in the United States and was a dual American and Canadian national. After 9/11, she sent out emails through the Muslim Student Association asking others to join her at vigils on Parliament Hill. I couldn't deny my job to her, so I told her that wearing the hijab and working for CSIS was great. I told her about the guards and the cafeteria lady but that my friends and colleagues had been largely supportive. I told her that CSIS doesn't investigate just anyone: "We target people who are a threat. There's a process, and a judge has to sign off on any intrusive method we would use." Faridah took out two CSIS business cards and handed them to me. "These officers came to ask me questions. They were polite, but how they spoke about Islamic fundamentalism and extremism made me uncomfortable. Their tone was kind of accusatory," she said. Faridah was an articulate university student. I trusted what she said. I gave her back the cards and told her she should keep them. I judged that her experience had been the result of a cross-cultural communication barrier and that no one had intended her harm. I trusted the investigators' professionalism and that they were doing their job, so I didn't say anything. Yet, I knew Faridah would have been more cooperative had she felt that the officers understood her religiosity and love of Islam. We never spoke about it again, both wanting to put the experience behind us.

One day, I walked directly to William's office with some documents, bypassing my direct supervisor, breaking with protocol. I was familiar with his office since it had been Marshall's, and we'd spent many hours chatting there. After I knocked, William fixed me with a piercing look. "You can leave it on my desk, Huda." His voice was deep and abrupt. He seemed different than he had when greeting me with a smile or when pulling out a chair for a friendly chat. I was taken aback by his tone and suspected something was wrong. I realized that I shouldn't have crossed the hierarchy or broken the chain of command, but I felt my information required his immediate attention. *I'm so stupid.* Perhaps William distrusted me because he'd learned that I had been, in university, a member of the Muslim Student Association, just like Khawaja. I wondered whether my Human Resources file and Internal Security records had been re-examined. Perhaps, in light of Khawaja, William or other managers doubted whether I deserved my security clearance and government employment. I also wondered whether I was being paranoid. Even if my Human Resources file had been revaluated, I had nothing to hide. I quietly returned to my office and tried not to worry, though I wondered whether I'd done something wrong. I hated myself.

When William called me into his office for "a chat" a week later, I wasn't surprised to learn significant changes were afoot. He wanted to discuss concerns about what he considered my conflicts of interest and my community involvement. William was a favourite of most progressive intelligence officers who knew him, yet he was cold and reserved with me. He asked me to disclose my activities in the Muslim community, at mosques or any place I might run into targets and or service sources. He also said that I required prior approval before attending events in the Muslim community. This shocked me. *Come again. Am I missing something? He can't be serious!* I told him that I felt uncomfortable discussing my outside activities with service managers. "Why aren't you sticking with policy? We're supposed to report any contact with service targets after and if they occur." This was a clear and reasonable policy. I'd followed it and would continue to follow it, to the letter.

"It's not enough," he replied. "You might be encountering subjects of interest or sources. Your best bet is to report everything." He clearly hadn't considered how this would impact me or what it meant to me to be viewed with suspicion. He also didn't seem to realize that his actions were discriminatory. "William, would you require a Sikh or a Jewish Canadian to disclose their private comings and goings in their respective communities?"

He lowered his tone and voice and tried to convince me the order wasn't personal. "Our targets, persons of interest, and sources may frequent the same mosques and halal shops as you." Then he offered a concrete example. He told me that several service agents had been monitoring targets at a lecture that I'd attended at an Ottawa-based public institution. I was embarrassed to learn this, but how could I have known? CSIS had strict need-to-know policies. I didn't have a complete list of targets under investigation or their upcoming activities. I hadn't noticed any targets, sources, or people of interest at the lecture. Besides, why weren't we discussing my impressions of the event and speakers? I began to question myself. *Maybe he's right. Maybe it's more complicated than I thought. I'm an intelligence officer. Maybe such exposure would limit my potential involvement in cover operations.* William must've sensed my weakness. He rushed to exploit it and said that his intention was to protect me and the service from controversy.

His use of *controversy* was interesting, I thought. If someone in the public or in the Muslim community linked me to the service, shouldn't it suffice to acknowledge that Muslims work for CSIS? Then I realized that CSIS neither confirms nor denies intelligence officer names. It also dawned on me that, under William's demands, there could really be no end to what I must report. Where would it stop? Schools? The University of Toronto, where there'd be many Muslims? Did that mean no intelligence officer should register for courses or be seen there? Clearly not.

I left the meeting confused and defeated. I didn't know what to make of William's directive. I had to stand up for myself. I hadn't done anything wrong and hadn't violated any service policies, yet I was being viewed with suspicion. *Is it my hijab? Am I being viewed the same as Khawaja, a young Muslim with security clearance?* How could I convince them that I was still the same intelligence officer who'd been fighting extremism for two and a half years? The more I thought about what William had said, the more I felt that he'd attacked my fundamental human rights to religion and privacy. Didn't CSIS understand that I greeted my family with *Alsamau Alaykum* the moment I walked into my home? Didn't they know I prayed? They knew I was a Muslim when I signed up. Now I had to obtain permission to attend events in my community. William's directive would cut me off from people I connected with most deeply. My mind raced. How could I meet a Muslim man if I couldn't go to Muslim events? What about our kids? We'd be completely isolated from our community. The situation seemed untenable. I was being forced to choose between being an intelligence officer and being a Muslim.

I loved being an intelligence officer. I was also Muslim. That wasn't going to change. When I discussed my concerns with a colleague, she felt the request was outrageous but thought William and I could solve our difference through communication. "Huda, communicate your concerns openly to your managers. Do it in writing to avoid being too emotional." She reminded me I was contributing excellently to Counter Terrorism and enabling others to do their jobs. She felt confident that the issue would be resolved through communication. So, I began to reach out.

I wrote an email listing all Ottawa-based Muslim organizations and asked the service to clarify which ones they didn't want me associating with. I thought that if we could establish parameters, I might feel better. It didn't go over well. William saw the email as a challenge to management and proof of my rebelliousness. Worse, in his eyes, I was no longer a loyal CSIS member. CSIS culture is like the military's – you do as you're told and don't question anything. That's what intelligence officers sign up for. Soon, William, Charles, and Roger all wanted to know what I was doing on my weekends and in my private life.

Slowly, many colleagues began distancing themselves from me. No one visited my office, and no one invited me to go for coffee. I wondered whether it was because I'd been wearing the hijab and whether people felt I'd changed. I felt isolated but blamed myself.

Despite our conflict, I admired many of William's leadership traits, even if I had to remind myself of them. Other intelligence officers held him in high regard. Some even called him Uncle William because of how much he'd supported and listened to their needs. Given this, I hoped that he and I could come to a workable agreement. I understood that he might be irked by what he perceived as my challenge to his authority, but I was confused about the reasons for his initial hostility. Did he dislike me? Was he really just trying to protect CSIS from controversy? Did he think Muslims, especially hijab-wearing ones, shouldn't work for CSIS?

I wondered whether William was being directed to harass me and thereby provoke me into quitting CSIS. I was certain that Jack Hooper, CSIS's deputy director, opposed my employment. One morning, Jack had frowned at me as I entered headquarters, making me feel unwelcome and insignificant. Jack was the embodiment of CSIS's old boys' club. He was a former RCMP officer and had transferred to CSIS in 1984. Jack is correctly described in a *Toronto Star* article as "cowboy-boot-wearing [and] plain-talking" and as at times using language that is misogynistic.[5] Except for the fact that I was a woman, I matched CSIS's profile of a "homegrown threat": young, Canadian, Muslim, an immigrant, could be radicalized on the Internet, and virtually indistinguishable from other youth. After 9/11, Jack had a lot to be nervous about. He was responsible for determining whether CSIS would use torture-obtained information, and he approved the decision to have Mohamed Jabarah, an alleged Al Qaeda member, apprehended in Oman and handed to American authorities without an extradition order.[6] He was also testifying on the Commission of Inquiry into the Actions of Canadian Officials in Relation to Maher Arar. Perhaps he received word that I met Maher's wife during that fundraising event and was threatened by the fact that I knew everything in the service's records, information that would prove Maher Arar's innocence.

In November 2004, Jim Judd, appointed by Paul Martin's Liberal government, became CSIS's director and Jack's boss. Jim was a seasoned public servant. He was reserved but friendly. In his first month, Jim conducted a meet-and-greet tour of each of the branch's offices. In his Counter Terrorism tour, he took particular notice of me with my hijab. Our eyes locked, and he walked over to shake my hand. I was proud to stand up and meet him. I was representing my values and identity while working to safeguard Canada, Canadian interests, and national security. Jim seemed to accept this.

Tension mounted between me and William and me and Charles, who had both stopped speaking to me. I continued performing my tasks, but the isolation I faced hurt me deeply. Roger had completed my third annual Counter Terrorism evaluation and sent it up the chain before I had a chance to review and sign it. William was only supposed to add comments, but he changed my scores and gave me a one on judgment and three on other competencies – no fours this time, as I'd received in the past. William wrote page-long comments indicating that I lacked judgment, as demonstrated by my continued engagement in the Muslim community. When I saw the evaluation, I was livid. *What?* I'd made tremendous contributions that year. I'd represented CSIS at CSE, produced and held a lunchtime lecture series on Islam, participated in training programs, and assisted other Counter Terrorism desks with translation and analysis. I'd completed my tasks, developed initiatives, and was fully engaged in my work. I was no longer a new intelligence officer seeking direction. I was training new recruits and was one of the most senior and knowledgeable intelligence officers in Counter Terrorism. I should have received more fours. I walked up to Roger, my direct supervisor, and told him I didn't agree with his assessment and evaluation of my work. I felt betrayed. I'd been doing both his work and mine. He said he'd rated my performance four, but William had changed the score and added the comment about my lack of judgment. I said that I wouldn't sign the document, given that it didn't reflect my performance. He spoke with Human Resources, who convinced him that signing wasn't agreement in itself. Still, I refused to sign. In this instance, I didn't care about service policy.

Why would William do this? I couldn't confront him on his escalation. He was acting within his power. I walked by his office and, for the first time, felt fearful. I then walked right back to my desk in shame. Discrimination was one thing, but to be seen as an ineffective intelligence officer who performed poorly hurt me deeply on an emotional level, and a negative evaluation would also hurt my career. As an immigrant child, I was raised to believe that, to prove myself, I needed a career. I still feel that way. I wish it were different. As a child in Cairo, I once received a negative midterm report card. As my mother was driving home, I threw the report out the window. I told my parents that I'd never received it and told my teacher that my parents had kept it. Soon it was out of everyone's minds. I would do that here too – I'd ignore the report and focus on my career.

In early 2005, I was under William's and Charles's supervision but on a new file – Counter Terrorism Afghanistan. I'd asked for the transfer and was relieved to receive it. Shortly before, though, Charles, in a closed-door meeting, warned me that I should "check my attitude." He told me that I didn't seem to understand the CSIS culture and that I took things too personally. With a stern and patronizing tone, he said that there was a hierarchy that I didn't seem to respect and that failing to meet the RCMP- and military-influenced expectations would hurt my career. Stupefied, I asked, "Charles, how can you say that? This organization was created as a civilian organization, as per the Macdonald Commission. Doesn't that mean anything?" He looked at me as if I were hopeless. He saw that I had a textbook understanding of CSIS and wasn't working within the realities of the workplace – and hadn't from early on, to my detriment.

My new supervisor, Dean, welcomed me to his desk and introduced me to the team, comprised of some of the brightest new Counter Terrorism intelligence officers. We supported the Canadian military's command of the International Security Assistance Force under NATO in Afghanistan. The desk was fast-paced and demanding. My colleagues were extremely busy, but Charles and Dean hadn't granted me access to sensitive source files relating to the desk, as they should have. I kept waiting, not knowing why it was taking so long. Tired of me asking why, Charles and Dean had me work on low-priority tasks, including Arabic translations for my old Counter Terrorism Middle East desk. My officemate Ryan suggested that I ask Dean once again. He and others couldn't understand why I wasn't getting access to files I was expected to work on. Dean repeatedly told me I'd be granted access shortly, offering excuses about why approvals hadn't been obtained. I was embarrassingly underworked compared to my overburdened colleagues. I felt my reputation as a competent, respected, and valued intelligence officer was eroding. No one, neither managers nor colleagues, seemed to support me, and I didn't know why. Was it the hijab, personality clashes, or both? I wondered whether they trusted me.

I tried to rebuild my relationship with William and to engage him in day-to-day conversations about work – he was still my chief, after all. I'd visit his office, talk to him about Middle East politics, and relay my theories about Islamic radicalization. Somehow, the conversations always turned personal. He'd guide the conversation back to me, his tone hostile and suspicious. Occasionally, he said things that were just plain offensive. When I spoke of my aspirations to work as an investigator in Toronto, for instance, he asked whether my father would "allow" me to move out of Ottawa.

Looking back, I wonder whether William had already officially recommended my dismissal. Especially hurtful was something he said during an offhand conversation between the two of us. He asked, flat out, how I could support Muslim human rights organizations that are critical of the service. I replied that they have a job to do that is more substantive than just challenging CSIS and that I didn't see the friction the same way he did. In response, he suggested that during my interactions with these groups, I may divulge CSIS investigative methods to Muslim community members. I was speechless. His assertion meant that he didn't believe I was loyal. That he thought I might break my oath and commit a criminal act. Through one short conversation, he'd revealed how little he trusted me in an organization where loyalty and trust were paramount. He viewed me as an internal threat and a risk to the service. For me, this was intensely painful to process. My brain tucked away what I'd heard to protect itself. I told myself that I'd undergone the same vigorous security clearance as anyone else. I was as loyal, trustworthy, and deserving of respect and equality as anyone in CSIS. I never told anyone what he said.

I didn't know it then, but William had engaged Internal Security, the branch that investigates service employees to ensure that they aren't selling state secrets to foreign governments or the private sector. It reviews, investigates, and makes final decisions on security breaches, conflicts of interest, and employee misconduct and determines employee loyalty and reliability to Canada and CSIS.

Revoking an employee's security clearance results in a dismissal from their position within CSIS and arguably a career within national security altogether. Most national security organizations who value CSIS training and experience would require at the very least a secret level of clearance obtained through an assessment by the CSIS government security screening program. Except for routine updates conducted every five years, which all employees undergo, the stakes are high for employees being investigated by Internal Security.

That spring of 2005, when my world was turning upside down, I began to conduct research on Muslims who fought terrorism in the US. I found articles on Captain James Yee, an army chaplain at Guantanamo Bay, who had been falsely arrested and deemed a threat. Yee was later released without charges, but the circumstances of why he was arrested in the first place were not clear to me at the time; however, I do recall feeling sick to my stomach and instinctually knowing his innocence. Reading this information in the news and feeling that something similar was going to happen to me made me feel like I had to fight for my reputation and be on guard. Everything that was happening led me to believe that a similar fate awaited me.

I once again emailed William about which Ottawa Muslim organizations I should stay away from, hoping to keep the channels of communication open and transparent. I wanted reasonable and established parameters. Because I was also afraid – no, petrified – about what might happen to me if they deemed me a threat, I wanted our communication documented. William never replied to that email. Instead, he called a formal meeting with the Human Resources director general, two Internal Security representatives, and me. The meeting was for nine o'clock on a Monday morning in April 2005. William had escalated the conflict again. If I refused to report my outside activities, I'd lose my job. I perceived William's request for the meeting as a threat to me as a Muslim woman.

That weekend, I tried and failed to get my mind off work. I declined a coffee with a university friend, a Muslim woman. I wanted to be alone. I was frustrated and didn't know what would become of my CSIS career. I couldn't talk to anyone about it, including my parents. I was sure that they'd tell me to stop working at CSIS and find another job. I didn't want to hear that. I tried to do other things, but nothing else mattered. Tensions were high. By Monday, I hadn't slept and was exhausted. What was about to happen would forever change my world.

I walked into the meeting room with my chest burning and thoughts racing. The false allegation about James Yee, that he, the Guantanamo Bay chaplain, was a traitor, frightened me. He was an insider accused of the worst crimes, and here I was, an insider, also standing accused. I read a prayer and walked in, thankful that it was early and many of my colleagues were not yet roaming the halls of the Counter Terrorism branch.

There sat three middle-aged white male managers: a director general, a chief, and William, all in crisp white shirts and suits and acting casually. A female analyst from Internal Security was also present, but I felt she was there merely for gender-related optics. The boardroom was crowded, tight, and unfriendly. William sat at the head like a man on a mission. He greeted everyone as if they'd just entered, like me, and welcomed me. He got to the point, directly accusing me of a conflict of interest in attending Muslim events in Ottawa. My blood rushed, my heart beat fast, and my lips locked. The meeting was serious from the start. They didn't waste time threatening to revoke my security clearance. They focused on two organizations from my list. One was the National Council on Canadian Muslims, a non-profit Muslim advocacy organization that many of my university friends, including Riad Saloojee, supported. I cannot legally name the other. Both organizations had charitable status and were not known to support violence of any kind. Still, I was directed not to associate, attend events, or maintain contact with anyone from these organizations. If I did, I'd lose my security clearance. I was puzzled. My relationship with Riad or any other members of these organizations wasn't intimate – I'd never tell them where I worked. Further, William and those at the meeting didn't understand that these charitable organizations attended many Muslim events to raise funds. CSIS's demand that I stay away from these organizations meant that I couldn't attend Muslim events or be part of my Muslim community. It wasn't reasonable or sustainable. As an expert counterterrorism analyst, I also didn't assess the two organizations as security threats to Canada.

I was terrified to sit before men who wielded so much power over me but refused to understand me. The experience reminded me of high school when I got in trouble even though I was the one being bullied. They were threatening my livelihood and my career. My career was my calling, and it meant the world to me. I was outraged at their ignorance. I wanted to shout, *I'm a Muslim! You knew that when you hired me! You're a bunch of ignorant, clueless white men who can't see anything beyond the walls of this institution!* But I held myself in check. Many times, I resisted the desire to leave the room. Knowing that they'd win if I walked away, I forced myself to remain seated. I sat and listened. I told them I'd comply, though I felt they were asking the impossible. In my head, I ran through the people I knew who worked at the two selected organizations, as well as their families and friends. I went to university with them. They were young, educated, principled, and moderate Muslims – the kind of people I enjoyed. They were my friends and good people. You could connect almost any Muslim in Ottawa to this network. The directive meant I couldn't attend the Eid festival, Ramadan parties, or Muslim community summer picnics. CSIS was asking me to completely disconnect from the Muslim community. *So be it*, I thought, convincing myself I'd be okay. I accepted their demands but committed myself to overcoming the conflict between my career and my community. More than ever, I had to prove my commitment and loyalty to CSIS. I told them I'd comply and left the meeting.

I was never the same after that day. All the glitter surrounding the organization, the excuses I was making for their discrimination, evaporated. I began to see CSIS for what it was – an organization steeped in white bias, one that refuses to regard Muslims and other minorities as equal citizens. I felt betrayed. They'd ganged up on me on a sensitive, personal subject. I felt powerless, misunderstood, and confused. I went back to my desk. They'd won, I thought. But perhaps with the Internal Security meeting behind us, they'd trust me again. I'd now have access to the files I was entitled to receive. I'd bury myself in work and turn the page on all this. I'd keep what had happened secret from my colleagues, parents, and everyone else. If I buried it deep in my soul, I could pretend it never happened.

12 | LOYALTY

Farah, my sister, has often envied my resilience and how I can tune troubles out. I once fell from a friend's motorcycle and hurt my knee badly, but I jumped away and pretended I was okay. "Huda, cry! Tell people when you're hurt," she encouraged me. But I'm one of those people who just takes pain, physical or emotional, and lives with it. At work, I was pretending the dark storm around me wasn't there. The alternative was to walk away and find another calling. I figured that if I didn't acknowledge what was happening, no one would see it. But they did. My lack of contribution became contentious among my desk colleagues. For two months, I'd been begging for access to files. Fed up, I walked straight into the office of my supervisor, Dean, to confront him. "What's going on? Why don't I have access yet? Why is everyone overworked while I'm working as a translator?" I asked with a fixed expression. I refused to calm down.

"Could you sit down, Huda?" Dean asked.

"No, I'm not sitting down. Tell me what's going on," I insisted. I was determined to get answers. "I can't pretend something isn't happening."

Then the revelation came. Dean admitted that William and Charles had instructed him to not grant me access to any source files due to my involvement with a specific Muslim organization – this was after I'd agreed to their terms. Stunned, I marched into the office of Counter Terrorism's director general, Daniel. Surely, Daniel had seen my commitment over the three years that we'd worked together. He'd read and signed my last two performance evaluations from Richard and Marshall, who'd given me fours for professionalism, work ethic, and being a team player. He knew that I loved my job and that I'd been bringing value to his branch for years. I told him that I had an urgent matter to discuss. "Yes, Huda. Come in," he said in his heavy Quebecois accent. I explained the situation, including the directive from Internal Security that I limit my outside activities in the Muslim community. I told him that I had and did. I hadn't attended any Muslim community function in months. I pleaded: "I can't do my work like this. I feel like they don't trust me. They scrutinize me and block my access to files I need to do my job. My reputation among colleagues is being damaged." Tears flooded my face. I hadn't admitted this aloud before.

"Huda, I understand your frustration. You must realize your managers are simply trying to ensure that you're fully aware of your responsibilities as an intelligence officer and how complicated and controversial being a member of the Muslim community can be. These are difficult times. We have young Muslims, ah, Canadians, first- and second-generation Canadians, who want to undermine our democracy. We're really fighting for democracy here in CT. You know, I mean, look at what happened in Madrid, London, and here, in Ottawa," he said. I stopped listening. I repeated his words – *first- and second-generation, young Muslims*, people like me who fit in. I'd become "them." I was being seen in the same light as the people we were investigating. I felt betrayed. When he said that we were fighting for democracy, wasn't I included? Wasn't I on the front line too? What was he talking about? He didn't get it. No one did. My blood boiled.

"Daniel, I can't work for you in Counter Terrorism if these are your views. I won't work under the supervision of William or Charles either, for that matter. This has gone on too long."

Rather than correct the situation, Daniel said, "Huda, why don't you take the week off? I'll sort things out. Clearly, you're very upset."

Feeling hopeless, I stood and said, "If you don't trust me, I can't contribute to this work environment. I'll no longer work at CT." He didn't react as I expected him to. I wanted him to say that CSIS needed me in Counter Terrorism. He didn't. He was silent. I agreed to take the week off. Wiping my flooding eyes, I left his office. Ryan saw my distress as I arrived at my office. "Are you okay?" I refused to look at him and didn't answer. I logged out of my desktop computer, secured my documents in the cabinet, took my spring coat, and dashed out. I hoped none of my other colleagues would see me as I ran down the staircase. I felt ashamed. I couldn't share the details of what was happening with colleagues or my parents. I went to a café so I wouldn't have to face my mother at home – she'd surely sense my distress.

Over coffee, I tried to make sense of what was going on. I told myself that I'd never go back to CSIS. Then I saw two Counter Intelligence employees having coffee next to me. I recalled one of them running out of the building behind me. I wondered whether he was following me. I left my coffee, hot as it was, and walked away. At home, I told my parents that I'd be going to Toronto to work for a week. I packed my suitcase and left. I didn't want my parents to know that my career with the service was ending. They'd be heartbroken. They knew that I loved my work. In Toronto, I stayed at Eman's place. Farah came out from New York for the weekend. I told them how I felt and how I was being treated as an inside threat for being a Muslim woman who wears a hijab. They said, "Find another job. This is too much." My sisters had always been my source of strength and true role models. Both were strong feminists, and they gave me solid advice that I took seriously. I knew they had my well-being in mind. I told them that I liked my work and was damn good at it. I'd advanced important investigations, and my colleagues relied on me. "Do they think you sympathize with terrorists?" Farah asked.

"No way. That'd be dumb," I responded. "Why would they?" I knew my colleagues didn't have such ridiculous ideas. But she'd struck a chord. Why didn't they trust me anymore? Was it my decision to wear a hijab? In despair, I walked Toronto's streets. I cried silently in public. I sat in coffee shops and ruminated over my predicament. There was no way in hell I was going back. *I should just go tell them that I want to resign. No, I should write a letter instead of going. But how will I pick up my stuff?* I wondered whether my service friends would think I'd lost clearance or, worse, broken the law. Would they think that I'd betrayed my country? *How can I face anyone after this? How can I face myself? Should I have taken off my hijab? Would that have made things better? What can I do? Who can I talk to? Who'll understand my pain?*

I fell into a depression and was glad that I wasn't at my parents' house where my mom would freak out. I couldn't get out of bed in the mornings. I felt mentally and physically exhausted. I wanted to sleep but couldn't. I suffered headaches and insomnia. My body was racked with pain. *How can I go to work after all this? And how will I quit?* I didn't know. In the mirror, I was surprised by how puffy my eyes were and by how bad my face looked.

As my more-or-less involuntary paid week off came to an end, Daniel called. It was Friday afternoon, and I was still in Toronto singing the blues. I was supposed to report back to work on Monday, but I still wasn't sure what my decision or fate would be. "Hello, Huda," he said clearing his throat and preparing for a long conversation.

"Hi, Daniel," I replied. I wasn't going to speak before him. Maybe I'd hear an apology or an expression of regret. Maybe there was a chance that all this would go away.

"Huda, how are you feeling?"

"I'm well," I replied. Silence doesn't make me uncomfortable. I use it as a strategy to make others uncomfortable and sometimes to force them to talk and break the tension.

"Huda, I'm transferring you out of Counter Terrorism to Counter Intelligence. Please, report to your supervisor, George, Monday morning," Daniel said.

I was baffled. I'd thought that I was valued in Counter Terrorism and that I'd provided knowledge and language skills needed for service operations. For the first time in my service, I felt devalued and dispensable. I was no longer the Arabic-speaking intelligence officer whom everyone fought over to get into their branches. What had changed? They'd changed. I'd changed. Everything had changed.

On Monday, I parked and sat in the CSIS lot in a state of fear and panic. My stomach hurt, as if it was the first day of school. I forced myself up the headquarters staircase. I was confused, heartbroken, and afraid of how I'd be received. Would people in Counter Intelligence know about the conflict? Would they accept me? Would they harass and bully me too? What about my former Counter Terrorism colleagues? What had they been told? How could I face them? What should I say? With all these thoughts rushing through my head, I reluctantly swiped my building pass, took the first elevator, avoided the cafeteria, and walked through Counter Intelligence in search of George's office. I didn't want to go to Counter Terrorism to get his location. I didn't want to go to Counter Terrorism period. I was entering a new division – Counter Intelligence Russia, a new world with a different investigative culture.

George's office door was open. If someone I cared about had been there, I would've burst into tears. But there wasn't, and I didn't. George greeted me. I said, "I'm Huda," wishing I wasn't. He didn't let on that he knew about what had happened in Counter Terrorism. George must've been in his late fifties or early sixties. He had grey hair, was reasonably fit, and looked tough, but he was kind. He clearly knew why I'd been transferred, but he avoided all conversation about it. He simply welcomed me to the desk and assigned me a low-priority investigation with piles of background documents to read.

My office was across from his. I shared it with another intelligence officer, a young Montrealer named Melanie. She was a long-time service employee who'd worked in physical surveillance before becoming an intelligence officer. She came in early every morning, was organized, and chatted little until she'd finished some work. Within days, I spilled the beans and told her what had happened. She was upset for me. Her attitude gave me hope that not everyone was ready to ostracize me. Some friendly and welcoming intelligence officers from my new branch came to visit during my first few weeks. I wondered what they'd heard and what they thought about me. I was afraid, awkward, and quiet in the same way as when my family moved to Montreal. Without English or French and with unfamiliar feelings, I'd had to study the others' faces for clues of what they knew, felt, and meant. It was the same among my new colleagues. I envied their privilege, which they were oblivious to, and how they were unhindered by their backgrounds. Surely, they hadn't experienced anything like what I had.

Their small talk about spring vacations and summer cottages was too much. It felt like they were screaming. It was all noise. Overwhelmed, I sat on the staircase and held my head in my hands trying to keep it together. I couldn't process anything. My mind was relentlessly pulled back to the humiliation and betrayal that I'd suffered. These feelings plagued me as I tried to adjust to my new role. In the mornings I'd tell myself that I had every right to be there – just like William, Charles, Daniel, and everyone else did. In the afternoons, once I had socialized with colleagues, I'd become overwhelmed with shame and pain, unable to leave my desk. I avoided the cafeteria and Information Centre. I wondered why no one asked me what had happened and why no one had stood up for me or complained about my treatment. What had they been told about me? Some former Counter Terrorism colleagues would call from time to time, but many didn't. One of them, a fierce supporter of William, even stopped greeting me.

One morning, I received an email from Marie, the Counter Terrorism administrator, with whom I'd had many positive interactions before. She forwarded me an email from Charles instructing her not to issue a Counter Terrorism certificate with my name. "No CT certificate for Huda," he wrote. Certificates were generally issued to all intelligence officers leaving a branch. An intelligence officer was eligible for one after spending at least two years there. I'd spent more than three years in Counter Terrorism and fully deserved one. They were hurriedly issued to leaving intelligence officers so everyone in the branch, including all management levels, could acknowledge and celebrate the intelligence officer's achievements and contributions. Usually, there'd be a lunch party at a local restaurant. Marie didn't think it fair that I wouldn't be receiving a certificate. She sent me the email so that I'd know it wasn't her call. I appreciated her gesture and acknowledged her honesty and courage, two traits I didn't see in my management team.

George sent me an email requesting that I present myself to Counter Intelligence's chief, Victor, who wanted to welcome me to the branch. When I told Victor what had happened in Counter Terrorism, he looked genuinely surprised but not outraged. Service managers and trained intelligence officers knew to hide their real reactions. He shifted the conversation. He told me great things about the Counter Intelligence work culture and my manager George's expertise in Russian operations and asked me to report concerns to himself directly. By the end of our meeting, I saw him as supportive and friendly, though I had difficulty believing it. I had difficulty trusting anyone anymore, especially managers. But for years, he continued to support me, which is why I feel his reaction and extended hand were genuine.

Days later, Jeff Yaworski, Counter Intelligence's deputy director, asked to meet with me, also with the pretext of welcoming me into his branch. He asked questions, including how much notice I'd been given before the transfer – Counter Intelligence had only been given notice the Friday before I'd shown up, but transferring intelligence officers were usually given weeks. I felt that he wanted me to tell him everything, so I did. I tried to hold back my tears, but they betrayed me and fell. He was uncomfortable and couldn't comment. He asked about my management team and changed the subject. Like Victor, he spoke about Counter Intelligence – the people and the work. I heard nothing. The flipping of pages and dismissal hurt. I felt small for having complained too long and for having detailed my experience.

For weeks, every morning, I wanted to call in sick, though I never had before. Still, I managed to get up, get dressed, and go to work. My parents, with whom I was living, had no idea what was going on. I couldn't shatter their world. They were proud that I was making our country safer. But they also saw that I no longer wanted to socialize and that I spent my afternoons until bedtime on the computer. They knew something was up at work and guessed it was because I wore a hijab. They told me that patience was part of faith – *Al Sabr min al Iman*, a famous Islamic hadith narrative. I felt that I'd somehow get over my troubles. I had no idea that they were just beginning.

In May 2005, a month after my appointment to Counter Intelligence, I received a call from an Internal Security investigator, Bruce, who asked me to report for an interview. Bruce asked what time I usually came in in the morning. I was always in by eight-thirty, but I said nine because I didn't want to be late to the interview. He asked me to come directly to Internal Security. "Yes, will do," I replied. I told my officemate and my supervisor. Seeing my pain and confusion, George and Melanie each expressed disappointment that the service would treat someone like this. I hoped that they meant that. I desperately wanted to be supported.

The morning of the Internal Security interview, I woke up early. I'd only slept three hours – I was nervous about what they'd ask. I wondered what the interview and Bruce would be like. When I walked into the building, I kept telling myself that Internal Security was impartial and fair. Even if Counter Terrorism managers saw me as no different than their targets, Internal Security wouldn't be so closed-minded. They'd hear my version and side with me. It was only eight-fifteen when I got to the office – way too early to show up to Internal Security. I took the elevator, walked to my office, and logged into my computer to go through emails, like I did every morning. I couldn't log in. I tried again and a third time. My account had been deactivated. Alarm bells went off in my head. *I'm going to be walked out of the building after my interview. They're going to fire me.* Melanie wasn't there that morning to console me. Neither was George.

I felt trapped in my office and numb. I couldn't move from my chair. I didn't want anyone to see me. I wished that I were invisible. I regretted ever walking into CSIS. I panicked again. I wanted to rush home, go to bed, cry my heart out, and forget everything.

"Come in, Huda," Bruce said when I walked into the Internal Security interview room. His voice was loud and unsuited to his thin, frail, and compact body. He asked me to read over some documents and sign them. I sat and read them carefully, looking for clues about how things would end. One of the documents was an agreement to be interviewed, the other an agreement to be polygraphed. Adrenaline surged through me – I went into fight-or-flight mode. I wasn't afraid anymore. *I must prove my loyalty. This is what Internal Security does – they assess employee reliability and loyalty.* "My five-year polygraph isn't due until 2007," I said. "Every IO is polygraphed every five years. You said you had questions. I'm here to answer them. I'm not prepared to take a polygraph examination and won't agree to one."

I'd learned a lot about polygraphs since recruitment. Heightened emotion and life crisis produce unreliable results. I was mentally and emotionally drained. I was anxious that my job was on the line. I was sure Internal Security wanted a deceptive or inconclusive result that didn't consider my mental state, either of which would be used against me. They failed to realize that the reason I'd made it through the lengthy and demanding recruitment process was because I was smart and in command of myself and because I can anticipate reasonable outcomes in new and challenging situations, which this clearly was.

Everyone had revealed their cards. I upped the tension. "Bruce, I'll only answer your questions with an Employee Association representative here." His small pale face turned angry and red. He was fuming over my attempt to protect myself by having a witness in the room. It was my way of taking control over a difficult situation. It worked. He threw his hands in the air and said, "Go call EA then."

"No, I'm going to sit right here while you do it," I said. He looked at me in disbelief, like I'd just outsmarted him. He hadn't prepared for that.

I told him that I'd already discovered my account had been deactivated and that I had no way of contacting an Employee Association representative. I looked at him carefully. I wanted to see his reaction to how I hadn't listened to his instructions about not going to my office. He asked that I leave the interview room and wait by the vending machines. "Certainly." I walked out and waited until the representative, my old supervisor Roger, arrived to attend the interview – apparently, he was the EA representative for both CT and CI. I guessed that it wasn't a demanding role. I knew Roger wouldn't protect me. William had changed my evaluations, but like most CSIS managers, Roger wasn't going to challenge a senior manager's decisions. That would be the kiss of death to career advancement. Still, I needed a witness in case things got worse with Bruce, who was angry and jumpy. Roger sat with us for a full day, listening, pretending to take notes, and saying nothing as Bruce asked his questions.

I'd prepared to answer all of Bruce's questions truthfully. Hopefully, I'd exonerate myself once and for all. I had a chance to prove my loyalty, and I'd use it. I decided that they wouldn't be revoking my clearance and that I sure as hell wasn't going to quit. I knew deep in my heart that I'd resign one day, but it was going to be my choice and on my terms.

The interview was more of an interrogation. Bruce questioned me about my faith, my level of religiosity, why I decided to wear a hijab, how often I prayed, and my contacts in the Muslim community. He said that these questions hadn't been asked in my first security screening interview because that interview was pre-9/11. CSIS wasn't interested in those things back then and had even incorrectly analyzed some of the information I'd provided. For example, I'd told them that I made $20 donations to the Canadian chapter of the Council on American Islamic Relations, which they assumed was CARE, a completely different international human-development organization. Apparently, he'd reviewed my interview tapes.

He asked how I felt about Canadian troops in Afghanistan, suicide bombings, and the Muslim Brotherhood and what my views about various well-known Islamic leaders in the Middle East were. I answered truthfully. I don't and didn't support any kind of violence. Suicide bombers are unjustifiable. I told him that having grown up in Egypt doesn't mean I supported the Muslim Brotherhood. I didn't have any connections with anyone in that organization. Bruce walked out of the room and came back with a printed logo of the Muslim Brotherhood and asked why their symbol has two crossed swords. I said that I didn't know. Then he asked how I arrived to work in the mornings. I told him I drove my Honda Civic. He asked whether I owned the car. I confirmed this. Then he said the car showed as owned by my father. I quickly remembered that the car had been my first big purchase and that I'd had no credit then, so my father had co-signed for me. Bruce then asked about my father, who he suggested would know many Lebanese cab drivers. "Okay," I said. Then he asked whether my father knew anyone who supported Hezbollah. My mouth dropped – my father was being linked to Hezbollah?! He had to be joking! I was disgusted by his lack of interviewing skills, questions, insinuations, and lack of knowledge. I wondered what kind of assessment he'd write about me. I'd met intelligence officers like him and always thought they should stay in the office to not embarrass themselves or the service. CSIS is wrong – not all intelligence officers can be investigators.

After seven hours of interrogation and three more the following day, Bruce seemed to admit defeat. He hadn't found evidence in my religious beliefs that I posed a security threat to CSIS. He didn't because there wasn't any. He told me to return to work and my accounts were reactivated. *What work? I haven't been able to work for five months.* I was mentally, physically, and emotionally exhausted. I couldn't talk to anyone about what had happened. Like a woman abused by her trusted life partner, I didn't want to report this to anyone. I felt that I'd brought it on myself. *I didn't have to wear a hijab. I didn't have to tell people I was Muslim. Heck, they didn't have to know I spoke Arabic. I could've simply explained my accent as Ethiopian and my culture as African and avoided all this nonsense.*

Alone in my bedroom that evening, I felt relieved and frustrated. I was exhausted. I hadn't slept well in days. As I analyzed what had happened, tears dripped onto my pillow, and I slowly fell asleep. But I couldn't skip a meal without Mom noticing. She came in at eight that evening. "Huda, get up and eat," she said in Harari, her voice comforting and smooth. My chest and heart were pained, and my stomach empty. She touched my hair as she always did and saw my eyes were red and puffy. She knew I didn't want to talk. She said, "You'll get through this. God's with you. Maybe, you can get another job. You have an education. You're bilingual. You could go anywhere else. You're creative and brilliant." I got up, took a long shower, ate dinner, and watched the evening news with Peter Mansbridge on *The National*, as I did most nights. I was glad that Dad had already gone to sleep for his early morning shift. I asked Mom not to say anything to him. He would've been outraged by the way CSIS men were treating me. He would've said, "There are laws in this country, and they can't do this to you."

I wasn't a quitter. I wouldn't be my father's daughter if I quit. I wasn't going to make it easy for them to get rid of me either. I had three annual evaluation reports, one from training and two from Counter Terrorism, and they were all stellar. On a four-point scale, I'd received threes and fours for knowledge, task completion, teamwork, and professionalism. Supervisors always commented that I'd excelled at my work, was motivated, and added value. It isn't arrogant to say that I was a model employee who hardly took time off. But I was still on my five-year probation. If they demonstrated legitimate concern about my performance, they could easily fire me.

At work, I received an email that Internal Security had no further concerns. I forwarded that email to George and said that my nightmare might finally and officially be over. I told Melanie too. I wanted my supporters to know that I was never a security concern and that I was as loyal as them. Then I fought back. I emailed Internal Security, asking to see their assessment. I thought that it would be biased. I was told that I had to make an official request through the Access to Information and Privacy Act. I didn't know how to do that, so I booked a meeting with the Employee Association president. She called what happened to me a "witch hunt" and told me that she too had been harassed and bypassed for promotions, not because of who she was but because she'd married a Black man. I learned from our conversation that reprisal was common and that I must select my battles. I told her that I'd think about her offer to help me write a complaint to the assistant director of Human Resources, who reported to the director.

A week later, I received a call from Human Resources indicating that a Muslim applicant had requested to speak with a Muslim intelligence officer before signing on. Human Resources said that the applicant had "concerns" about working as a Muslim for CSIS, including how the service would impact his personal life. First, I wondered whether it was a joke. Then, I wondered whether I was reading the email right. I was upset that Internal Security, or whoever was behind this, figured that I'd be so stupid. But my anger turned to amusement when I realized how desperate they were. When I told Melanie and George, they rolled their eyes at how ridiculous the ploy was. George told me that I didn't have to speak to the guy. "Just say you aren't interested." Nevertheless, I agreed and called the "applicant," who turned out to be a South Asian Muslim man with a heavy accent. "Hi, Ahmad," I said when I called. I didn't say *Al Salamu Alaykum* (Peace be upon you), the standard greeting between Muslims. I didn't want the transaction to be authentic. We spoke in English because he didn't speak Arabic. I used an alias, Heba, and told him that I'd been working for the service for four years and had worked Counter Terrorism investigations. I told him that I was happy to answer his questions about being a Muslim intelligence officer at CSIS. He asked, "How are you received as a Muslim intelligence officer? What do you tell your family, and what do you say to your friends? How does being an intelligence officer impact your personal and social life?"

"As a Muslim, you'll realize that the service has established thresholds, policies, and procedures to determine which organizations and individuals to target for investigation. Once in, you'll see the process is transparent. There's accountability through our review body, SIRC. As a Muslim, you'd contribute immensely to investigations because you'd have insights and language abilities others don't. Once you're an investigator in our regional offices, you'd build rapport with people and obtain information to advance investigations." I told him that CSIS employees are under strict obligations not to mention anything to family and friends about the job. "Except for the building you work in, your family shouldn't know anything about your work."

In June 2005, I forwarded a written complaint about three men – William, my former chief; Charles, my former deputy chief; and Bruce, the Internal Security interviewer – to the Employee Association president and the Human Resources assistant director, who responded unimpressively, saying cultural awareness was already part of the service's training program and that management was confident the service was providing first-class training to all employees. Clearly, the assistant director wasn't taking my complaint seriously. In the end, I backed down. I was worried about reprisal and figured that I'd won anyway. I'd proven I was loyal and reliable and would continue to prove it. I'd shown them that I had the same mission as everyone else in the service – to safeguard our country. I confirmed that you could be both Muslim and loyal.

Later that June, Marshall called me to his office. "Hi, Huda, have a seat." Not wanting to speak and holding my tears back, I locked my lips. I didn't know what to expect from him. I was upset at him for not interfering earlier and for having allowed my conflicts to persist. Where had he been when I was transferred? I showed him Marie's email about Charles denying me my Counter Terrorism certificate. "Do you see how immature Charles is?" I asked. "Do you know he often yells at IOs and no one speaks up?" Tears fell down my face. "Why, Marshall? Internal Security cleared me! Why was I treated this way? Because I'm a Muslim woman?"

Marshall said, "Huda, I'd be honoured to present you with a Counter Terrorism certificate. I'll have one prepared. As for what happened, I'm sincerely sorry. I'll make a note on their files about how badly this was handled. I'm also going to write a comment on your last performance evaluation, which William changed. How is George? How are your colleagues in CI? You have a few months until your intelligence officer investigations course." It was an uncomfortable conversation, and we both needed to distract ourselves by talking about work. To ease the tension, he went on about Counter Intelligence culture and told me interesting stories about my new managers.

In spring 2005, as the muddy snow melted, so did my wounds. I worked unenthusiastically and tried to make sense of all that had happened. I told myself that I belonged and had a right to be there. It was hard, but I became more resilient and less emotional. I also behaved like victims of abusive relationships do – I convinced myself that things had changed and that what I'd endured was because of my own poor judgment. I wanted to win back CSIS's trust and approval. I even felt remorse for fighting back, and I justified the abuse that they'd thrust upon me. *I'm a Muslim working at CSIS post-9/11. I have contacts in the Muslim community. Of course, they were going to be suspicious. They don't know what to do with me. But things have changed. They've changed. I've changed – for the better.*

My difficulties taught me a lot about myself. I'd known since high school that I wasn't a pushover, but this experience taught me not to act impulsively. I learned that patience can pay off. I learned that I had personal dignity and the strength to demand it. I owned my fate. I continued to contribute to the service and to my country, despite the harassment. Though I was cleared by Internal Security, for the rest of my time at CSIS, a bitter taste remained. I learned that bias, distrust, and miscommunication can ruin lives. Had I felt Internal Security was independent, impartial, and fair, I would've respected their request for an interview and further scrutiny.

13 | LONDON

In the summer of 2005, humbled by my colleagues' and managers' expertise on the Russia investigation file, I had no choice but to dig in my heels. "What makes a good Counter Intelligence analyst?" I asked George, my supervisor and a long-time expert on the Russia files.

"Attention to detail, patience, and a whole lot of vodka." He smiled. "It takes years to crack a case." One such case was of two spies sent by Russian intelligence to Toronto to assume Canadian identities and then lie low for decades. They were to infiltrate academia and obtain Western intelligence from policy makers, military, and intelligence officials.

I found George's calm demeanour and language intriguing – he used words like illegals, sleeper agents, defection, spy tradecraft, official and unofficial covers, diplomatic immunity, and expulsions. His language demonstrated respect for our adversaries as professionals in the trade: we had to outsmart them while they needed to be steps ahead and discreet in their craft. I suddenly felt as if I were just starting out as an intelligence officer. This was a refreshing and much-needed change from my previous investigations of Islamist extremists, a job that felt more like law enforcement work. Attempting to catch unsophisticated criminals made me feel like a police officer or something similar, but instead of hunting for criminals after they committed a crime, it was our mission to find them before their crimes were perpetrated. There is a lot of grey area when it came to searching for Islamist extremists, while the work in Counter Intelligence seemed more cut and dry.

At my desk, I read backgrounds on the Russian intelligence agencies – the Foreign Intelligence Service, the Main

Intelligence Directorate, and the Federal Security Service – and on emerging threats from Russia. But I still didn't feel knowledgeable on my file. And I didn't believe I'd get there. Others knew their cases like the back of their hands, and some even spoke Russian. I felt like an observer and wondered how long it would take me to get into the swing of things in Counter Intelligence. I realized that the zest and excitement I'd developed for my Counter Terrorism investigations hadn't transferred with me to my new role.

Then on Thursday, 7 July 2005, four terrorists carried out a series of coordinated attacks in London, England. They detonated bombs on two underground trains and one double-decker bus at three locations in Tavistock Square – London's first and most lethal Islamist-inspired terrorist attacks. They killed fifty-two people and injured more than seven hundred. The London transit system was shut down for fear the attack was chemical or biological. Police and emergency sirens rang out as journalists scrambled to make sense of what had happened. I watched news of the attack with my colleagues and recalled the Crevice operation and how CSIS had feared there were other groups like Crevice out there. I immediately wondered what my Counter Terrorism colleagues were working on and felt frustrated I wasn't there to help.

I followed the BBC news breaks and was saddened for the Londoners who'd just been celebrating having beaten France's bid to host the 2012 Olympics. Fear, grief, and heightened anxiety hit the city. Just like after 9/11, charts of the names of the missing emerged as people tried to locate their loved ones. Against the loud sounds of sirens and yellow crime scene tape, British security and intelligence organizations, police, and emergency responders worked around the clock to respond to the attacks.

Just two weeks later, on 21 July, five more terrorists tried to replicate the incident. Police responded to calls of explosions and panic at three underground stations: Shepherd's Bush, Warren Street, and the Oval. Police also received reports of a fourth explosion aboard a double-decker bus in Shoreditch. A fifth bomber, later learned to have lost his nerve, abandoned his weapon in a park. Fortunately, there were no casualties. All the 21/7 explosives failed to detonate because of faulty construction. Police recovered forensic material from the scenes of the attacks, collected witness statements, and riffled through thousands of closed-circuit television images to identify the terrorists.

I was in Ottawa following the news. My parents and I were surprised to learn that the terrorists included East Africans, Somalis, Eritreans, and Ethiopians. The terrorists were from our part of the world. I didn't know that I'd soon be dispatched to support efforts in London and that my work would help in the eventual conviction of these terrorists and their network.

The British security establishment had sent a special communique out across the Five-Eye Intelligence community: the United States, Canada, Britain, New Zealand, and Australia. The British were seeking intelligence officers and communications analysts with enhanced, top-secret clearance and East African linguistic and cultural backgrounds to assist with their 7/7 and 21/7 investigations. I'd served as CSIS's Counter Terrorism liaison to the Communications Security Establishment (CSE) in 2004. CSE had a record of my linguistic profile and had reached out to CSIS international language department with my name.

With a sense of urgency to offer the British Security Service timely assistance, director Jim Judd approved my deployment to London. This ignited conversations, across the two time zones, between Jeff Yaworski, my deputy director general, and David, the CSIS head-of-station in London. David, who couldn't contain his excitement, called at my desk to confirm my availability. An hour later, when Jeff called me into his office and formally asked, I accepted the deployment and said I wanted to be on the first plane out of Canada to the UK. There were, of course, procedures and paperwork that needed to be fulfilled first. I learned that I had to get a special passport, which took the service about a day to arrange for my pickup. David was impatient. He wanted me there yesterday. I was surprised to receive a call directly from him at home the day of my departure as I was packing.

"Huda, it's a man from your work, David," shouted my dad as he handed me the phone and turned down the volume on Al Jazeera, the channel that seemed to be on whenever he was home. I cleared my throat and took a deep breath before answering: "Hi, David. It's Huda."

"Hi, Huda. Did you finally manage to buy your ticket?" he asked.

"Yes, I got my special passport, bought my ticket, and will be flying this afternoon. Should arrive by 5 p.m. your time."

"Okay, great," he replied. "I'm really looking forward to having you here. I can't say much, but the security situation is very tense. It's really sad. People are feeling, well, you'll see it on everyone's faces. We're shaken up by the attacks – understandably so."

"I can only imagine, David." I could feel the stress of the situation settling into little lines across my forehead. "At least they've captured the ones who were on the run. I guess the worry is there may be more of them out there?"

"You'll see when you get here, but there's definitely a lot of fear on the streets," he coughed. "By the way, a prominent Muslim leader, Zaki Badawi, issued a fatwa that Muslim women don't have to wear a hijab, given the rising attacks on them," he paused. "That may be something for you to consider, if you choose to." Though he spoked respectfully, I could tell there was hesitation in his voice, and how he ended this part of the discussion only verified my assumption: "Erm, just thought I should tell you."

My heart skipped a beat. "Ah, yeah, I heard about that. I'm certainly open to it, if necessary." I promised to call him as soon as I arrived.

My cab ride from the London airport to the hotel reminded me of my childhood school commutes in Cairo. I had always loved taking in the historic architecture of the city, and apparently still did, watching famous sites pass me by from the cab to downtown London. There were vehicles driving on the left side of the road, red double-decker buses, black taxi cabs, churches, historic landmarks, and the rushing Thames River.

Shortly after I checked into my small, Victorian-style downtown hotel, I met David in the lobby. We talked for an hour, using code words so as not to alert anyone nearby. He told me a meeting was scheduled for nine the next morning at MI5 headquarters. Then, over Lebanese *manakeesh*, we spoke of many things, business and personal. David had east-coast charm. He was a world traveller who looked and spoke more like a diplomat than a spy, dressing in expensive suits with a certain affinity for fancy ties. He was into yoga, kept fit, and his handshake and posture were as deliberate as his words. Unlike most CSIS top brass, he hadn't served in the RCMP or military before CSIS – a rarity.

While we chatted, I was surprised to learn that David had been in Dire Dawa, Ethiopia, where I was born. I'd never met a service member who'd heard of it, let alone one who could locate it on a map. He was well-travelled in the Middle East, and when I told him that I grew up in Cairo, he couldn't help but joke. "So, tell me, why the heck are all Egyptians, at least the ones I've encountered, so damn full of themselves?"

I laughed bemusedly. "Look, Egyptians are like Americans, in a way," I said. "They have history and culture and outnumber other Arab populations. They hold power and influence over millions of Arabs and Muslims. All other Arabs change accents and speak the Egyptian dialect, but most Egyptians make no effort to learn other Arab cultures. They train international imams at Al-Azhar University and send their own all over the world, including to Canada."

David smiled. I spoke with the waiter in Arabic and exchanged jokes. David continued smiling. I wanted David to like me. I assumed he'd already spoken with my director general and perhaps others who held similar, shall I say, unsavoury opinions of me. It made sense that our dinner meeting was more than a simple "welcome to the team." It was also about rapport building and perhaps intelligence gathering, to see where my head was at. I found myself opening up to him. I told him how CSIS had treated me but played down how hurt I was. I did my best to contain my emotions, but revisiting the story caused me much anguish. Then I took a deep breath and said that I'd felt scrutinized for being a hijab-wearing Muslim woman. "It's not like they didn't know I was Muslim when they hired me. Suddenly, after three years and all my hard work, they wanted to know my reasoning for wearing a hijab and all about my activities outside the office. Why? In case I turn on them? It took a lot to clear my name and reputation."

David assured me that if the service had any doubts about me, they wouldn't have sent me to London. "You've been vindicated," he said. *Vindicated* – the word reverberated in my mind. I repeated it aloud. I hoped it was true, but I knew not to trust anyone. Even David's substantial charm couldn't restore my shattered innocence. David, kind as he seemed, could never understand what it was like to be *other*. "Right," I said, not wanting to show him how angry I still was. I judged that David would never understand what it was like to be a racialized Muslim working in Counter Terrorism at CSIS after 9/11.

"Are you up for heading to Thames House now?" he asked, as we walked out of the restaurant. "Maybe we could go in and introduce you?"

"Of course," I replied.

"Okay, pay close attention because you'll be on your own tomorrow morning," he said.

We took the tube to Westminster station and walked past Parliament, Big Ben, and the Richard I statue. I was tired. David kept asking what I knew about London and the security issues they were currently facing. It was midnight when we finally arrived. We stood beneath the arched entrance of Thames House, also known as MI5, the headquarters of Britain's spy agency. Its white exterior glowed in the moonlight, which stirred the butterflies dancing around in my chest even further. David opened the heavy metal door and ushered me in. With my ocean blue hijab around my hair, I was smiling and full of curiosity. This moment was meaningful for me – I was about to embark on one of the most important chapters of my career as an intelligence officer representing Canada.

"Stop! Freeze!" shouted one of two armed officers moving quickly towards me from both sides, guns pointed right in my direction. Bent at their knees for ultimate flexibility, they gestured with their hands, awaiting my response. Fearful, I stood perfectly still. My adrenaline rushed, my heart raced, and my body tensed. I couldn't risk even turning to ask my colleague for help.

"No, no!" David shouted, rushing in behind me, guarding me with his hands, and telling them we were from Canada's security service. I stood, dazed, as David gave the two armed, stern-looking men our information. Their weapons were soon back at their sides.

"Oh my God, David," I exclaimed as we waited to speak to his MI5 contacts. I remember thinking, *Maybe now he'll have an idea of what it feels like to be a Muslim intelligence officer.*

We took the elevator up to the glass-walled foreign-language office. Mike, an MI5 manager, welcomed us and apologized for what had occurred. The other foreign-language analysts stood to greet me. Mike introduced us and selected Asma to mentor me on the computer applications I'd be using to translate. She logged me in and pulled up the lines. I put headphones on and began listening. "The first dialect was Oromo, the next Amharic, then Somali, Tigrinya, and the last one was Harari." Mike, eyes open wide, was blown away. "I can also work on any Arabic lines, if you like," I added. "I'm familiar with most Arabic dialects.

"Right then, I've got my work cut out for me for the next few days," Mike said. I'd classified the languages and dialects on the recordings for translation, and it was now up to Mike to send them off for translation. The Harari and some of the Arabic lines were for me to work on. They'd become associated with Hussain Osman, one of the 21/7 attackers.

On 21 July, Osman, riding the tube at Shepherd's Bush, had reached into his bag to detonate a homemade explosive. The device failed and he got flustered as smoke filled the air. Then, everyone panicked. He managed to escape in the chaos, but police identified him on camera and proceeded to hunt him down, along with the five other terrorists who'd also attempted to detonate explosives. A day later, police mistakenly identified Jean Charles de Menezes, a Brazilian student, as Osman at Stockwell Station and fatally shot him. Osman had gone into hiding at a friend's home and later escaped aboard a train to Europe. Osman was eventually arrested in Italy after police traced his mobile device to his older brother's house, where he was hiding. It was up to me to transcribe the tapes and determine how he'd become a terrorist, who his support network was, and who was involved with him, willingly or unwillingly. Government Communications Headquarters, MI6, MI5, the Metropolitan Police Service (i.e., the Met or Scotland Yard), and Italian security and law enforcement agencies, all investigating the 21/7 attacks, were eagerly awaiting my findings. I was to answer crucial, urgent questions: how and why Osman had gone to Rome; whether his brother, also arrested, or family knew about the attacks; whether they supported him; and whether another terrorist network existed in Italy. Answers to these questions could be used to prevent another attack, hold Osman accountable, and determine the extent of his terrorist network. I told Mike I could begin transcribing immediately, but he saw how tired I was and insisted we start the next morning after a scheduled meeting with Counter Terrorism executive managers. Mike, smiling ear to ear, escorted me and David out and the two of us took the tube from Westminster. *What a day*, I thought as my head hit the pillow.

14 | THE CANADIAN SPY

I woke the next morning full of energy to meet the MI5 executive managers at nine. When I got to the tube entrance, dozens of people were leaving the station, some running. I was confused but kept walking. Police rushed past, but still I kept going. A civilian hurriedly walking out of the station gave me a venomous look. I thought he was going to spit in my face. I was confused until a transit security officer asked me to exit the station. She informed me that the tube was being evacuated. An unattended knapsack had been found, and officials feared that it might be another bomb attack. The panic on everyone's face suddenly made sense. I became afraid. *What if I die in London, alone and away from my family?*

I found myself on the street with no idea how to get to work. I hadn't written the address down, and my cheap cell phone didn't have Internet. I was horrified that I was going to be late on my first day at MI5. *How embarrassing!* I frantically searched for a cab. I told a driver that I wanted to get to the Security Service, MI5. He looked at me blankly. "I beg your pardon?"

"The Security Service, please." This time he looked at me like I was from another planet and said he had no idea what I was saying. I told him to take me to Parliament and I'd walk from there. *Unreal!* As he drove, I willed the cab to move faster through London's busy streets. My impatience was getting the best of me.

I made it to the meeting on time and did my best to look unfazed. David was waiting for me in the lobby. We were escorted to a large meeting room, where the executive Counter Terrorism managers were waiting. They welcomed us and thanked me and the service for my quick involvement. They'd spoken to Mike and knew I'd be transcribing on the project. They asked that I focus on the timeline of events, which was crucial. "You also speak Arabic?" Mike asked.

"I do. I grew up in Cairo, and my father's side is Yemeni." They were fascinated. Asma asked that I speak to her directly if I needed assistance or had concerns. Sarah and Mike would take care of me as well. They briefed me and David on the threat environment and the latest developments on the 7/7 and 21/7 investigations.

The meeting ended. David went back to his office at the Canadian High Commission. Mike walked me over to Sarah, the team leader. "This is Huda from Canada. She's here to help transcribe some of the Arabic and East African lines connected to the 7/7 and 21/7 investigations." Everyone walked up to shake my hand. They asked what part of Canada I was from, and some expressed their desire to visit someday. It felt like the first day in a new school, a recurring feeling in my life. Asma and Sarah, who'd already set up an account with my name, ushered me back to my cubicle.

I soon found myself alone at my desk, headphones on, transcribing the recordings. I began producing summary reports for MI5 to forward to the Met. I was transcribing actionable information to be used during the questioning of Osman and other suspects and for Osman's extradition to England from Italy, where he was held. My chilling reports detailed how he'd been radicalized, how he and others had planned their operation, and how he'd involved his family and a friend to help him flee the country. Once my reports had been sent up, case analysts came down to garner more context and to provide updates.

During my first week, as I walked through the MI5 canteen at lunch, I felt everyone's eyes on me, but as I realized their looks were positive, I was all smiles. I heard whispers: "She's Canadian, from their security service." Some of the staff working at the canteen pointed out that they were also Muslim and suggested some halal options. I was proud to offer my valuable skills to MI5 and pleased to represent my country and religion. Given the horrific terrorist attacks, I was hoping to provide a positive representation of Muslims. I felt like I was walking on a cloud. Returning to work, I plugged away into the night like everyone else. I was gratified to know that my contribution would be essential to the investigation and that I was once again a trusted member of a team working to safeguard a country – not my own, but one I'd come to love.

Over the next weeks, I worked diligently, putting in long hours and producing reports. Many MI5 analysts and investigators asked to meet with me to get my insights on the file – this was the icing on my cake. I was impressed by the MI5 analysts' dedication and expertise. I loved how they used the word *brilliant* so generously and would greet me with a casual "Hiya!" in the elevators. It took a lot of practice to offer a "Hiya" back, and I couldn't help but be uncomfortable at first. I loved being "the Canadian." I wore it like a badge of honour. Soon, I was invited to office lunches, colleagues' homes, and for drinks at bars. I would not come to know my colleagues' last names, but they did make a concerted effort to make me feel welcome, on one occasion even taking me for a night out on Edgeware Road, the Arab part of the city. We went to an Arab café with loud Arabic music and smoked shisha while exchanging stories. It seemed unreal. I was hanging out with British spies in London!

I was surprised to learn that my "fame" had spread beyond Thames House. One day, John Prescott, the British deputy prime minister, walked in with an entourage of politicians and beelined to my desk. "So, you're the famous Canadian here to help us?" he began. I stood tall and proud to greet him.

"Young lady, I hear you speak several languages. That's quite the talent you have. Where are you from in Canada?" I told him that I'd grown up in Montreal and had later moved to Ottawa. He told me that he'd spent time in Western Canada and added, "CSIS is lucky to have you. We all are."

Humbled, I nodded. "I'm happy to be here. I'm falling in love with London and its people," I said.

"Splendid," he replied, offering his hand again while continuing. "Well, I want to thank you on behalf of the British government for your service."

After Mr Prescott left, I immediately called David to tell him. He congratulated me and asked that I come meet the Canadian High Commissioner that afternoon – news about my encounter with the British deputy prime minister spread throughout Global Affairs Canada and Canada's Ministry of Public Safety. I was feeling a bit overwhelmed by the honours. Two in one day! I also received an invitation to meet with managers at the British Secret Intelligence Service (BSIS or MI6), a massive organization with centuries-old history and a spectacular building that's home base to the fictional James Bond. I couldn't wait to tell my colleagues that I had been there.

Once work became more manageable, David invited me to dinner. He bought halal meat and cooked a delicious meal at his home. I met his wife and son. I told them I'd visited the British Museum and seen the Rosetta Stone, and we debated whether the Brits should keep the stone or repatriate it to Egypt. David thought the stone should be preserved in Britain. He argued for its international significance. His wife and son thought it belonged to Egypt. I couldn't agree more.

I returned to CSIS headquarters in September 2005 for five weeks to complete my scheduled IOIC training with the rest of my class. David knew I would return to London after my training and asked that I bring him back some of his favourite crunchy peanut butter upon my return. At headquarters, I was expected to fold right back into the role of an officer-in-training, under watchful eyes. I was excited to undergo the IOIC training program, not just for the specific skills I would be gaining but also because I would do so with my head held high after such a successful period in London. It amused me how much my success irritated some of the haters and racists at CSIS. I identified them based on tone and the snide comments they'd make about me around the office. Being able to catch them and call them out in a meaningful way was futile – it's easy to pretend to have good intentions when faced with the consequences of uttering a discriminatory remark.

In training, I learned how to conduct effective interviews and detect deception, much of it based on police methods of investigation. They first asked us all to lie in an interview with an experienced officer and revealed to us some physical signs of ourselves lying. Mine was looking up for a split second before answering and then smiling. We also trained in how to plan and execute cover operations, including direct training with senior officers who have taken part in one. We learned basic surveillance and countersurveillance to ensure that we weren't followed when we met with our sources, and so that we could properly train sources to do the same for their own security. Additionally, we spent a considerable amount of time on human-source recruitment, development, and termination. What motivates someone to work for the service, betraying an ideology or country? How can we check and double-check a source's credibility, especially in a situation when the threat is imminent? These remain unanswered questions here, as I can't share information about the program that would reveal classified information and service investigative methods. Suffice it to say, I successfully completed the training. Upon graduation, I was posted to the Toronto Region to work as an investigator – but first, I had to return to London to continue my assignment with MI5, who were still sending me material to work on while I was in training.

In October 2005, following the end of my investigative training, I returned to work as an intelligence analyst on MI5's Counter Terrorism East Africa desk. I can't discuss the investigations that my colleagues and I worked on during this time, but I can share a surveillance exercise that I took part in with seasoned MI5 and Met surveillance officers. The team lead gave me a road map and asked me to follow an officer without being detected. I was to report back if the source or anyone else acted suspiciously. Fearing that I'd lose the source in the unfamiliar city, I followed closely but without being discovered. We walked downtown, stopped at the British Museum, and returned to the city's business district. Afterward, when I walked into the debriefing meeting, I was surprised by how large the team was. A few officers burst out laughing in awe and disbelief. I smiled back, not understanding. They all recalled seeing me but had quickly dismissed me as a member of the public. They'd thought that there was no way a Muslim woman with a headscarf would be part of the exercise. It was brilliant, as the British say.

My most magical night in London was the 2005 Canada House Christmas party, attended by international diplomats, MI6 and MI5 Security Service officials, Director Judd, and MI5 director Eliza Manningham-Buller. She had sent me a letter thanking me for my contributions to MI5, but here I would see her in person. She was wearing a glamorous, sparkling greyish dress. She made a star-like appearance, gave a wonderful toast, and then simply disappeared. She was a woman running a national security agency during a critical time, so I really admired her and was excited to be in the same room with her. The MI5 executive managers I'd met on my first day were also there and wanted to hear about my experience. Given my unique profile and linguistic abilities, European security officials were encouraging me to set up a consulting firm in London. I smiled. So did David, who offered me more compliments. That evening,

I was invited to dinner at a central London Thai restaurant with Director Judd, David, and other CSIS colleagues he worked alongside.

At dinner, I sat next to Director Judd. I wanted him to know me, just as David had come to know me. We seemed to hit it off. I gave him the Coles Notes version of my life – where I was born; where I grew up; how I immigrated to Montreal, his hometown, at a young age; how I learned French and English, etc. We discovered that we're both Carleton University alumni. He told me about his travels, spoke about immigration trends in Canada, and offered his political views. I felt like we made a connection.

As my time in London neared its end, my officemate Peppe asked whether I wanted to extend my secondment. Despite how much fun I was having and how fulfilling the work was, I was homesick. I was excited about returning to Canada to work in Toronto as an investigator with the skills I'd acquired at MI5. My London colleagues organized a farewell dinner party for me, reserving half the seats at a local restaurant. It seemed every colleague I'd interacted with during my year in London came to say goodbye. I was flooded with memories of my time there and overwhelmed by emotions. A colleague asked why I was so fond of British culture. "How could I not be? You all made me feel like I belong." I don't think they understood how deeply my gratitude ran. The British understand Arab culture and Islamic civilization. They didn't say to me the ignorant things North Americans sometimes do.

On my last day at MI5, I met with an executive manager who thanked me for my service. I told him it was a privilege to work with his incredible team. David entered as I was leaving. "We should get you a hijab with a Canadian flag on it so they know you're ours," he said grinning. I smiled and gave him a gentle push for being silly and protective. I liked it. I liked him.

That day, management and colleagues presented me with a unique merit award. I was honoured. They gave me goodbye gifts and many hugs. I was sad to leave, and my tears flowed freely. *I should stay!* I was torn. I was going to miss these people dearly, but I was eager to start in Toronto as an investigator. I knew that I'd look back and appreciate every minute of my time in London. I still do. My MI5 deskmate Mark stood beside me, held my shoulders, and in an American accent said, "Hold it together, girl." He liked my accent and often made me repeat words and expressions so he could get them right. We had an inside joke about the term "security violation." Every day, I would check twice that I had placed my top-secret files in the cabinet and double-check that it was locked. Mark looked at me as though I was being strange. I said, "What? I don't want to get a security violation here."

"A 'violation'? That is *sooo* American," he laughed. "Like in football? I think you mean, a security *breach*," he said playfully.

"Oh, right. A *breach*," I repeated. From that day forward, I would say "breach" instead of "violation."

Following my departure from London, I took a couple weeks off and travelled to Jordan, Israel, and the occupied territories. With a Canadian friend living in Amman, Jordan, we visited the capital city's old quarters, the Dead Sea, and Petra, and then crossed over into Israel via the King Hussein Bridge. In Jerusalem, I prayed at the Al Aqsa Mosque. I also visited Bethlehem, Ramallah, Hebron, and Tel Aviv.

After returning to Canada in May 2006, I spent a week in Ottawa at headquarters and then relocated to Toronto. In Ottawa, I received a call from Director Judd's secretary, who told me that the director would like to thank me in person. I was excited to talk to him again.

Service executives work on headquarters' X floor, which unsurprisingly is better maintained with improved lighting, polished marble floors, and thicker carpets. The walls are decorated with long glass cases for memorabilia, including gifts from foreign intelligence organizations, some with inscriptions in Arabic and some in languages I didn't know. On the left wall preceding the director's office were photographs of service employees who'd made significant contributions to CSIS and Canada's safety and security. I recognized many employees, including my former supervisor, Richard. I wondered what I needed to do to get my picture up there. I was still hopeful that I'd make such contributions to my country and its national intelligence agency. As I lingered over the photos, my cynicism overcame me. *They should put my picture up there for all the harassment I've endured because of my hijab. I weathered that storm and made CSIS look good to MI5.* My resentment passed. *It's over.* My work in London and the praise I received from MI5 would surely pave the way for CSIS to once again recognize and value my expertise. I honestly thought London had changed all that.

With anxiety and excitement, I presented myself to Director Judd's secretary and waited to be escorted in. The director's office was large and imposing. His desk was well back from his reception area, which was furnished with comfortable seating – an arrangement meant to protect sensitive documents from prying eyes, since the materials on his desk were often highly classified and related to Canada's most sensitive national security concerns. The director welcomed me to the reception area and sat across from me. He leaned in with a warm friendly smile. "How are you, Huda?" He was known as a man of few words who shied away from the spotlight, but he was also an engaging conversationalist. He asked about my family and my recent travels to Jordan and Israel. We spoke at length about Petra, a historic city in southern Jordan, famous for its centuries-old rock-cut architecture and its complex water conduit system. The director had been to Jordan but not Petra. He listened to my stories with interest and shared his thoughts about the fascinating Moroccan mosques he'd visited. After a half-hour of small talk, he abruptly adopted a formal tone. He thanked me on behalf of the service for assisting MI5 with their investigations of the July 2005 terrorist attacks. My contributions, he said, were greatly valued by MI5, and this had given CSIS real-time access to relevant information. Of course, the relationship between the two agencies was strong and well established, but the director made clear that CSIS had received exclusive access to timely intelligence due to my presence at MI5. He stood and shook my hand, wishing me well at my new posting in Toronto.

I told him that it had been an honour to help both agencies. I also said that I'd enjoyed working with MI5 and appreciated the opportunity the service had provided me. As I said this, I couldn't help but wonder what he thought about the harassment and discrimination complaints I'd sent through the Employee Association to Human Resources. David had told me that Director Judd had been briefed about these incidents. I'd heard the director speak about the need to value diversity in the organization, but I thought it best not to ask him directly about my complaints.

I then had one last meeting at headquarters with Internal Security – a routine interview for all relocating and deploying CSIS employees. After my Internal Security ordeal in 2005, I had contempt for the department. I was bitter about their inappropriate questions concerning my faith, their inferences that I was a possible radical Muslim because I wore a hijab, and, worst of all, the damage they did to my career by questioning my loyalty. I didn't trust them to form an unbiased assessment of me. My chest tightened as I walked the corridors of Internal Security. This time, my interactions with them were vastly different. I was greeted by John, a slim man with glasses who had a meticulous air and was close to retirement. I liked those close-to-retirement guys – they had nothing to lose and always gave me useful insights into CSIS's people and culture. "I heard you just met with the director," he said.

"Yes, Director Judd thanked me for my work with the British Security Service in London," I replied, reminding myself to keep it brief with Internal Security.

"Well, I'm going to ask you a few questions about your time in London and your travels across Europe and the Middle East," John said matter-of-factly. "Then I have a few documents for you to sign." Despite John's friendly tone, I didn't trust anyone from Internal Security. We spoke for an hour. As I signed the documents, John sensed my anxiety and coldness. He then said something I'll never forget: "They've got nothing on you, you know, from the last time you met with Internal Security."

"I know!" I responded abruptly to show this should be obvious.

"My advice is to watch for the phone calls," he said, mimicking a phone to his head.

"The phone calls?"

John let me know that sometimes managers informally seek information about incoming intelligence officers through internal reference checks. They want to know the good, the bad, and the ugly about an IO before they meet them. They'll ask about everything – who their friends are, what the employee wants to accomplish, and what makes them tick. I'd heard these checks were frequent but assumed they focused on employee conduct, work ethic, professionalism, etc. I didn't think they pried into personal lives. I was wrong.

15 | TORONTO REGION

In May 2006, I was elated to receive my transfer papers for the Toronto Region and to get to use my CSIS badge. After four years as a case officer, and having successfully completed my IOIC training program, I was finally an investigator. I was excited to sign out service vehicles, get out and talk to sources, and collect information that could help save lives. Though I got a taste of this type of work in London, I was excited to be doing it in my own country and, more specifically, in Toronto, the most diverse city in the world. As a single, adventurous, and curious thirty-year-old woman, I thought there was nothing but clear skies ahead for me. I'd meet people from all walks of life. Every day would be different. I couldn't believe that I would be getting paid to do this. My dreams were all coming true.

Because of widespread fear of another terrorist attack like London's and the global surge in radicalization following the Iraq War, the Toronto Region was then focused on Islamist extremism. My training had taught me interview techniques, deception indicators, spy tradecraft, firearms use, and self-defence. I had experience and skillsets others didn't, including cross-cultural communication abilities and my familiarity with Middle Eastern languages. These would set me apart from other intelligence officers, I was sure of it. On top of all those positives, I had just successfully worked on a high-profile international MI5 investigation in London. This boosted my confidence about my ability to work towards the CSIS mandate.

The Toronto Region is CSIS's largest office outside headquarters. It's where ambitious career managers and new intelligence officers go to establish names for themselves. It's also where the most legendary CSIS files unfolded. There, CSIS source Grant Bristow had infiltrated the Heritage Front, Canada's most influential white supremacist organization. CSIS Toronto had also uncovered Russian spies living undercover as a married couple. Ian and Laurie Lambert were unmasked as Yelena Olshevskaya and Dmitry Olshevsky, spies who were later deported to Russia. They'd taken their identities from Canadians who'd died as infants. Plus, after 9/11, the Toronto desk ran many Al Qaeda–linked investigations and was where the Toronto 18 investigation started.

I was determined to re-establish my service credibility and help stop terrorism in Canada's most populated city. My focus was on gaining as much experience as possible so I could qualify for a foreign officer position, which would bring my work overseas – I'd have to be especially careful not to trip up and make mistakes that would ruin my chances. There were rules every intelligence officer was advised to follow: use your spy tradecraft every time you meet a source, don't get sloppy, don't fall in love with your subjects of interest (even if they fall in love with you), ensure your sources sign the receipt when you pay them, and never accept gifts.

A colleague in a regional office once recounted to me how difficult it is to speak with members of the Muslim community. Many Muslims interpreted the war on terror as a pretext for open discrimination against Muslims and thought that security agencies unfairly focused on their communities in police-state countries. Many didn't want anything to do with the service. My colleague was a culturally sensitive, soft-spoken, articulate man whom I looked up to. He told me that he once walked into the house of a Canadian Saudi family to conduct a routine interview. The parents welcomed him in; he took off his shoes as a sign of respect and sat down. Just as he was getting comfortable, the family's son walked in and asked who my colleague was and what he thought he was doing talking to his parents. When he told him that he worked for CSIS, the son brought my colleague's shoes to the living room, placed them on the fancy carpet – where perhaps no other pair of shoes had ever been placed – and asked him to leave immediately. My colleague tried to reason with the young man and explain CSIS's mandate and the routine nature of the interview, but the young man didn't want to hear it. He asked that the meeting be conducted in the presence of a lawyer.

Although most people were cooperative, some weren't. Muslims were being profiled as terrorists at airports, border crossings, and places of work. They were seeing their religion tarnished with the media linking Islam to terrorism. Worse, the war on terror was being used as a pretext to justify the Iraq War and to further repress freedoms and justice in certain dictator-run countries. For many Canadians, Maher Arar's wrongful charge of terrorism and rendering by the United States to Syria, where he was tortured, demonstrated how innocent people can get caught up and tortured for no reason at all. The inquiry into Maher Arar's case, including the roles the RCMP and CSIS played, revealed the dark side of national security.

My colleague's story about the young Saudi spoke volumes about my work. I understood how the young man felt. He was doing what he thought was right and protecting his parents. He was doing what I so often did for my parents as a young immigrant in Canada – he was taking charge. My immigrant parents didn't have a command of English or French. They had strong accents and limited vocabulary. So, I completed forms on their behalf, paid their accounts to cashiers, and explained to them Canadian culture. Children of immigrants who were hurt in the developing world often feel a need to protect their parents. Those feelings run deep. Some people are fragile, so their children take it upon themselves to take charge in Canada, where their parents still feel like guests. I couldn't wait to transcend these communication barriers.

In Toronto, my sister Eman was working as a computer hardware engineer for the company AMD. When I confirmed my upcoming transfer, she moved from her one-bedroom apartment to a luxurious, modern, two-bedroom apartment on Harrison Gardens in North York – it had a gym, a sauna, and private security – so we could live together. The highrise building was ideally located, close to Sheppard subway station and Highway 401 at Yonge Street. Eman had a complete set of furniture, so we agreed that she'd take the primary bedroom, and I settled for the smaller bedroom with modern windows overlooking Yonge and the 401. I felt refreshed to be in Toronto, a city where nearly half the population, like me, was born outside Canada, spoke a foreign language, and was working hard to contribute to society.

Eman was younger than I and didn't enjoy cooking, so I got groceries, cooked, and cleaned. She supplied the company, including her gifted and talented engineering friends who worked with her at AMD. They were mostly men since women make up only about 10 per cent of engineers in Canada. Some were white Canadians and others were Canadians of diverse backgrounds: Taiwanese, Pakistani, and Portuguese. I enjoyed entertaining. I liked their geeky-techy vibe and it was refreshing that they were completely apolitical. It was really nice getting to know my now-adult younger sister. She had accountant-like organizational skills, strict financial goals, and impatience for nonsense. I was a morning person, but she lived by night. Eman would reluctantly rise only to the smell of fresh coffee. We spoke English at home but Arabic in the elevators, to keep our conversations private. "Are you coming home right after work?" I'd ask, to her annoyance. "Not sure, Huda. I'll call you, okay?" I knew she wasn't into morning conversations, but I was feeling homesick.

"Okay, have a great day, little one," she'd say to me, lovingly. She loved feeling like she was older and wiser, and she loved taking care of me. I enjoyed it too. "Bye, sis. Let the boys down easy." Colleagues were always confessing their love to Eman, who is a beauty.

On the subway, sandwiched between Torontonians, I listened to music or recitations from the Quran on my white iPod. I was excited for my first day at the office on Front Street. I knew a few colleagues from Counter Terrorism, plus five intelligence officers from my class had arrived at the same time as me. I didn't know who my manager or the chain of command were. I'd just returned from London and hadn't accessed the service computer system in months. It would all be a delicious surprise. I hoped my manager would be as welcoming as Marshall.

First, I reported to Internal Security to obtain my building pass and to sign documents. James, Internal Security's chief, a long-time service employee of Irish descent, had a Stephen Colbert sense of humour – smart jokes and half-truths. We quickly established an amicable relationship. After that, I viewed James as someone to go to when I wanted to lighten up. While briefing me on building-entry procedures, James made up elaborate ways to come into work unnoticed by the public and tried to convince me of them with a straight face. James provided a refreshing icebreaker after my rocky history with Internal Security at headquarters.

I soon discovered that Toronto's regional director general was Martin, my former Counter Terrorism director general from headquarters, the man who claimed to defend democracy by upholding discrimination and who'd so willingly approved my transfer to Counter Intelligence. In Toronto, he once again placed me in Counter Intelligence, this time at the Asia desk on an investigation that was wrapping up – i.e., a file that no longer represented a threat and which required more desk work than field interviews. I was livid. After my Counter Terrorism experience both on Crevice and with MI5, he was putting me on a dead Counter Intelligence investigation, as if there were no pressing Counter Terrorism investigations, like the Toronto 18.

At the time, CSIS and the RCMP were investigating a group of young men, popularly named the Toronto 18. Some were later convicted of plotting terrorist attacks in Toronto and Ottawa. I could have contributed significantly to that major Counter Terrorism investigation. I felt that Martin had excluded me to put me in my place and deflate the confidence I'd built on a pressing international case. This was typical of CSIS culture and management's contempt for minorities; nothing minorities do should ever be celebrated, recognized, or awarded. For example, another racialized colleague, a male Muslim strategic analyst with a doctorate degree, was taken off the Toronto 18 investigation for no apparent reason. Furthermore, a Christian Lebanese Canadian IO didn't receive awards after a dangerous deployment while every other IO who worked on the case did.

What bothered me most was the office's lack of diversity. There was no one I could talk to, learn from, or share my frustrations with. For a month, I wrote warrant termination reports for our warrant coordinator and her court submissions. This meant conducting a full review of the investigation, identifying useful information derived from the use of Section 21 warrant powers, and determining how that information furthered the investigation. It was slow, painful, analytical work on an investigation that I was learning about only so it could be terminated. Slowly, my excitement was waning, and my spirit was being crushed – again.

My supervisor Jared had spent five years in the Toronto Region. He was a supportive and great mentor who brightened the days of everyone he worked with. I accompanied him on interviews and thought the world of him.

"Huda, it doesn't matter if you don't get all the information you need in a single interview," he explained. "Rapport building is more important. It leaves the door open to future contact and discussion. Take your time, explain the service mandate well, and you'll find most people are receptive to our goals. Most people want to help." Wise advice from a mentoring legend. Jared had a thing for Asian food, and as a team-building exercise, we'd walk down Spadina Avenue in Toronto's Chinatown, a couple blocks from the office, to enjoy delicious egg rolls, sesame chicken, dim sum, and more. We also went to Korean restaurants for thinly sliced steaks, barbecued on our tables. The aroma stuck to our clothes all afternoon. Toronto changed my tastes. I began to explore authentic, delicious foods from all over the world.

To celebrate being in the same region, five of my training class colleagues and I would go for lunch downtown. We were on different desks, but it was great fun to gossip and exchange experiences and stories. We shared our frustrations about the bureaucracy and paperwork required for every interview and outing. My colleagues wanted to hear all the details about London. They were proud of me and wanted to know how they could land opportunities overseas, too. I felt validated when they openly recognized how unreasonable it was for the service to place me on the Asia desk.

That was when I reached out to Margaret, head of the Toronto Region branch. She was a seasoned, close-to-retirement officer famous for getting people applying for status in Canada to cough up the truth. Margaret had a stern reputation, which I figured was the result of the challenges women of her generation faced while having to prove themselves useful outside the home to former RCMP officers, now service managers. It couldn't have been easy establishing credibility and demanding a seat at the table in such a male-dominated environment. She was a remarkable, strong woman.

Margaret had complained of not having enough investigators on her desk, even though Security Screening Toronto had been inundated with immigration and refugee files of people coming from war zones and countries that might want to target Canadian national security. Security Screening was the service's first line of defence against spies and terrorists wanting to gain status in Canada. For these reasons, immigrants required national security interviews and assessments. Security Screening assessed files of national security interest, including permanent residency and citizenship applications with possible links to terrorism, weapons procurement, or foreign intelligence. Investigators conduct interviews and research, analyze findings, and issue decisions. In summer 2006, Martin had issued a directive to intelligence officers to assist Toronto's Security Screening. In this context, I approached Margaret to offer my help. I also wanted to get out and conduct as many interviews as I could.

I told Margaret that I'd heard she was an effective interviewer and that I wanted to watch and learn. She was taken aback at first but then agreeable, even a little flattered. She took it as her mission to be a great mentor to me. I valued her openness. Everyone I talked to described her as tough and uncompromising. Somehow, despite our age difference, Margaret and I clicked and enjoyed our time together. She was articulate and hoped to, upon retirement, write a book about Canada's contributions in World War II. Our first interview together was of an Iranian refugee claimant who we suspected was under the direction of the Iranian government. He claimed that he was gay and because homosexuality was a crime in his country, he was fearful for his life. Following our interview, Margaret and I spoke of the cruel realities and aspirations of many refugees and immigrants seeking a peaceful life in Canada. I didn't tell Margaret about my family's experience in Ethiopia. I'd always painted a rosy picture of my childhood in Egypt to everyone at the service. Everything else was secret. Margaret and I empathized with many refugees, though we felt others were untruthful or embellished their stories. Aware of our privilege, we sipped our coffee and agreed the young Iranian man was a legitimate refugee.

Something came over me that day, though. I don't know why, but I sensed the approach of failure. Like the young man escaping Iran, I wanted to escape from my daily reality. Because of my identity, I felt neither accepted nor a full member of CSIS. I told Margaret that I wanted to quit the service. I hadn't planned to say it, it just came out. Margaret routinely met with Citizenship and Immigration Canada. I thought employment in that organization would be secure and more ideal. I was frustrated at having to fight for my place at CSIS. "What? Why would you do that?" She leaned over to hear my thoughts.

"I was really excited about coming here, but I don't know – I don't feel welcome. I'm working a dead, low-priority investigation, while there's the big Toronto 18 investigation going on. I should be in Counter Terrorism. What am I doing in Counter Intelligence, or here?" I felt that I'd offended her. I didn't tell her about my history with Martin or the harassment I'd faced. Let bygones be bygones, I'd convinced myself. The service had changed and was becoming more diverse, I believed. But Margaret didn't want me to quit. I told her I was disillusioned with CSIS and its managers. "Something just doesn't feel right when I'm in the office. I've always been likeable – in school, university, socially, and my other jobs – but not in the service. I don't think I'm welcome here. I don't think they care to have me."

"You've got to find your way," she said. Then she narrated how, when she started, her trainers, all ex-police, had expected her to raise her voice, intimidate, and be forceful with investigations subjects. "'Bang the table,' they'd say." Margaret did no such thing. She developed her own techniques for eliciting information – dialogue, more reliable deception indicators, and analytical tools. She built her reputation one success at a time. Margaret encouraged me to improve my performance and worth. She showed me that it hadn't been easy for other women too. I promised her that I'd continue to try. I felt that I owed it to myself to give it time. I returned to my desk and continued pushing through paperwork.

The winds of change were blowing in Toronto Region. Martin was on his way out, and his former assistant, Evan, who'd enviously waited for the promotion, would replace him. In the process, I got a new supervisor. Daryl was the region's only visible minority manager. He was smart, focused, and completely emotionally detached. But he also operated within the white, misogynistic law-enforcement culture at CSIS. Exerting power within one's area of control was normalized. Thus, I was under his command and he felt he could raise his voice and intimidate. He failed to realize that I had developed a thick skin over the years. We immediately clashed. He told me that he'd "asked around" and knew "I was less than liked by some of my managers in Ottawa." He asked me directly what the conflict was about. My answer was simply that it had been resolved. He said that he'd Googled me. I wasn't surprised. I knew that our relationship wouldn't last long.

While I was writing a warrant termination, Daryl asked that I send some files to our communication analyst for translation. I did. The analyst saw my request as low priority and refused to spend any time on it. I forwarded this refusal to Daryl. He called me into his office and berated me for not having included the material that should've been translated in my analysis. His tone was accusatory, as if I hadn't done my job or hadn't put enough effort in. I was upset. I'd learned a thing or two about fighting back. I walked out of his office, wrote a detailed email about the incident, and CC'd everyone concerned, including the Toronto Region Asia chief, Daryl's supervisor. I sent it after he left the office.

On the subway that night I reflected on how I wasn't upset that I had just sent an explosive email that would have the attention of service managers at so many levels. My experience fighting back at headquarters taught me that calling out harassment officially in an email would trigger positive action on their part. I wasn't intimidated anymore by the allure of their power over new employees and the fear of burning bridges for future career success. I learned that whatever I get I would earn with my hard work and talent. While Daryl is a racialized man, I guess he played into the service culture and understood his ability to use intimidation tactics. I wasn't playing anymore, and I certainly wasn't afraid of being fired, knowing that I had a positive relationship with David and Director Judd. My plan was to drive to Ottawa if necessary. Even the regional director general was close to the boys' club (guys like Jack Hooper) and so he had never welcomed me, spoken to me, or even acknowledged my presence. I would go above him, if I had to!

I came in early the next morning to see where the dust would settle. As I was walking into my office, the Asia chief called me for a talk. "Huda, thank you for your email. I realize you and Daryl have butted heads, and it may be difficult to resolve your personality disputes. I've spoken with Spencer, chief of CT, and he'd be happy to have you on his desk. You're being transferred as of today. Pack your stuff up and head on to CT," he said, winking. I could've jumped up to hug him and said "Habibi ya, boss," but I settled for a polite and firm "Thank you, sir." I found a box, packed what was mine, waved goodbye to my colleagues, and ran off to Counter Terrorism, where I belonged in the first place.

The Counter Terrorism Middle East bullpen was a large room with small desks, a couple of Internet kiosks, and printers. Intelligence officers came and went at odd hours. Someone was always on the phone scheduling an interview or a debriefing with headquarters. Across from us were the offices of the chief of Counter Terrorism, the region's deputy director, and the director general. They pressed us for the latest developments on our cases. The intelligence officers on this desk had uncovered and recruited sources against the Toronto 18, a case that was being led by the RCMP at the time. There was no shortage of investigative cases to follow up on, sources to develop, interviews to conduct, addresses to check, incoming suspected foreign fighters to investigate at airports, and poison-pen letters alleging terrorism between family members, co-workers, and neighbours to decipher.

Nick was the most accomplished investigator in Toronto and a senior colleague on my desk. He was a stunning, tall, handsome, young man with deep hazel eyes, a hawkish nose, and a concrete jaw. His voice was deep. He was undoubtedly an intelligent man who read for pleasure. His awareness of others had earned him the respect of almost everyone in the region – middle managers, specialists, support staff, and, especially, women. He and I developed a special relationship that I believe was the envy of many. Nick understood the office's conservative, police-like culture and cleverly navigated it. Given his investigative accomplishments, I wanted to impress him. I'd spend long hours reading through cases, including his, to add insight. He believed in my abilities and sought out my views, which he considered original and insightful.

Finally, I selected an Al Qaeda-linked case that felt worthy of pursuit and wrote an elaborate cover-operation proposal. Nick pushed the proposal through the bureaucracy chain, and it received approval and support from the regional director general and the director general in Counter Terrorism at headquarters. When it got to the deputy director of operations Luc Portelance, it was rejected. I wasn't sure whether the proposal was dismissed because I'd written it and would be executing it or because it was just too risky of an operation. This kind of insecurity really got to me. But I knew it wasn't just paranoia. Luc had visited the London-based Canadian High Commission while I was there with MI5. At a CSIS staff lunch date, instead of encouraging me, he stated that he wanted a detailed report about the exact nature of my work at MI5 and whether it justified all the money the service was spending on me in London. I couldn't believe my ears and didn't tell a soul. His comments chilled me. It was very clear by his request and the way he spoke to me versus the way he spoke to other intelligence officers that he didn't like me. Luc was former RCMP who had replaced Jack, another former RCMP, who, as I explained earlier, wanted me out. Maybe Jack had convinced him that I shouldn't be there. I didn't know what to believe. I became emotional when I received the news that Luc hadn't approved the cover operation after so many director generals had given their approval.

After the proposal rejection, I concentrated my efforts on source-recruitment operations. I thought that I'd excel there. At first, I went out on interviews with male colleagues. I appreciated how they conducted interviews but usually felt I shouldn't interject. I often noticed that they didn't take time to build rapport, contemplate how they were being received, or consider the cultural and linguistic differences at play during their interviews. They usually only interviewed men, as if women don't have valuable information to provide. Management had, ludicrously, convinced the previous generation of women intelligence officers that Asian, Russian, and Middle Eastern men aren't comfortable talking to women investigators. This kept women from entering CSIS roles that would lead to future promotions. I once listened to a deskmate try to schedule an interview over the phone. He kept saying, "in your neck of the woods." He repeated it three times until he realized that the other person didn't understand the idiom – a very obvious communication error.

When I began conducting more interviews alone, I developed my own style the same way Margaret had. It quickly became apparent to me, and later to my colleagues and managers, that I had a "way" with the people I interviewed who were mostly Canadian immigrants or first-generation Canadians. My linguistic skills gave me an edge as a subject-matter expert in my field. Slowly, I stopped thinking about leaving the service. I stopped looking for work elsewhere. I enjoyed coming into the office and I felt valued. I thought that I was fulfilling both the service's mandate and my aspirations for being a capable intelligence officer and investigator.

My deputy chief, Ben, for reasons beyond my understanding, hated me. Anytime I was about to conduct an interview, an address check, or anything else, he had to know, approve, and add his perspective. His micromanagement, from what I could tell, only applied to me and my interviews, not to those of other investigators. His tone was discouraging. He questioned my abilities and communication style. He'd ask me how I, a Muslim woman, was perceived by Muslim men or leaders in the Muslim community. I answered that respect and professionalism go a long way. I didn't want his micromanagement and ignorance impacting or overwhelming me, so I often ignored it, choosing to instead focus on my work. Ultimately, he was always begrudgingly satisfied with the results I produced, so I soldiered on with my mission to prove myself and make an impact.

16 | MARITAL STATUS

Many of my Toronto Region colleagues dated among themselves, including one classmate who'd soon marry another colleague. We were all in our late twenties, early thirties, and I too was looking to meet Mr Right. Unfortunately for me, he wasn't going to be an intelligence officer. As a practising Muslim woman, I wanted to marry a Muslim man. But there were hardly any Muslims my age working in national security. None that I knew of anyway. And my service directive to not be seen in the Muslim community still stood. I wished to respect the directive and to continue my life as an intelligence officer, but it created a unique challenge for me.

I thought about online dating, though it scared me at first. Reading through profiles, I wondered whether any of the men were sources or service targets and whether by contacting them, my name would pop up in a report – basically, career suicide. *I would be the joke of the office and there would be no recovery*, I thought. Nevertheless, I setup an online profile through a paid-only Muslim matrimonial site. I didn't use a picture since someone online could potentially recognize me as a CSIS intelligence officer who'd interviewed them. I hoped that only serious and mature candidates would pay for a membership when free sites were also available. After long days at the office, I delighted in finding messages waiting for me. I hoped to connect with someone like in the 1998 Tom Hanks and Meg Ryan movie, *You've Got Mail*. I'd go through the messages, sometimes chuckling away with my sister. I wasn't sure whether she was laughing at me or at how I'd dramatize meeting strangers. Ahhh, Internet dating!

Among those messages, I found Ali. His profile said that he was an Egyptian pharmacist from a traditional family and that he valued education. That sounded simple, authentic, and familiar. I placed a "like" on his profile, hoping he'd contact me. Ali, not the type to chat online, responded immediately and asked for my phone number. I liked his direct approach and missed the Egyptian dialect. Within minutes, he made me laugh with jokes about Egyptians. He wasn't a serious type and made fun of himself and where he came from. I liked that too. We spoke in Arabic and were pleasantly surprised at what we shared. When I told Ali that my background was Yemeni, he paused. Then he told me that his father and uncles had lived in Yemen, adding that his father had passed when he was only sixteen and away from home at a high school in the city. I felt his deep affection for his father and wanted to make him feel better, so I told him that his mother must be proud of his pharmacy degree, a significant accomplishment given how competitive Egypt's educational system is. He agreed and proudly added that five out of six of his siblings were educated and as teachers and nurses no less. "But Sherine, the youngest," he added, "has Down syndrome, so she's at home with my mom." I liked how open Ali was in our first twenty minutes of conversation. He told me that he had a photo of his late father dressed in Yemeni clothing, including a *gambia*, a traditional sword tucked into a belt and a symbol of Yemen. When I spoke about Cairo, he identified with my experiences, and we discovered that we'd watched the same Arabic-translated Western movies and Arabic series.

One of Ali's traits especially held weight for me. Ali is a *hafiz*, someone who has memorized the Quran. He spent his early childhood in traditional Quranic schools and held all thirty chapters of the holy text in his heart and mind. I felt that this was really special.

Ali was living in London, Ontario, then, and drove to Toronto to meet me, just a few days after our first conversation. I was standing in front of my apartment building when Ali drove up in a cracked, old, beige Honda Accord that made noise when he stopped. As we walked to a coffee shop, we noticed that we matched perfectly, each wearing beige pants and a blue shirt. He asked where I worked, and I said I worked in public safety, knowing that he'd be clueless about what that department did and where it was located. I added the word *government* and quickly changed the topic by telling him that I studied law and was a legal analyst, but not a lawyer. He looked impressed and didn't ask for details.

I learned that Ali was a foreign student working on a graduate degree in pharmacology. That sounded smart, but I was a little taken aback by him not being Canadian yet. "But are you planning to live in Canada?" I asked.

"Absolutely," he said, which I found reassuring. I opened my heart to knowing Ali. As an immigrant, I don't judge people by their circumstances. I was meeting Ali to determine his character, not his status in the country, but sadly, his status was important, nevertheless.

At the coffee shop, I let Ali do the talking. I was trying to analyze everything he said. I carefully connected dots, made assumptions, asked follow-up questions, and tried to detect deception. I realized that he was alone in the world and struggling to make something of himself. He was broke, worked at a pizza shop, and struggled with the English qualifying exams to become a pharmacist. He felt comfortable sharing this truth with me. My curse and gift is that I have a comforting demeanour, as many have told me. I'm also a trained intelligence officer who said little and asked the right questions. He was in over his head.

There was something innocent and childlike about him. He wanted to be loved and was insecure in life, just as I was. It gripped my heart. I judged that he was looking for something real and was being honest, forthcoming, and authentic. He spoke of his mother and sister in high regard. His mother had worked to successfully educate five children. I admired him for appreciating the remarkable women in his life.

Hours later, we walked to a Persian restaurant on Yonge Street. We enjoyed the sunset and warm Persian kebabs and shared what inspired us. We laughed at each other. He kept poking fun at me for being timid and listening more than talking. Then, just like that, the night ended. We walked back to my building slowly. He kept guessing how the night had gone and what I thought about him and his crazy stories. I wouldn't give a straight answer, so he asked directly, "Will I see you again?" I couldn't help but smile – a partial answer. Growing up in Egypt, I knew that I had to play hard to get. It came with the culture. I liked how smart, articulate, real, and vulnerable he was, but I wouldn't tell him, not just yet. Maybe I'd watched too many romantic Egyptian movies. I'd let him spend the night guessing. When we got to my building and I was preparing to go up, he called in Arabic, "Huda, do you need anything before I leave?" I looked back, smiled, and said, in Arabic, "Like what?" He said, "Anything, anything at all." I smiled and said I didn't. That moment stood out for me. He was a giver, a supporter, and a kind soul with a generous heart.

At home, my sister was waiting to hear all about my first date with Ali. We wondered whether he'd be the one and whether he'd get along with our parents, family, and friends. I told Eman I was concerned, given my work, that he was a foreign national. I also wondered how he'd feel if he found out that I was an intelligence officer in counterterrorism – a spy. Maybe he wouldn't want a complicated life with me. Perhaps CSIS wouldn't permit our union. Maybe I'd lose him or my job. "One thing at a time," Eman said. "You don't even know this guy." Still, I'd never had to think about these questions and complications.

At work, I told two colleagues about my exciting date with Ali. They were happy for me, which is when I realized how happy I was. I didn't dare tell them that he was a foreign national. I wondered why I told them anything, but they were friends and colleagues, and we were bonding during lunch and sharing a little of ourselves each day. I was excited about Ali, and they were curious, attentive, and friendly young women. One of them was also seeking love. I didn't understand why it was so hard for her – she was beautiful, sophisticated, Francophone, kind, smart, and looking for a real relationship. Her pool of potential mates was much larger than mine, plus there weren't restrictions placed on her personal life.

I told her that she'd be a great match for a friend of mine, Steve, also in Toronto and in Counter Terrorism. Steve and I had worked together in CT at headquarters for years and had each been transferred to Toronto around the same time. He was smart, sophisticated, and kind. He was also one of my students when I ran the Islamic discussion group. During the course, a woman intelligence officer had questioned me about how Muslims could believe Jesus wasn't crucified on a cross. She argued that the crucifixion was a public, historically established event. I simply explained the Muslim view. I told her that there were also Christian groups in the United States, Unitarians, who believed the same as Muslims. She was a practising Christian, and I'd somehow offended her. Her tone was hostile. After 9/11, threats and stereotypes about Islam and Muslims were constant and she couldn't take a view that didn't align with hers. I wondered how she was going to function as an investigator if she couldn't respect other people's views. Steve immediately backed me up and tried to defuse the tension. He said that he was aware of the Unitarians, adding that I was simply narrating a Muslim belief. Two years after my suggestion to Anna that she connect with Steve, they sent me an invitation to their wedding.

Over the next months, Ali and I got closer. He was still in London, Ontario, but he called daily and would make the two-hour drive to Toronto, sometimes just to spend an hour with me. I introduced Ali to my sister, her friends, and later to my family in Ottawa. I loved how he got along well with everyone. Dad was on cloud nine when I told him about Ali. He was also impressed that Ali was a hafiz and studying to become a pharmacist, like my uncle in the United States. Dad and Ali clicked immediately. They had a lot in common; they were both visionaries, hard-working, and responsible. They saw themselves as accountable for their families, dreamed of better futures, and were uninhibited by location, culture, and country. They'd also both chosen to come to Canada and shared intimate details about conversations they'd had with Canadian embassy officials in Cairo during their respective immigration, something I'd never discussed with Dad. Both Ali and Dad hung onto every interaction, word, and correspondence from the Canadian embassy. It was consequential. They knew many others in similar situations who'd failed to secure a Canadian visa – they were the lucky ones. During those conversations, I felt like a hopeful, privileged young woman who just happened to have landed in Canada without effort.

Given that Ali was becoming an essential part of my life, I had to tell him what I did and who I really was. I also had to tell work about Ali. I told Ali that I had something important to discuss with him. When we sat down, he was puzzled. What could it be? "Ali, I work for a government organization called CSIS. They're the Mukhabarat in Canada." I told him I was an investigator, had worked in Counter Terrorism. Ali was surprised, and his immediate reaction threw me off. He was smiling ear to ear. "Wow," he said. "That's amazing. Seriously amazing. I can totally see that. You never talk about yourself or your work."

"No, Ali," I tried to explain. "It's not that simple. I'm an intelligence officer with a spy service. I can never discuss my work with you. I can't speak to anyone about what I do. I must pretend I have some boring government job, but I must also keep a low profile. There are places I can't go and people I have to avoid interacting with. I have to relocate time to time or travel overseas for work, alone."

"I understand, Huda. I think it's amazing," Ali said.

He told me that he was proud of me and elated that I was such a strong woman. He didn't understand why I was so serious. "You could've told me earlier, no?" he asked.

"No, Ali. I couldn't have. I had to know we were serious about each other." Ali was super happy, smiling, and trying to joke about me being James Bond.

"Do you have a gun?" he asked. "I think female police officers are great," he said.

"*Aliiii*, I'm not a police officer. It's so different," I said. "No, I don't have a gun." I was tense and confused by his lack of understanding of the seriousness of what I was saying. Then I broke it to him. "The service will have a problem with you not being a Canadian national and with you working under the table." Silence followed.

"What? *I* am the problem?" he said. "Sorry, what are you saying? You can't be with me? You have to choose between your job and me?" He was still smiling, like he was confident that I would want him. His arrogance was kind of sexy. I was beginning to laugh at myself. It was hard enough that I had to choose between being a member of the Muslim community and an intelligence officer. Now I had to choose between Ali and remaining an intelligence officer. Ali didn't understand this yet. If I revealed my commitment to my job to him now, perhaps he'd move on. I wasn't ready for that. By the end of the night, I think he was trying to process what I'd said. He closed up a little in a way he never had in the past with me. He was quiet and reflective, and then he said that it was my decision. My heart sank.

In November 2006, I decided to do what I'd been avoiding for a month – inform Internal Security that I was in a serious relationship with a foreign national. I understood that the service and Internal Security would investigate whether Ali was trying to get close to me, as someone with sensitive information, for the benefit of another country. I knew that was not the case, but I had to provide his details to Internal Security and allow them to come to their own conclusions. It wasn't going to be easy, but I also wasn't the kind of woman to run away from challenges and I certainly didn't want to miss out on this beautiful, promising relationship. Ali and I were becoming emotionally attached, but I was also happy with my career then. The stakes were high on both sides. I decided that I was going to do the right thing: report my relationship and deal with the consequences. So, I took the elevator down to meet Paul, head of Internal Security, about my file. I knew Paul to be closed-minded and old school. Scott, chief of Internal Security was different, but I couldn't go to him. I had to respect the chain of command and hierarchy.

"Hey, Huda. What's up?" Paul said, looking curious.

"Hi, Paul. I have something to talk about. Is this a good time?"

"As good as ever. Come on in and close the door," he said. He knew that any time an employee reached out to Internal Security, the conversation had to be discreet and confidential and could potentially be of great consequence down the road. "So, what's up?" he repeated.

I smiled nervously and locked my lips. Suddenly, I didn't want to move forward with this, but it was too late. I was right in front of Paul. There was no going back. "Well, hmm, I have some information to report. It's too sensitive to just write in an email, you see. Hmm, so I'm here to talk to you in person," I said. A moment of silence passed, then the words just came out, inarticulately at best. "I met someone. I met him online. I'm interested in marrying him. I mean I'm considering marrying him. He's a great guy, but, but he isn't Canadian. He's Egyptian, ah, a foreign national, which may be an issue, as I understand from an Internal Security perspective. I mean, not like a threat, but he's a foreigner and stuff. Oh, he's Egyptian. He's an Egyptian national, hmm, right now." I stopped and, with big wide eyes, looked at Paul for his reaction to all I'd so incoherently reported.

"Huda, let's break this down a little," he said. "You've met an Egyptian man in Canada, online, and you'd like to marry," he said.

"Yes, sir, I did," I said, trying to own how crazy that sounded to a white man in his fifties who hadn't travelled beyond North America and probably married his high school sweetheart.

"So, how long have you known him?" he asked.

"Four to five months," I said. I felt uncomfortable that it had only been that long and then added, "I spoke to his mother and sisters over the phone. I believe he is who he says he is. My family has also met him."

"Huda, you know, generally, people tend to take these matters a little slower. What do you know about his finances, for example?" He paused, looking for an answer.

"He doesn't have a lot of money," I said. "Unlikely that someone is paying him to court me for information. He comes from a simple background and is currently working part time at a pizza shop." What I wanted Paul to do was to run his name and details on our system to uncover security concerns. I was unauthorized to conduct searches on my family or friends; there would need to be an operations reason. I would be risking my security clearance. They trusted me to make judgments on service targets – as a threat or not – so in my mind, they should as well have trusted me to know that Ali was of no security concern.

The meeting had been going well because of my transparency since I was disclosing information to Internal Security as per my obligations, but Paul was now questioning my judgment. Four months earlier, I'd spoken to Paul about my interest in going to Saudi Arabia with my dad. He'd questioned why I had to go with Dad, completely unaware that the Saudis would never issue an Umrah visa to a woman without her male guardian. "Go as a tourist," he said, not knowing the Saudis didn't, then, issue tourism visas either. I was now perceiving Paul as a threat to my happiness, and I became more defensive about what I thought he was thinking of me, my judgment, and my decision making. I hadn't expected the meeting to go smoothly, but I also didn't imagine it was going to be this bad. I wanted it to end fast.

I trusted my gut feelings about Ali. I was in love, and there was no stopping me. I was no longer attending Muslim community events, so I hardly had any Muslim friends. Ali would fill that void in my life – one I'd chosen, even after the harassment I'd faced from the department. Perhaps Ali would save me from my imposed isolation and loneliness.

Paul said, "My personal advice is you should know someone for at least two years. That's what I'd tell my daughter." But I wasn't his daughter, and I wasn't seeking his personal advice. Paul's words cut like a knife. I sat back in my chair.

"I appreciate your advice, Paul. I'm very serious about Ali, and I'll send you an email with his name, date of birth, address, and other personal details including family overseas, as per policy. If Internal Security has any security concerns, please let me know," I said.

I stood and left. I didn't like feeling judged or schooled like a little girl, but I had to accept that the service had a right to conduct background checks on Ali. I waited two months to hear from Paul. I never did, which caused me much stress. I didn't know how CSIS would react to my plans to marry my partner.

Ali and I wed in a civil ceremony in January 2007 but postponed the reception and living together until August. We married that winter because we were eager for Ali to gain Canadian status so he could continue his education. I also didn't want the service to distrust me for having a relationship with a non-Canadian. I sent Paul a follow-up email, per policy, advising of my new marital status – still no response. Later in 2017, when I received my personal information through the Access to Information Privacy Act, I found an email Paul had sent to our regional director general, Evan, in which he wrote, "She has gone ahead with it and got married."

17 | COMMON GROUND

With that huge challenge behind me, I couldn't have imagined that things in the office were about to get even more complicated. One morning, Nick walked in and saw me looking worried at my desk. He came over and asked, "Is it Ben?" as though it were common knowledge that Ben, my deputy chief, had a way of upsetting me. For instance, I'd recruited a source whom I thought was valuable, but Ben didn't agree, so he asked me to stop communicating with the source. I saw this as a move to exercise his power over my decision making. I complied with his request. Then a few months later I would be directed to open the file because Ben was wrong. The source *was* valuable.

But it wasn't Ben this time. As complicated as my relationship with Ben was, it paled in comparison to this. "It isn't," I replied. "Worse; close the door." I told him that I'd just read a service memo indicating that William, my former Counter Terrorism manager who'd tried to have me fired, had been appointed the chief of Counter Terrorism in Toronto. My heart was pounding. I finally felt fulfilled in my career. How could the service allow us to work together again? Why was he being transferred to this unit? Would I have to leave the desk, after all my effort and accomplishments? My deskmates looked up to me, but I feared that they'd soon learn of what had transpired at headquarters. I was afraid that I'd be an outcast again. I wondered whether William would still look for reasons to strip me of my clearance.

Nick was sympathetic but unsurprised. "The service is just too big to take into account past conflicts between managers and employees," he judged. He promised that it would be okay, given I had an established reputation and a number of accomplishments at this point in my career. He didn't think that William would be openly discriminatory since I'd previously complained about him. "Stay," he convinced me. Nick was like Ziad, my older brother. I felt like he'd look out for me and help me if I encountered problems again. I didn't tell him this, but I counted on him. I had many friends in the Toronto Region, but no one knew or understood me like Nick did.

By the time William finally arrived months later and had begun his assignment as Toronto's Counter Terrorism chief, I'd had time to digest the news and accept that he and I would be working together again. However, I knew that it would be hard for me. I'd have to watch my back and make sure no one but Nick found out about my history with William, while trying not to give William a reason to discredit me again. I was comforted by the fact that Director Judd had been openly critical of CSIS's lack of diversity, that he understood minorities like me added value to CSIS's mandate, and that he personally knew me and the value of my contributions. I was empowered by these things in ways I hadn't been before.

When William walked into the Counter Terrorism bullpen, I stood up with everyone to shake his hand. "Welcome," I said. He acted like nothing had happened between us. That Friday, after I'd shut down my computer and was preparing to take the subway home, I received a call from my supervisor directing me to go to Pearson International Airport to conduct an interview with a suspected extremist who'd been granted a tourist visa and was stopped upon arrival. Following my interview and report, William called to thank me for being available on short notice. He asked that I let him know how my interview went. His tone was respectful and professional. I decided that perhaps William and I could move past our conflict, though I couldn't stop myself from feeling guarded. I think he felt the same way.

David, who was, by then, CSIS's director general in the International Region, was in Toronto to give a presentation on his branch's expansion. I'd missed David, and we spent time catching up in the hall before taking the elevator up to Counter Terrorism. William walked into the elevator as it was about to close. David joked that William and I should talk more to create a better working relationship. His comment came out of the blue. William seemed, understandably, uncomfortable but said nothing and never offered to have a discussion. I wish that I'd had the courage to speak with him. I wish that he'd reached out to me. Neither of us did, and this perpetuated the tension between us.

William was a good manager – he always was. He pushed investigators to go out, interview, build contact networks in the intelligence and Muslim communities, seek out new threats, establish lines of communication, and recruit sources. He was an effective leader, and to an extent, I liked the energy he brought to the branch. As time progressed, I ran investigations as I saw fit. I didn't need to be encouraged to do what William wanted. We, the desk's investigators, were eager to get out of the office and equally eager to come back and share our experiences. We were also a little competitive.

In time, I developed recruitment initiatives that were recognized as unique, valuable, and well-executed. I also assisted investigators on other Counter Terrorism desks – East Africa, North Africa, and South Asia. I went out with them on interviews and helped to elicit cooperative relationships in those communities. Ironically, the reasons for my success as an investigator (my identity and skills) were also why I faced some resistance with sources. Some Muslims were, at first, skeptical of me, especially when they had things to hide. One source said that he didn't wish to be met by an Arab investigator, alleging that I'd make him uncomfortable. I was surprised but kept silent. I wondered why my supervisor would even ask a source for their preference. Why and how did that conversation happen? Why did the source have a say in who interviewed him? Then I learned that same source had been less than truthful with the service, so I reckoned he knew I would catch his lies faster.

A few Muslim men with security issues on their immigration files, which I was assessing, dropped their jaws when they realized that I'd be the CSIS investigator meeting them. One had already made up a story about being a Shia refugee from Pakistan, and the other had fabricated a story about how he was running away from a terrorist organization that was threatening to kill him and his family. Each realized that they couldn't give me a sappy, unrealistic story, as they would've with another investigator who neither understood nor could call them out on these details. These men were not a security threat: they were here, and they wanted to stay in Canada for a better future for themselves and their families.

Many Muslims trusted me, especially mothers and fathers whose sons had logged into extremist sites or come to our attention via their interest in radicalization. Such parents often compelled their loved ones to cooperate with me, so I was on the same page as them – we wanted to warn their youngsters about going down a dangerous path that would ruin their lives, families, and communities. Those parents trusted me, so by extension, they also trusted that CSIS wasn't out to get them. I generally impressed the mostly young men I interviewed and worked closely with. I was like them, an immigrant, but I represented the government, which is, I think, one of the reasons that they agreed to listen to me. They recognized that an authority and security figure was on their side and wanted what was best for them. This made them feel better. They weren't worried that I was investigating and profiling their community. There was one young man that I felt was lost, and I wanted to help. He was broke, so I broke service protocol to drive him to his high school to get his certificate, booked him an appointment with a college counsellor, and tried to get his life back on track and away from harm.

I also learned that investigators in outreach programs in Toronto and Ottawa sometimes mentioned that CSIS had a Muslim investigator who wore a hijab. They did this to dispel the view that CSIS was profiling Muslims, and it usually interested people. That I was being used in such a manner was aggravating. It excused profiling and looking into the real concerns the community had.

Though I was doing good and impactful work, Evan, the Toronto regional director general, kept refusing to recognize my achievements internally. He'd attribute my successes to a host of other reasons, such as luck, but not to my skills and good judgment. He maintained and fed a toxic office culture, ironically under the pretext of being cool, open, and close to investigators. Every Friday afternoon, he'd invite selected intelligence officers to an office party with alcohol, held a stone's throw from my office. I was never invited, and neither did I know what one had to do to get an invitation. My friends believed the parties were essential to department networking since, at CSIS, a manager's approval trumped work accomplishments. I once placed my name in a pool of candidates to serve in Afghanistan. That pool included a woman colleague with military experience. We weren't selected, and all the selectees were men, one a great friend of mine with absolutely no counterterrorism work experience. I didn't like the way Evan constantly avoided looking at me. Surely, he'd read my Internal Security file. I was sure that he had judged me without getting to know me or my work commitment. But I also wouldn't feel comfortable at his parties. The Friday afternoon club gossiped about others in the office and made inappropriate sexual and racial comments. My colleagues and I would hear the rumours that emerged from the Friday party the following week about who was dating who, who was cheating on their partner, and who had made mistakes at work, like using a hotel room after a source debrief for other purposes or using a service vehicle for grocery shopping.

On 11 August 2007, Ali and I held our wedding reception party in Ottawa for 200 guests, mostly my family. Ali's family couldn't come, given how difficult it would've been for them to obtain visas. Instead, upon my request, his sister made a home video of herself and his mom, siblings, uncles, aunts, friends, and neighbours. They congratulated us and wished us a happy marriage. David, Nick, some other service employees, and my university friends came to the reception party. I hired a Lebanese dance group to perform as we entered. I was mortified that 400 eyeballs would be on me. Ali, enjoying the attention, danced most of the night, but he isn't a great dancer. My friend Mohammed came up and asked me, "Where the heck did you meet him? Definitely not a dance club."

"Shut up," I said, laughing among all the people who loved me. My parents, brothers, sisters, and extended family were emotional – I'd finally met my prince.

Ali and I were broke, even after the generous gifts and money from our reception party, so we honeymooned at the iconic Chateau Laurier for a couple days then a few days in Montreal and Quebec City. We returned to a new apartment that we hoped to slowly furnish. Our place wasn't as glamorous as Harrison Gardens. I was sad to leave Eman on her own but excited to begin my new life with Ali – that is, until he began leaving dirty socks on the couch after a hard day at work. I called Eman and screamed that I missed her and was frustrated to be living with a man who I had to remind to keep the house clean. "Aaaahh, I'm living with a boy!"

Ali, still studying, had begun attending the University of Toronto international pharmacy program. He was also still working part-time to cover our living costs and his tuition, books, and transportation. He was broke, so I paid the rent, which left no money for entertainment or anything else. I quickly realized that being married to someone in the process of becoming accomplished wasn't easy. When I came home, I wanted to go out with Ali, even if just for a walk or to the movies, but he didn't have time or money. "You've accomplished yourself, habibi. Just give me time, please. I have to study." "I have to work." "Wallahi, I know it's difficult. Wallahi, I do love you. I just have an exam next week." On and on into insignificance, I disappeared. I became bored and resentful after we married.

Naturally, work was my priority. The service's Counter Terrorism focus at the time was online radicalization. Open and classified information demonstrated that some Western youth were downloading violent videos of beheadings, killings, and bombings, including suicide bombings produced and propagated by extremist groups in Afghanistan and Iraq. Those images were meant to turn individuals and groups against societies. They served, enabled, perpetuated, affirmed, and accelerated radicalization. This radicalization process didn't require physical contact, and it provided an us-versus-them narrative. My experience is that religion can be a factor, but family relations, friends, political views, traumatic child/youth experiences, identity politics, and racism all contribute. What I brought to the table was my ability to filter through information in real time, add context otherwise unavailable, and decisively make sound judgment calls. As a Counter Terrorism investigator, I identified those logging onto such sites and assessed whether they'd been radicalized enough to carry out attacks against the public. Through research, I identified participants, knocked on doors, and methodically produced information and assessments. During this time, I recruited a source who became, arguably, one of the best sources Toronto Region ever had, since he had worked for an allied intelligence agency overseas in the past and had tons of helpful and useful information for CSIS.

I worked countless hours of overtime and drove around the Greater Toronto Area and beyond – London, Guelph, Waterloo, Barrie, and other cities – in vehicles that didn't always have winter tires. I hated sleeping in hotels far from home, so I made every effort to return the same night. Fortunately, Ali always made soup for when I returned home. I recall one night phoning my boss and telling him I was too tired to drive home after debriefing a source in a hotel room. He ordered that I not drive that night and to get to a different hotel just in case. That was costly and I appreciated his care.

When I asked Ali what he wanted for his birthday, he said, "more books." That hurt. I had hoped Ali would want to take a trip to Niagara Falls or share a romantic dinner outing. A break from the usual, which was him studying and me working overtime and weekends. I was disappointed that my experience as a newlywed was not as exciting and fun as I had imagined. Overwhelmed by his studies, Ali paid little attention to me or our marriage. It was frustrating. He appealed to my patience, arguing that I had accomplished myself professionally, and he had to do the same and complete his pharmacy program the University of Toronto. He would say, so lovingly, using the word "Habibi," and looking into my eyes, that our future together was bright and full of promise. I respected his position; still, I felt lonely. It was challenging to adjust to the reality that our first year would be financially and emotionally hard. Over time I learned to appreciate the little things like our morning hugs as Ali rushed to catch the subway, him picking up the groceries, his cooking, and his fantastic bright laughter. Ali has a big personality, and, even within our limited time together, his optimism and joyfulness helped ease things out.

For my birthday, he bought me an oud, a Middle Eastern musical instrument that looks like a guitar. I had always wanted one and he had been listening. No one else took my love of music seriously.

In the office, I worked on the 2007 Adel Arnaout case. Arnaout had been arrested in connection with three letter bombs that he'd sent to residents in the Greater Toronto Area in August 2007. He also sent four cases of poisoned water to a talent agency, a bank, and a judge. The water had been laced with the toxic industrial solvent dimethyl sulfite. At the time of his arrest, a rental car driven by him was found containing three similar explosives, which Toronto police destroyed in a controlled explosion. I worked closely with the police to determine whether there'd been any terrorist links, but we lacked sufficient information to establish his motive as political. Working with Toronto police over morning coffees in their offices or at Starbucks was thrilling. I made good friends with an officer on exchange from the New York Police Department. He loved how I'd try, unsuccessfully, to imitate his New York accent and how I'd call it sexy – he'd tease me that I found *him* sexy, not just his accent.

One day, I heard that William, in a town hall, had encouraged another officer to get out and uncover opportunities, "like the ones Huda Mukbil developed." However, I continued to doubt William's sincerity. I couldn't allow myself to trust him again, though I sometimes felt that his position towards me had changed. I kept telling myself that he saw me as a useful asset, but he probably still distrusted my identity and what I represented. I couldn't allow myself to put my guard down – not ever.

By mid-2008, Nick had completed his training for a foreign posting in the Middle East. I was envious – I'd long dreamed of working as an international service officer in the Middle East. I couldn't apply, though, since Ali and I were planning to start a family. I was in my mid-thirties, and it would've been unreasonable for me to wait another four years to start a family. Most foreign postings were, at the very least, a three-year commitment. I convinced myself that such a posting might be possible in the future but that for the time being I was newly married and should focus on my life with Ali.

At the time, Barack Obama was running for president with a message for change. That was all I talked about, in and out of the office and with my family, friends, and Ali. I desperately wanted to believe in positive change. I lived and breathed "Yes, we can." I followed the close race between Obama and Hillary Clinton and later, more carefully, the one between Obama and John McCain. I liked and continued to love and respect John McCain. I viewed him as a great experienced leader for the Republican Party, but I believed deeply in Obama's message. Republicans under Bush had done a great international disservice to America by starting a war in Iraq and by not completing the necessary work of peace in Afghanistan. They used terrorism as a pretext to advance political agendas, ideology, and war in the Middle East. They justified torture campaigns, violated international law with Guantanamo Bay, and unfairly imprisoned and targeted a great many Muslims, both in the US and internationally. Their war on terrorism was shameful. I wanted Bush out of office – yesterday. I viewed Obama as articulate, smart, and a new refreshing voice. I enjoyed his speeches, confident smile, and authenticity. After reading his memoir, *Dreams from My Father*, I loved him even more. Dad liked America but didn't want to go there while Bush was president. I didn't have that luxury. I was required to go to the US to conduct interviews at the Canadian consulate in Buffalo and to work with American security officials.

While Nick was in training at headquarters for his upcoming overseas assignment, I became the most senior investigator on the desk. Then, within months, my new supervisor was asked to work overseas. I was selected to replace him as acting supervisor. I was excited to be acting supervisor on the most critical regional desk in the service. For a month, I ran and directed operations. I trained two new intelligence officers and mentored and guided other investigators. I approved requests for warrant applications and investigative tools, including surveillance, and participated in budgeting decisions. I took on increased decision-making responsibilities, and with my supervisor and senior investigators on assignments, I interacted more with Ben, my deputy director. Ben and I didn't like one another, but I felt Ben had started to trust me and value my work. He knew that I was running the most interesting operations on the desk.

Evan was the ultimate boys' club guy. I just knew he'd received a "reference phone call" like the kind John, from Internal Security, had warned me about all those months prior. Evan didn't like me and made sure I knew it. On the rare occasions that he spoke with me, he would do so arrogantly and with formality. He always spoke to me at the tip of his nose, as we say in Arabic. But there was nothing I could do about it, so I avoided unnecessary conversations with him. Luckily, four managers were between us, so our interactions were limited – nevertheless, our occasional encounters made us both uncomfortable.

One day, I received a message from headquarters that the FBI required my assistance with a high-profile investigation in Amman, Jordan, into threats to the US. I was excited for yet another opportunity to help. I flew to Jordan and worked with the Jordanian General Intelligence Directorate and the FBI, who were most welcoming. Once I completed my assignment, headquarters sent a memo thanking me for my work. Of course, Evan was obligated to invite me to his office to ask about my contributions and excellent collaboration with national security–allied organizations. Without even a thank you, he listened and nodded to the details of the investigation. Encounters with him left me sick to my stomach. I was confused about why I worked for such an uninspiring leader and amused at how difficult it was for him to say I was amazing. His insincere meeting meant nothing to me. I cared about my work, my duty, and saving people's lives.

After Nick left, I had to face reality. Every manager up the chain disliked me. I didn't trust them. I'd, at some point, challenged every manager and proven them wrong. These were not men that would accept a challenge from a racialized woman like me. I couldn't rely on them to even acknowledge my skills. What if I made a mistake? Would I be forgiven as others were, like those who attended Evan's parties? Absolutely not. Then I'd think that I was just being paranoid and try to focus on family and my wonderful relationships in the office.

I was approaching my mid-thirties, and Ali and I wanted a family. I was anxious to have a baby. I felt my biological clock ticking. I was excited when I got pregnant, but even if Ali was excited too, he wasn't ready for a baby. I wanted to be a mother and have a house and everything that came with it. I figured Ali would have graduated and be working by the time of the birth. I began reading about pregnancy. I wanted to know how my body, baby, and life would change. I hid the large books in my purse and only read them on the subway. Nick saw them but, so as not to embarrass me, didn't say anything. When I realized he knew, he said that he'd seen my books and that his wife had read the same ones. He congratulated me. I didn't tell anyone in the office for a month, which any working woman would wisely advise. I was nervous about whether I'd carry a baby to term – I'd faced early complications already – and I didn't want to miss work opportunities. Much of my work involved travelling across Southern Ontario, and I didn't want to give those files away. Not yet.

Friends at work organized a baby shower for me, a very kind gesture. Colleagues of all professional backgrounds – intelligence officers, communications analysts, surveillance professionals, and warrant coordinators from Counter Intelligence, Counter Proliferation, and Counter Terrorism – came to my shower in the largest boardroom, right next to Evan's office. The entire region seemed to be there. I couldn't believe that so many people had taken time to purchase presents, pause essential work, and think of me. I was touched. It brought me to tears to know so many people cared about me. William and Evan didn't come, of course, but Ben did and made jokes. He had come around to liking me. The deputy director of operations came. He reported to Evan and William reported to him. It was nice having him in between them. We had a somewhat kind and professional relationship. He was timid and reasonable. He asked whether I was having a girl or a boy. I told him a girl. He said, "Consider yourself lucky. I have two of each, and girls are really great. Much easier to raise."

As much as I appreciated how liked I was in the office, I'd already decided that I couldn't work there anymore – not when every manager up the hierarchy wouldn't support me and not without Nick there. Daryl was transferred to Counter Terrorism too. How lovely, I thought. As I was wrestling with these thoughts, Andrew, a manager I had never reported to, bumped into me in the hallway without apology. I was startled and my paperwork fell. This was a manager that would never respond to a good morning directed at him in the elevator. And it wasn't just me. My racialized friend who worked as a communications analyst also took notice that he didn't reply or speak to them. Andrew was odd but totally accepted amongst the IOs. He walked by without helping me. I wanted to complain to someone, anyone, but I couldn't. He was close to Evan, and no one would acknowledge or listen. Then I made my decision: I would leave Toronto Region.

At the end of October, I gave birth and, in the same month, Ali finished his national licensing exams and became a pharmacist. He'd secured employment with a Shoppers Drug Mart in Ottawa, where we agreed to move. We found a small apartment close to my parents and started looking to purchase a home for our small family. All this happened during my parental leave and before I could find the words to speak to my managers at work.

Then I received a message from Ben. When I called back, he asked whose number I was calling from. I explained I was in Ottawa. Ben said that they needed me to come in for a week to work on an urgent file. CSIS, though, wasn't going to pay for my travel and accommodation. I was still a Toronto Region employee. I explained that my daughter was less than four months and I'd be doing CSIS a favour by working on parental leave. Ben said that he'd speak with management and call back. When he did, his tone was completely different. He said management would set me up in a hotel with my daughter if I came in to support the investigation.

Of course, I complied. I travelled with my little girl. When I walked into the office with her, Ben joked "Did she go through Internal? Is she cleared to be here?" He'd missed teasing me. William was nice to me too. He'd grown a white beard and looked at me kindly. I wondered what had changed. Was I looking at them differently because I was no longer under their command, or was it because we'd worked together for years and had finally got to know one another? That's one question, among many, that I'll never have an answer to.

18 | OFFICIAL COMPLAINTS AND REPERCUSSIONS

In October 2009, upon return from parental leave, I was placed at the Integrated Terrorism Assessment Centre (ITAC), a CSIS headquarters-housed organization that included representatives from other national security organizations, namely, the national defence, Global Affairs Canada, and Transport Canada amongst others, on a two-year rotational basis. Derek, my officemate, was a seasoned military police officer with years of service in Afghanistan. While we shared criticism of the Harper government's handling of Afghan detainees arrested by Canadian forces, our roles within ITAC did not intersect. He was to produce a threat assessment on the Arctic, and I worked on fictitious terrorism exercise scenarios in preparation for the 2010 Olympic and Paralympic Winter Games in British Columbia.

My daughter was in daycare, but even at the office, I would catch traces of her beautiful soft scent on my clothes and miss her. We were inseparable for a year, and pregnant again, I was looking forward to another parental leave in six months. I was glad to be in Ottawa. My friend Susan and I took leave at the same time and frequented all the indoor playgrounds that year. Ali and I bought a new-build house in the south end of the city, close to my parents. Given the hefty financial requirements for new homeowners, he worked twelve-hour shifts, six days a week, to save money for a decent down payment and the associated fees. We took great pleasure visiting the site of our home to witness the development as it was being built, dreaming of greater stability for our growing, young family.

My colleague, Saul, the only Black man at ITAC, was experiencing harassment. When he opened up about his experience, I shared mine with him and encouraged him to challenge his aggressors in written format and through the Employee Association. I judged that he was strong enough for it, but we were both disheartened that it had to be us, racialized employees, who took on powerful managers in the organization. I thought about him a lot during my parental leave and wondered if he was okay. Later I learned that he transferred out. That thought made me tremble. Based now on both my own experiences and Saul's, I strongly believed that there was no winning through complaint mechanisms at CSIS.

Following my second parental leave, I returned to work with the appetite to refocus on my career. Having a nanny at home alleviated the physical demands of caring for toddlers and the family–life balance was working well for me. This time, I was placed on the Counter Intelligence People's Republic of China (PRC) investigations where we were mandated to investigate spies sent to acquire sensitive military technologies from Canada, amongst other national security threats posed by the Chinese government. The PRC's intelligence operations were ongoing but more politically sensitive than today. My role involved establishing connections with officials from Global Affairs and the Controlled Goods Directorate to investigate potential violations of export laws on dual use technologies and any unauthorized defence goods to PRC. Part of that role was also uncovering PRC military or intelligence front companies internationally. My supervisor, Nelson, had worked on PRC investigations for many years and I benefited from his experience. I also benefited from his personal experience and struggles as a gay man at CSIS, which I won't go into here in respect for his privacy. Suffice to say he was more compassionate, balanced, and professional than any of my previous managers. As a senior intelligence officer and a mother, I needed this style of leadership. My deskmates were millennials, and I enjoyed how they often questioned our policies on mobility and the lack of transparency on management's decision making. In not-so-subtle ways, they also demanded a better work–life balance. Whiffs of a new culture were starting to emerge at CSIS as result of their efforts. For example, for a supervisory competition where mobility was being enforced, IOs dropped out of the competition in great numbers and the service had a limited number of applicants.

My files on the PRC counterintelligence were interesting, and I enjoyed learning about the different types of threats that permeated this investigation. But my heart was set on finding a way to get a foreign posting. That spring, when the annual call letter for foreign postings came out, I jumped out of my seat and ran into Nelson's office. We walked over to Richard's office and discussed the vacancies with excitement. Richard and Nelson both thought I would be one of the strongest candidates for a posting in the Middle East or East Africa. I took a deep breath and felt I had to have a serious discussion with Ali at home.

I painted a picture-perfect tale about me working abroad and got his support: "Ali, you could continue studying online towards your doctorate. You'd have time to spend with the kids. You could enjoy their childhood, cook your Alexandrian seafood recipes, and maybe travel more." As a bonus, our traditional roles would be reversed – I'd be the primary breadwinner and Ali would be home. That ought to balance things out.

At work, every morning, I logged into my computer and studied every word on the call letter, the essential and desired qualifications, screening processes, and timelines. I scanned the Global Affairs website to learn what working overseas would be like. I imagined working abroad at a Canadian embassy. I recalled my temporary-duty assignments in London and Jordan and how thrilled I'd been to work in international settings, proudly representing CSIS and Canada. After checking my email for anything pressing, I'd then get to work on a cover letter and resume.

And, sent! Now it was time to network, and luckily, I knew just the right executive manager to call – David, my former supervisor in London. I was disheartened that as a racialized woman, I couldn't count on the support and sponsorship of the many managers whom I'd served well, like Evan. Others could, but I couldn't. The process was predicated on who you knew, which at CSIS meant privilege, not merit. Marshall and David were my only sponsors. Marshall had retired, and David was serving in Washington. I called David, who had direct contact with the International Region's director general and with service executives at headquarters. He provided useful insight about how to demonstrate confidence and professionalism. Fully supportive of me, he recommended that I schedule a meeting with the International Region director to introduce myself, demonstrate my credentials, and inform the director that I had David's support and confidence. David said that he'd be happy to act as a reference for me. I followed his advice to the letter.

I met with Kelly, the International Region director. I hadn't worked for him and didn't know what kind of man he was, which at the service is a good thing. Kelly provided a kind reception. We sat on sofas, at a distance from his desk. I introduced myself and gave my credentials for a foreign posting. I narrated my achievements, hoping he'd be impressed. I gave a copy of my cover letter and resume and thanked him for meeting me. Glancing at my resume, he asked about my accomplishments as recruiter in Toronto. He seemed pleased with my answers about having recruited and developed highly productive Arab-speaking sources. Then he asked permission to ask a personal question. "Of course," I said, happy he felt comfortable to do so. I saw it as a signal for real consideration. He asked how many children I had. My heart dropped. I'd prepared for a question about how my family, which now included two children, was going to adapt to the change or survive on one income while my husband put his career on hold for me. I told Kelly that I had two young children and that my husband would be home with them. When I left his office, I was nevertheless confident that I'd be at the top of the consideration list.

The day of the interview, I opened the meeting door and wanted to leave. My interviewer, Sean, was at the heart of CSIS's old boys' club culture. He had been a Counter Terrorism supervisor in Toronto during 9/11, travelled to Afghanistan, and made a name for himself being tough on terror. He was also the same man who travelled to Guantanamo Bay to interview Omar Khadr, with whom I had always sympathized.[1] I followed the case at CSIS and in open source intimately and I knew that Mr Khadr, at just fifteen years old, suffered tremendously in Guantanamo Bay. Many did not see him as a child soldier. Images of him crying calling for his mom came to mind as I sat across from Sean, and I could feel my chest trying hard to breath. I dreaded the idea of Sean having access to my Human Resources and Internal Security files and the pleasure to ask any question he liked. I hated that men like Sean stood at every corner of career advancement and opportunity in CSIS.

The interview didn't go well. He asked how I'd prioritize work. To show I was willing to disappoint family and friends for the sake of work priorities, I recounted missing my best friend's wedding for an overseas assignment. Sean interpreted this as a complaint or regret and docked motivation marks, which he told me about when I met with him later to determine what went wrong. When I spoke of my Europe and Middle East travels, I was pointing out my experience travelling alone and that I'd do so for CSIS. Service officers stationed internationally frequently move country to country, as required. To demonstrate my understanding of the cultures and languages of Amman and Jerusalem and that I could be effective in male-dominated cultures and difficult circumstances, I told Sean about my travels to those regions. Sean questioned why I'd travel to Jerusalem as a tourist. I judged that, in my Internal Security files, he saw I attended a pro-Palestine demonstration back when I was at university. I felt scrutinized, so I didn't answer but said that all my travel had been reported to Internal Security.

Months later, I received an email saying I was no longer being considered for a foreign posting. I was disappointed. When I saw the list of successful candidates, I was surprised to learn applicants with less than four years' experience had received postings – some had never even held a successful liaison post or been on temporary duty abroad. Almost all were men, some totally untested. I decided then to submit an official grievance. I complained. No one that wished to have a successful career at CSIS complains. This is one of the unwritten rules for all CSIS unionized intelligence officers who live and breathe at the discretion of the powerful. Statements provided by the Federal Public Sector Labour Relations and Employment Board reveal that, at CSIS, "employees refrain from filing grievances because no legal basis supports them, apart from the employer's [management's] goodwill. Since the CSIS is a small organization and the possibilities for advancement are few, employees generally fear that filing a grievance or challenging a performance evaluation may compromise their careers."[2]

Still, I hoped that if an executive on the sixth floor learned of my determination, then I'd undoubtedly obtain a posting, even if it was as distant as a year later. I waited. According to service policy, the grievance process is supposed to take ten working days. I didn't hear back for five months. My complaint disappeared into the bureaucracy of the system. I thought they must all be saying "how dare she?" Colleagues I told widened their eyes in disbelief that I had complained.

Meanwhile, I applied for a supervisory position. Again, I was interviewed by a panel of white men and my interview was unsuccessful. The young white men in these interviews supported and promoted young men they saw themselves in, but there was no minority manager at CSIS for me to either speak with or count on for support. All I could do was hope for a breakthrough.

All this hit me hard. I fell into a familiar depression. Frustrated and feeling unheard and unseen by CSIS and its managers, I began experiencing migraine and tension headaches. I internalized all the unfair treatment and felt alone and less confident. I judged that I should accept my glass ceiling at CSIS. But I couldn't stop myself from dreaming and wanting more. It's part of who I am – I wouldn't have made it as far as I did otherwise.

My attitude at work changed. My exclusion compelled me to further exclude myself, since I felt more in control by doing so. I asked my supervisor to let me sit in a cubicle by the corner, alone. Permission granted. I went to work, communicated by email, and returned home. I was no longer me. I didn't come in chatty or smiling. I just wanted to get through the day. Living without a professional goal in an institution I'd served for many years was hard on my spirit. I felt foolish. At night, I'd pray to not have a migraine again. I'd take my migraine meds, lock myself in my dark room, and weather the pain. My children worried. Though they usually nagged me to tuck them into bed, on migraine nights, they stood sad in their pajamas with Ali and hoped that I was all right.

I wanted to take care of my mental health and for my depression and headaches to go away. I consulted the service psychologist. I was reluctant because of stigma surrounding mental health and depression. I knew he'd draft a report, a permanent record that would be used against me. This scared me. What if it further kept me from advancing my career? What options did I have? I couldn't seek a psychologist outside CSIS, as I wouldn't be able to tell them anything about work. Plus, they'd never understand the culture and therefore would never understand me or my struggles. I did the brave thing and scheduled an appointment. I told the service psychologist – of course, another white man – that I hated some service managers and felt they hated me. They were like wolves, one at every corner. They held power, and I couldn't overcome the challenges they threw at me. I told him that I wished to belong at CSIS. "They aren't gods, you know," he replied. "Tell me who, and maybe I can schedule a meeting where we can all discuss your concerns." *What a fool. A meeting? Just announce to them I dislike their attitudes, decisions, and actions? Show my fear? Why don't I just give him a bullet to shoot me now?*

"No, that isn't necessary – how long have you been working here?" I asked.

"A little less than a year," he replied.

"That explains it." I told him reprisal was real at CSIS and that the faster he learned that, the better he'd be able to help people. But I wasn't going to school him on CSIS culture. Let him figure it out – I needed help and was too tired to explain. The psychologist said that I was stressed and anxious. He recommended anti-anxiety medication. When I told Ali, a clinical pharmacist, he was upset. He said the psychologist had no right to recommend meds. He told me about the serious side effects. "That's the last resort. You must try everything else first," he said. "Talk to people. Exercise. I'll help you. I'll give you all the time in the evenings," he promised.

Ali became much more attuned to what I was experiencing at work and the impact it was having on me. He felt bad about what I'd experienced and regretted not having been there to help. He also encouraged me to stand up for myself. He realized that I was being pushed around. What was most uplifting was that he believed in me and my abilities. He never questioned whether I should've been promoted or received a posting or that work culture wasn't as it should've been. When I least believed in myself, he believed in me. *That was everything.*

They say God never forgets a faithful subject. Lo and behold, a fascinating Counter Intelligence investigation landed on my desk, exactly what I needed to get out of my depressive state. It was a classic CI investigation: politically sensitive, sexy, and requiring daily liaising with the regional office and service intelligence partners, including my friends at the CSE. I was selected because of my seniority on the desk and was trusted to progress the file and brief my management team, which included my chief and deputy director general.

After the investigation, the deputy director general thanked me for a job well done. I was then selected to work on a huge project that required me to research and write the warrant renewal report on all of CSIS's China investigations. The project took three months to research, draft, and analyze. It required levels of approval and coordination between three departments. I was busy and fulfilled. Slowly but surely, the migraines became manageable.

Later in the summer of 2012, I received a transfer to work on the Counter Proliferation Iran desk. On my last day in Counter Intelligence, my deputy director general called everyone for a huddle. To all who'd worked on the China investigation, he said kind words about me, my professionalism, and my great contribution to a sensitive investigation that hardly anyone knew about. I was profoundly touched but found it ironic that this was happening in Counter Intelligence and not in Counter Terrorism, where I'd made even more impactful contributions.

That night, fulfilled and confident to tackle my next position, I slept more peacefully than I had in months.

19 | LEAN IN

In July 2012, I worked on Counter Proliferation Iran investigations. I felt good about my transfer, even though Charles, my former Counter Terrorism manager whom we nicknamed Napoleon for his authoritative style, would become my deputy director general. He had been promoted two levels up since our last encounter and my informal complaints against him in 2005. Above him was the first woman director general I had encountered at CSIS, Rachel. She called me in for a meeting first thing and spoke about how satisfied she was to have climbed the career ladder at the service. I agreed. I was happy for her success and glad she was personable. I felt she'd appreciate the difficulties of navigating CSIS culture. I sensed that she had heard about my reputation challenging Charles and liked that. I walked from her office straight to Charles, who was curious about my and Rachel's closed-door meeting. I was a little nervous, naturally – he was in a position of power, and I'd previously complained about his conduct and judgment. But I was in my late thirties by then and felt better equipped to deal with challenges. *The enemy you know is better than the one you don't.* Besides, I'd managed to work with William again after our difficult past. "Come in, Huda," Charles said.

"Hi Charles." I sat in his large office.

"Huda, did you ask for a transfer to CP?"

"No, I asked for CT, but CP needed resources more, so here I am, happy to be here."

"Happy," he repeated. "Exactly, Huda. I want you to be happy. There's nothing worse than coming in every day and not being happy. I know there's history between us, and if you decide you don't want this transfer, I'd be glad to help you transfer to another branch."

"That isn't necessary, Charles. I'm happy to be here. I'm sure we can work together, so long as we're able to leave the past behind us. I've moved on." I knew he didn't want me there, but he also knew he couldn't refuse me – he wanted me to ask for an out. It's as if he was hoping that I'd quit so he wouldn't be challenged or accused of discrimination. I told him that I looked forward to contributing to Counter Proliferation and its Iran investigation. Reluctantly, he leaned forward. "Great, welcome aboard. Let me know if you need anything." And that was that.

I adored my officemate Phillipe, a brilliant, knowledgeable Francophone with a confident smile and an applied-sciences background like most of my siblings and friends. There was no office space for me in the Iran bullpen, so I shared a small office with Philippe, who was on the Syria file. Phillipe knew everything about Syria, the Bashar Al Assad leadership, and its access to chemical and biological weapons. He took his responsibilities to heart and humbly admitted to any blind spots in his analyses. Over the years, I've learned that admitting our weaknesses with humility is key to becoming knowledgeable. He hadn't worked in a regional office yet, but I sensed he'd be a star there, just as he was in our office. His eyes lit up every time I spoke to him about my time in Toronto.

Since I was already a seasoned intelligence officer, my first assignment was large and noteworthy; I was to draft a direction statement, which meant providing national direction to regional offices on their Counter Proliferation Iran investigations. This was a monstrous task for a new analyst on the desk. I was given six weeks. I began reading and researching. My direct supervisor, Justine, was impressed by my ability to articulate national security threats, identify gaps, and map paths to overcoming challenges. I loved owning and running with projects. My Iran desk colleagues each had less than three years' experience as intelligence officers, and I enjoyed sharing my knowledge and insight on how to run sources in the field.

I was also preparing to try to advance my career again. My sisters each had MBAs, had both become engineers in the US, and held managerial positions. Even Ali had a few years' management experience. My sisters recommended that I read *Lean In* by Facebook executive Sheryl Sandberg. Reading her book, I was encouraged to compartmentalize CSIS's old boys' club culture and my gender and path to career advancement. Sandberg explained that in boardroom meetings, men often grab plates of food and sit at large tables while women take food last and sit in chairs to the side.[1] At CSIS, less experienced white men without source-recruitment experience, travel experience, and cross-cultural communication skills were being given opportunities that I'd worked hard for. Sandberg encouraged women to underestimate neither themselves nor their accomplishments and to feel worthy of success. I learned that I had to expect gender bias and navigate it. Her book doesn't address race, intersectionality, and systemic barriers. Sandberg's suggestion that women shouldn't underestimate themselves is valid, but there are bigger challenges for racialized women – systemic racism trumps a racialized woman's efforts for career advancement.

Still, I thought that if I wanted something, I'd have to make it happen. I was a determined Type A person, after all. So, I booked an appointment with a Human Resources advisor and expressed my interest in working as a foreign service officer. The advisor suggested that I write an interest statement to the director general of the International Region highlighting my qualifications, linguistic abilities, and work experiences abroad. Less than two days later, the International Region director general sent a response to Human Resources indicating that the branch was full. My advisor and I were puzzled, as this wasn't true. I was disheartened, but my advisor encouraged me by telling me that the director general would be switching branches within the year. She recommended that I gain as much qualifying experience for these postings as possible in the meantime. We both agreed that I was only missing security screening experience on immigration files. While service officers with foreign postings often assist immigration and CBSA partners with security screening, many of my colleagues hadn't obtained this experience prior to being posted. Nevertheless, I figured that, as a female minority, I should check off every possible box that could aid my career advancement.

In preparation, I spoke with many returning foreign service officers, including Rick, from a class close to mine all those years ago when I first started my career with CSIS. He'd had two postings and had won a supervisory promotion. Rick told me I needed to demonstrate my loyalty. *Here we go again – it always boils down to managers who can't conceive that a Muslim could be a loyal Canadian citizen.* "What, because I'm different?" I asked him, without specifically referencing that I was Muslim or Black.

"No, Huda, that isn't what I mean. You have to be loyal, like Paul and Jeff. Show decision-making managers they can trust you with anything."

He added that Jeff was like a son to the director general of the International Region, and although Jeff lacked experience, he was, yet again, going on another posting. I thanked Rick for his honesty and walked back to my office. That Jeff was like the director general's son rang in my ears. The white men at CSIS trusted and looked out for one another. Women at CSIS could tap into this culture selectively.

On my desk in Counter Proliferation, Iran a critical operation was coming into play due to the Harper government's decision to suspend diplomatic ties with Iran, close the Canadian embassy there, and expel Iranian diplomats from Canada. My deskmates and I were working closely with Global Affairs Canada and the decision impacted some of our investigations. Upon successful completion, my unit manager brought alcohol to our office on a Friday afternoon to mark the occasion and thank everyone for having diligently worked many late afternoons and evenings. In one of the division's more spacious offices, managers and intelligence officers in Counter Proliferation gathered, shared some light conversation and laughter, and exchanged noteworthy observations and reflections. The mood was collegial and relaxed when a manager asked Erica, one of the female managers on the desk, if she was sipping orange juice. It was a microaggression meant to tease her, perhaps embarrass her, and communicate that the space she, we, were holding there at CSIS was for men, those who can handle a drink or two in the afternoon. Erica pushed back saying, "Orange juice my ass," suggesting that her drink did contain alcohol. I enjoyed watching her be assertive and use her voice to reclaim the space. However, there was nothing gender neutral about what she said, nor was that space racially neutral.

Fitting into CSIS culture and, specifically, gaining the personal trust of CSIS managers was necessary to secure career progression. But as a Black Muslim woman, I, unlike Erica, could not just accept the status quo and make it work for me. I wondered, besides my accomplishments at work, how I could compete professionally with my colleague whose gender and race served to benefit her. These kinds of impossible calculations always drove me to want to leave CSIS. *Do I keep on trying or leave the service altogether and find work in other federal government departments? Is it different elsewhere?* I wasn't ready to leave. I liked working in national security, so I had to figure out how to advance my career, one way or another.

20 | SECURITY SCREENING

CSIS's Security Screening branch is divided into Immigration and Government Security Screening. The government side investigates and provides security assessments on those whose Canadian government employment requires lawful access to classified information or sensitive sites, such as nuclear facilities. The Immigration program provides in-depth investigations into immigration, visa, and permanent citizen applications to Canada. The program is aimed at preventing non-Canadians with security concerns from entering or gaining status in Canada. At CSIS, we called it Canada's first line of defence against terrorists and spies.

"Who did you piss off?" said Karter, my chief in Immigration Security Screening, as I sat on my desk training with a security screening expert. "No one ever asks to come to Security Screening by choice," he said authoritatively.

What is up his ass? He was on to me from the start! He was a complicated character whom I enjoyed dissecting. He'd wrapped the director general around his fingers by complimenting, lunching, and joking with him. He was an ambitious former military officer, a Calgarian, and a self-made man. At first, I thought, wrongly, that he was a bully, but I soon liked working for him. He was unique. I came to learn that former military guys were different than former law enforcement guys. When they liked you, they liked you and would at least feel bad about betraying your trust. Brotherly comradery trumped the frequent cunning of the intelligence world. I explained that I needed security screening experience to land a foreign posting. "You don't need it, but sure, I will accept that," he said. He knew that many intelligence officers serving abroad couldn't possibly have checked off all the requirements listed in the foreign posting call letters. I did too, but still, I felt that as a visible minority and woman, I had to meet every requirement and then some.

I slowly showed Karter that I was open to dialogue and willing to joke. I enjoyed watching him, including how he demanded authority, craved power, and read everyone well. He spoke and acted without hesitation and was uncompromising and opinionated.

My new boss, Randy, a surveillance officer turned intelligence officer – later promoted to supervisor – was disengaged and disgruntled with the service. He often romanticized his time after 9/11 as a Toronto intelligence officer recruiting Counter Terrorism sources.

Once I learned how to process, research, investigate, and make decisions on security screening files, I was unstoppable. With my extensive Counter Terrorism experience, I was able to easily establish the necessary background security thresholds for accepting or denying permanent resident, refugee, and citizenship applications. I was processing more files than anyone on the desk. "What's everyone else doing?" Randy would comment as I processed file after file.

Three months into my position, Karter and Randy called me into a meeting and said that they wanted to transfer me to Security Screening's Iran desk. Karter explained that he needed a knowledgeable, experienced intelligence officer like me to work in the program. I was taken aback. I'd settled into my Counter Terrorism file, and there was going to be an influx of new intelligence officers soon. I also understood that I shouldn't question Karter's decision, given that I'd need his recommendation for applications to foreign postings or other opportunities. I complied but demanded that Randy write a three-month performance evaluation of me. "Consider it done, Huda," Randy said. He wrote:

> Her SSB Middle East file is characterized by a high volume of files, and Ms. Mukbil has demonstrated the ability to adapt to changing priorities; she readily takes responsibility and her work is accurate and detailed. She demonstrated a continuing positive approach toward achieving set expectations and corporate goals. In this regard, she is consulted widely, and her knowledge of the subject

matter indicated through preparations. She suggested appropriate courses of action and enacted them, furthering the work of the unit. She is very well regarded by her colleagues and works very well in a team environment where she [has] promoted positive and productive working relationships. Ms. Mukbil takes personal initiatives; she had completed online courses in critical incident stress management and communicating with diplomacy and tact. She is also the fire warden for the Branch.

I was pleased. This was the type of evaluation that I could provide to any selection committee. I'd been working above and beyond by volunteering as the branch's lead on the Government of Canada Workplace Charitable Campaign and as one of the branch's fire wardens.

Liz, my new supervisor, was enthusiastic about having me on her team. She'd worked in the Toronto Region before me, and we knew many of the same people. She saw me as seasoned, experienced, and an asset to her team. During meetings or chatter, she'd put me and other intelligence officers up on a pedestal, so to speak. My officemate Lisa was an experienced intelligence officer who'd worked in Afghanistan and was no pushover. She ate healthy, kept fit, kept it real, and wasn't as pretentious as other intelligence officers her age. Liz was of German and Polish descent and loved travelling in Europe. After every trip, she'd bring boxes of decadent European chocolate to share us with. Mary, another intelligence officer, also shared the office. She was a young and timid security screening officer turned intelligence officer and a great analyst and researcher, but she was untested as an investigator. She wanted to recruit sources and run operations and would soon leave for Toronto.

Liz was a true leader. She built her team by demanding we take courses and receive more training. She supported us in every way possible. She was dedicated to her work and to her team. She'd drive to work in her BMW at nine every morning and, looking sharp as a button, greet us all warmly before burying herself in work. When we were ready for a break, she'd come in with her fancy chocolate, share about her last date, and light up our hearts. We were lucky to have her. Liz is a phenomenal woman. I began counting on her. I even sought her advice on career and husband troubles. She'd laugh at my willingness to open up about the most intimate things.

On her team, I quickly became a subject-matter expert on Iranian weaponization. I processed thousands of applications and provided security assessments to the CBSA and IRCC. I led presentations at the CBSA and IRCC on the inner workings of our branch and trained new CSIS employees. Additionally given the complexity of the Iran WMD file, I conducted interviews across the country and landed an interview overseas as well.

That spring of 2014, when the annual call letter for supervisory positions and foreign roles was posted, Liz, Lisa, and I decided, excitedly, to compete. We each had headquarters, regional, and overseas experience. We supported each other, which meant a lot to me. I also sought assistance from two other former Toronto Region colleagues. I had all the support I could wish for. When I approached Karter about my intent to work abroad, he encouraged me to apply to both.

Ali was fully supportive. He knew that I lived and breathed to work overseas for CSIS. We agreed that the kids were young enough, still being in grade school, that such a position wouldn't interfere with their secondary school studies, which are important for post-secondary education. In July 2014, I took a week off work to spend time with my kids at home. That week, Karter called me. I was surprised. "Huda, I know you're on your holidays, but I have something important to ask of you. How would you like to go to Ankara, Turkey, to conduct security screening interviews?"

"Karter, are you serious? I want to say 'yes, absolutely,' but when and for how long?"

"You would leave in August, in two weeks, for a month. I'm calling you this week because I need an answer right away."

"All right, it's a tentative yes, but let me speak with my nanny. I'll confirm soon."

Karter laughed and said, "Don't you mean your husband, Huda?"

"Yes, Karter, my husband *too*, but honestly, it's in the nanny's hands. She's who I trust to take care of my kids," I said, smiling. It amused me that Karter and I got along. The man had a portrait of Prime Minister Stephen Harper in his office and joked that Justin Trudeau was a kid with nothing but his dad's legacy. Yet Karter and I worked well together, despite our political differences. It didn't surprise me that some managers didn't avoid politics or overt displays of partisanship. Many managers supported the Conservatives. I didn't care. I knew that Karter and I had the service's interest at heart, and we respected one another for the skills we each brought to the mission.

I was frustrated to have little time to prepare for the temporary-duty assignment, and I worried my kids would be disappointed with me for not spending summer holidays with them. But I had to go. I had to prove that I, a female intelligence officer, could put family considerations aside to get the job done, especially if I wanted the service to take my foreign posting application seriously. So off I went.

Once in Ankara, I conducted many interviews and assessed candidates whose permanent residency files demonstrated security concerns. I sat across the table from possible Daesh members and supporters, people who'd worked for the Syrian government under Bashar, people who'd deserted the Syrian military, and Iranians who'd worked in sensitive Iranian institutions. I conducted my interviews precisely, wrote reports, and sent my assessments to the branch. I identified threats to national security and proposed remedies. Karter was pleased when I returned. He took me to the deputy director general's office to recount my many and exciting finds. He knew I was a good storyteller.

To prepare for my position applications, I met with a Human Resources advisor, colleagues, and supervisors from across CSIS. They all supported my candidacy and shared with me their experiences and advice. I also teamed up with Stacey, a former Toronto Region intelligence officer. She didn't have Counter Terrorism experience, hadn't recruited sources, and hadn't been abroad, but she was great with people, and she networked by attending many private parties that colleagues held, and that was something I never did. Stacey was loud, strong-minded, provocative, and famous for wearing unconventional clothes. I got along well with her. She was real, spoke her mind with clarity, and didn't take anything too seriously, which had been my problem. For months, Stacey and I took coffee breaks together. Eyes rolled when people saw us laughing and whispering together. We looked so different yet were similar in many ways. Stacey was free-spirited and unapologetically against marriage, institutionalized religion, and patriarchy. I was a married, traditional Muslim woman who chose to live by a strict set of rules, and I'd never strayed from that, not even for a sip of wine. Liz used to chuckle about how Stacey and I were buddies.

Our respective supervisory position interviews were the same week. Afterward, we spoke about how we'd answered the questions. The results were to be posted in two months, but given the approaching summer holidays, we knew it would be more like three. Liz, Lisa, and I all had foreign postings interviews. For mine, I entered a massive boardroom in a navy blue suit and a crisp white shirt. There were two white men – Robert, a senior executive and the decision maker, and Phil, a supervisor – and a Human Resources advisor, Celine. "Huda, please tell us about yourself and why you applied for a foreign posting. Narrate your experience, qualifications, and achievements." For twenty minutes, I detailed my Counter Terrorism experience, which related heavily to the posts. I also spoke of my Counter Intelligence and Counter Proliferation experience; my liaisons with CSE, the CBSA, and IRCC; and my three temporary-duty assignments overseas. I added that I spoke four languages and had travel experience in Europe and the Middle East. The panel was clearly impressed. I knew that Phil, who'd already been on a posting, didn't have the exposure and opportunities I did.

Then Robert asked me peculiar questions. "Huda, I know you applied for CT-centric posts in the Middle East, but an officer must remain flexible. How would you fit in if we sent you to, say, Europe?" I doubted whether he'd been paying attention earlier when I'd spent ten minutes discussing my London work. I told him that I was aware many of my colleagues preferred European countries, as I did, but given my linguistic abilities and expertise in counterterrorism, I felt I had a better chance applying to represent the service in Middle Eastern countries.

Then, Celine asked whether I held any other citizenship. I told her I didn't – I'd been on my father's Yemeni passport as a child but hadn't sought my own citizenship, passport, or status there. I told her my husband held Egyptian citizenship in addition to his Canadian citizenship. To uphold diplomatic status, Global Affairs has a strict policy of not sending dual Canadian citizens to countries where they hold status. Then Celine asked how many children I had. I told her three but was bothered that she'd ask that during an interview and enter it into their decision making. I'm sure the two white men, the decision makers in that room, saw me then as a mom and not an intelligence officer. I smiled uncomfortably. I figured that I'd be adding gasoline to the fire if I said my husband would be taking care of my children, but I did say my husband was fully supportive of our possible relocation. Maybe that would reassure them, I thought.

After the interview, Liz and Lisa said Robert was less inclined to give opportunities to people who don't look like him. "I felt uncomfortable talking about my female partner to Robert in an interview," Lisa said. "I feel like I may not end up getting anything," she added.

I said, "You know what else was weird? They asked how I'd fit in in Europe, even after what I'd said about London, MI5, and how I went to dinner parties with members of other intelligence organizations and met with the Canadian high commissioner."

"I guess they were wondering if you'd go out to bars with the CIA and Brits while on the post. It would be part of liaison relationship building, you know?" Liz explained.

"I get that, Liz, and I did that in London. Going to the local bar was a weekly thing. I'd order a coke. Big deal. But how do I say this in an interview setting?" I asked.

"Oh, Huda, they'll never find anyone as qualified as you. I'm sure you'll get a posting this time, and we'll come out and visit you," Liz said, sounding serious.

Liz, Karter, and my new chief, Lucy, all spoke as if I already had a supervisory promotion or posting – apparently, I was an intelligence officer on her way out. I hated hearing this. It put my hopes up, but I sensed all wasn't well.

I received my rejection letter for the supervisory position first. Stacey succeeded. I was happy for her and a little envious, but I was surprised. I had passing scores for knowledge, abilities, and supervisory functions but was docked points for work ethic and leadership. I was perplexed. I'd been a mentor to many intelligence officers and was a branch fire warden and a Government of Canada Workplace Charitable Campaign volunteer. On performance evaluations, I'd always been commended for my work ethic, relationship-building, and leadership abilities. I called the interviewing manager, another white male, and explained. I invited him to review my performance evaluations. He replied that I hadn't clearly demonstrated leadership abilities during the interview. I thought I had. I argued. I reminded him the call letter required him to consider my application comprehensively. He stuck to his guns and wished me better luck next time. "Look, I like you, Huda. I know you'd be a great supervisor. I'll be happy to help next year."

When I returned defeated to my desk, my new chief apologized. "I'm sorry, Huda. I don't know what happened, but you'll get it next time," she said. My officemates Denny and Sarah and others came to express their disappointment too, which was unbearable for me. I realized many people cared about me, but I felt I'd disappointed them all. I felt ashamed of myself.

A month later, I received another rejection letter, this one for the foreign posting. "You were not selected by the committee." I read this again and again. I was docked points on motivation and flexibility – again, subjective categories – not knowledge, qualifications, or ability. I felt hopeless. I'd given my best performance, rehearsed my answers with intelligence officers who'd had foreign postings, and checked all the essential qualifications and desirable attributes. I'd gained experience in previous interviews (five by that time). I had great relationships with all my managers and had volunteered on many committees. What was I missing?

Liz had received 100 per cent on required categories, and Lisa had scored better than I did, yet we were all unsuccessful. Liz argued that they were crazy for not selecting me. I was puzzled as to why they wouldn't have chosen her given that she was a single woman and that her only commitment would be to the service. We all agreed that the International Region was the embodiment of old boys' club culture. The selection process was a sham. In the end, it was relationships, not merit, that prevailed.

My dreams were crushed. I felt small, defeated, and disheartened. A foreign posting had been my motivation for years. Now that was impossible. *Will I apply again, knowing I don't stand a chance? Will I go through the motions, believing a different set of managers can change the outcome?* I felt lost. *It isn't fair.*

When the foreign postings selectees list came out, I quickly printed it, called Lisa into Liz's office, and closed the door. "Look at this!" The list was 90 per cent men and 0 per cent minorities – no surprise! We went through the names and determined that some selectees didn't have the exposure, training, or experience we did. Some were selected for a second time, as if no other intelligence officer could've benefitted from overseas experience. Some knew members of the panel. Men had children too, but it was easy to think that their wives would be home with them. I figured that the old white International Region managers saw themselves in these men. "I can't believe this. This isn't right!" I said. Liz and Lisa agreed but weren't as passionate. "I'm filing an official complaint again," I said, determined to turn the table on the International Region and its selection process. It was a daring move and would come with consequences. My experience was that CSIS management did not like to be officially challenged particularly with a paper trail that would force them to acknowledge their decision-making processes.

I marched back to my office with determination, wrote the names of everyone already at post and everyone who'd been selected, drew up a pie chart to create visuals, and drafted a detailed grievance complaint. I already knew that the International Region's call letter, unlike other service call letters, didn't have a diversity clause. I included this information in my complaint and fired it off to Labour Relations. I argued that there was a systemic bias for white men that disadvantaged qualified, experienced female intelligence officers. I argued that my application had been treated unfairly and inequitably, contrary to service policies. Labour Relations forwarded my complaint to the assistant director of operations, Jeanne.

I was supposed to receive a reply in ten days. It took three months. I understood that they weren't going to freeze the entire selection process because of my complaint and findings as they should have, but I felt strongly and sent out a monthly email demanding at least some kind of action. Labour Relations kept assuring me that I'd receive a response shortly. My colleagues warned me that I'd never get a posting after questioning the International Region's decision making. I decided the risk was worth the reprisal.

In the meantime, I received news that a selectee for an unadvertised posting hadn't met the post's requirements, including the necessary interviewing and liaison experience. She was the spouse of the head of station for the post she was going to. This was wrong on so many levels – the post was unadvertised, she was unqualified, and she'd be reporting to her husband. I reached out to the Employee Association president and expressed my outrage. At first, they were as concerned as I about the inappropriate selection and said that they'd meet with International Region executive managers. After their meeting, they responded via email that they no longer wished to pursue the matter. They also explained that new policies coming into effect would allow the selectee to temporarily report to headquarters. The International Region hoped that their decision would save the cost of having another intelligence officer at post. This was a breach of policy and detrimental to national security. Why would the service want an untrained, inexperienced officer interviewing and making decisions on counterterrorism and ISIS-linked files, just to save a few dollars?

My colleague Stacey, who was shortlisted for the supervisory position, was running into trouble of her own with management. Given the personal nature of that struggle, I won't get into it. However, it had upset some top guys at CSIS. She ultimately lost her promotion, and her name was removed from the supervisory list as a result. This angered me tremendously and made me feel that every wrong at CSIS was deliberate and calculated. By that point, I'd lost all my faith in the system, institution, and its management.

Jeanne finally replied to my grievance. It read, "Your application was treated equitably" and "your complaint is not upheld." She apologized for not including the diversity clause in the call letter and noted it would be included in all subsequent International Region call letters. Jeanne didn't acknowledge or discuss what I'd brought forward regarding the International Region as a "white boys' club" or the systemic nature of the problem. Jeanne was the first and only woman to fill the position of assistant director of operations. I'd held her in high regard, but she failed me. CSIS culture always won out over merit. Had she invited me for a discussion, explained herself, or indicated that change was possible, I could've held on to my dreams. I would've consoled myself by saying "not today, but one day." Leadership demanded that.

I plugged away at work – what else could I do? But I felt hopeless. The system had failed me, and I couldn't imagine walking into an interview room or grieving another missed promotional opportunity. I found the idea of a glass ceiling hard to stomach.

Suddenly, Stacey and I had even more in common. We were women facing reprisal who were hoping for meaningful career advancement in a male-dominated culture and who were surely on a blacklist that doomed our careers. Over coffees, we shared our frustrations. When friends, puzzled by our relationship, wondered what we were whispering about, we'd say, "diversity in the service." We passionately disagreed about many things – marriage, sex, religion, and children – however, we both agreed we wanted out of Security Screening. But on to where and what?

Though I continued to perform my job effortlessly, managers who'd been supportive of me were now irritated by my relationship with Stacey. They said that she was too loud when coming to get me. So, I had her wait downstairs, to the disappointment of officemates who loved our gossip. That winter, Stacey correctly predicted that Donald Trump would win the presidency. "It's Trump mania, man," she told me and Liz. She brought a red hat with his name from her trip to Florida. I didn't think he'd ever be elected. I was furious with Stacey, but we continued our friendship, each aware that we were on opposite ends of the political spectrum. When Trump said that he'd "implement a database for tracking Muslims in the United States,"[1] falsely claimed "thousands and thousands" of Muslims had cheered in New Jersey when the World Trade Center collapsed, and called for a ban on all Muslims entering the United States, I was deeply upset.[2] I judged Islamophobia, racism, and bigotry would intensify under a Trump presidency. I worried about another wave of militancy in American national security organizations, something Trump threatened. Islamophobia, of course, was not limited to events in the US. Here in Canada, during the federal election campaign in the fall of 2015, I often listened to CBC Radio. Prime Minister Harper and the Conservative Party were espousing hate against Muslims. The Conservatives were hoping to use their politics of fear to materialize support for their party. They argued that women who wore the niqab, clothing that covers the face but not the eyes, violated Canadian values. They also wanted to strip Canadian citizenship from those Canadians convicted of terrorism. Answering questions about terrorism suspects, Harper said, "it doesn't matter what the age of the person is, or whether they're in a basement, or whether they're in a mosque or somewhere else."[3] Muslim Canadians read this as Harper casting mosques as "venues of terrorism" and were concerned that his remarks would result in increased attacks on mosques.[4] Liberal leader Justin Trudeau called out the Conservatives and Harper on their fear mongering. In one public debate, he said, "A Canadian is a Canadian is a Canadian."[5] Every time I hear that statement, I get emotional. My whole family does. Canada is our home, and many members of my family serve Canada. I served and continued to serve Canada.

One day in the office, one of my colleagues said that she'd take out a gun and go on a shooting spree if Justin Trudeau won. Her husband was a cop, and I believed she might have access to a registered gun. I looked at her and said, "If I made the same comment about the Conservatives, Liberals, or *anyone*, I'd be escorted out of this building in no time. Check your privilege." She regretted her comments but that Karter had a portrait of Harper in his office must have emboldened her to make these inflammatory remarks. I felt that we at CSIS were all wrong for not speaking up and standing against inappropriate behaviour. Trudeau won the election with a majority government. I celebrated his win, as many Canadians did. I felt even more patriotic, if that's possible, and more optimistic about where my country was heading. Hope is a beautiful thing.

21 | FIGHT-OR-FLIGHT

In October 2016, on a sunny Saturday morning family drive near the end of my final parental leave, I realized how happy and secure I was in my marriage. It had been ten years since Ali and I had met and nine years of marriage. Though we bickered daily, we always looked forward to talking to each other and counted on one another's support. With time and life's challenges – financial pressures, career navigations, and parenting – we'd grown closer and more intimate, but I wondered sometimes whether he loved me more than I him. On weekends, he'd touch my back flirtatiously as we made breakfast, making sure the kids never saw the boyish look in his eyes. He was "old school" in front of the kids about these things and instantly shied away. I enjoyed these interactions. His firm, broad shoulders gave me the security I needed.

This time, it wasn't an ordinary parental leave. My daughter was born at twenty-four weeks of gestation. She was weak and fragile at less than a pound but had a strong will to survive. For four months, I stood amidst dimmed lighting and the beeping sound of ventilators, watching her miraculous journey, experiencing the agony that comes with surprise diagnosis and medical setbacks in her health. I never appreciated science more than when she was returned to me and was under my care at home. She taught me how brave a little girl can be and how tough I am. All of us were tested in this way. I learned that I had an incredibly resilient husband, children, and extended family. I was going to be all right no matter what life threw at me.

I had mixed feelings about returning to work that fall. I was one of the most senior intelligence officers in the Security

Screening branch and had been selected to work on complex Counter Proliferation files – Iranian weapons of mass destruction. That meant a lot to me. I missed the rush of learning a new case's details, using necessary investigative techniques, making decisions on files, and liaising with security partners in the CBSA, IRCC, and other domestic and international agencies. Most of all, I missed my friends at work – small talk, coffee breaks, gossip, and snapshot details of my colleagues' lives when we chatted about marriage, children, schools, Halloween costumes, or Christmas parties.

I started my preparations by calling Denny, my former officemate. I was nervous. I hadn't spoken to him for almost a year, but he heard the smile in my voice. I told him that I was coming back and asked how the new Counter Proliferation supervisor, Debra, was. He said that her management style was different from Liz's but that I'd be working for Leslie in Counter Intelligence. "Leslie is a new manager there. This is her first Level 9 position, but I've only heard great things about her."

"Denny, I don't want to work CI. I've built expertise for CP Iran. I'm not meant to work CI. I'm not happy, Denny, not happy."

"I wouldn't want to go there either, but even the CP file isn't as interesting as it was. Listen, I'm trying out for a Level 9 promotion coming up. Once you're here, we'll all prepare together. Wherever you land is temporary."

I called Leslie. She picked up quickly. I was unprepared to speak with someone I didn't know. Leslie thanked me for calling and welcomed me to her team. She didn't want to say too much over the phone but made it clear she looked forward to working with me given my experience. She also said that I'd be the most senior investigator on her desk. She forgot to mention that I was many classes ahead of her and that she was my junior by perhaps half of the time I'd spent with CSIS (which totalled more than fourteen years at that point). I liked Leslie's professionalism and humbleness, though. Maybe Denny was right.

On 17 October, my first day back, I walked into CSIS, relieved to finally be getting on with what was making me anxious. No one was in my office yet, so I walked to Denny's office. I learned that Denny had gained enormous experience in the branch, including travel experience. I recalled his first trip to a Muslim-majority country and his nervousness about going until we'd spoken. I'd missed much while on parental leave.

I really missed my girls Liz, Stacey, Lisa, and Mary, but they'd all moved on to bigger and better things in other regions. I was happy for them, but Security Screening wasn't the same with them gone.

When Leslie walked into my bullpen, she adjusted her casual jacket and swung her long black hair. She stopped directly in front of me then coughed and sneezed. I stood up to shake her hands. "Huda," I said, smiling. She apologized for not being able to shake my hand, as she had a cold. She said she'd only come in to welcome me to the team and write a few emails.

Later, over coffee, Denny told me that he and Victor, one of my classmates, would be applying for a supervisory position. "Huda, we'd love to have you in our prep group."

"Let me think about it," I said. The thought upset me. I didn't know whether I believed in the process anymore. I added, "It would depend who's on the panel." We agreed to look out for one another. Denny informed me that Alex, our common friend in Toronto Region, the same Alex who was with me from almost the beginning of my career, had been in conflict with some of the most senior managers there. I was curious. I knew almost everyone in the Toronto office, so I made some calls to learn what Alex's troubles were. I was surprised to learn that a colleague from my class who'd failed the investigator's course was a chief. I left her a message. She never replied. I later learned that she hung around with Alex's harassers. She must've known that I was fishing for information and had likely decided to keep her mouth shut. Others called back, and I was shocked to hear Alex had filed a xenophobia complaint against the deputy director of Toronto Region and had won but wasn't well and was off work. *A daring move*, I thought.

The files I worked on were unchallenging and routine. I was bored and unmotivated. In November, I completed my five-year security clearance forms, the first part of a comprehensive Internal Security review to assess my continued loyalty. The process included checks on financial records, criminal records, mental health, drug dependency, information that could be used as blackmail, and contact with foreign nationals who know where the employee works. It took me a week and a half to complete the form, as I had to provide information on where my four siblings lived and worked. The second step was an interview and the third a polygraph. I was ready for both and then waited to hear back. My last encounter with Internal Security, in 2011, had gone well. The interviewer was friendly and courteous and made a real effort to hear, but not act on, all my concerns.

One day, browsing our Intranet server, I noticed an "Ask the Director" webpage. This new communication forum must have begun while I was on leave. I scrolled through the topics and found a question on diversity and minorities. An unknown questioner asked something along the lines of the following:

Director Coulombe,
The Service has come a long way towards addressing gender inequality in the workplace. For example, all operational and non-operational hiring is at or close to 50 per cent. We must continue to work on making progress in gender representation at the managerial and executive levels. That being said, the Service could do more in terms of representation on visible minorities. A high percentage of visible minorities in the Service occupy administrative and manual labour positions, and there is a lack of representation in operational support roles. Perhaps more effort needs to be afforded to hiring visible minorities in the future.

I remember the answer, stated similarly to this, being unsatisfactory at best:

Thank you for your question. The Service is committed to a workforce that is representative of the Canadian population. As you have mentioned, we have achieved targeted gender hiring quotas and representation and through our Human Resources and the Diversity Coordinator, in consultation with the Canadian Human Rights Commission, we are working towards representation for all employment equity groups. I encourage you to review the CHRC Employment Equity Report of 2014 accessible through the Diversity Coordinator.

I reread the question and the answer. I saw it as a slap in the face. The message was clear: diversity isn't a service priority – we have other, more important things to tackle.

I suddenly recalled the first-generation Canadian immigrants at the service: the Portuguese lady who cleaned our office and the handsome Ethiopian guy who always carried stuff up and down in the elevators. *Is this a scheme to get the minority numbers higher?* I sent out an email requesting a copy of the 2014 Canadian Human Rights Commission's employment equity report on CSIS. I received a peculiar email that left my hair standing on end: "Hello Huda, I hope all is well. I have received your request for the CHRC EE Audit for 2014. There is an approval process for distributing it, so hold tight, and you will hear from me soon," the CSIS diversity coordinator wrote. A week later, she sent me a printed copy and a follow-up email requesting I not distribute it. When I read the document, I understood exactly why she was so concerned.

I walked into my supervisor's office and showed it to her. She was shocked – there were 0 per cent visible minorities in managerial positions. "It seems like a systemic problem," I said. "I was under the impression it was only Toronto Region and International Region. It seems it's the entire system. It's service-wide and national."

While browsing through career call letters for service positions, I saw a Security Screening call letter for a CBSA liaison position. I wanted to find out more. I knew the hiring manager, Kevin, so I went to his office. Kevin, a seasoned manager, was the service's legendary breaking-and-entry specialist. He was also known for his significant contributions in Afghanistan. You couldn't bullshit Kevin. He'd cleverly call you out on it. He knew most of the service's executives, including the director, and didn't kiss anyone's ass. With Kevin, what you see is what you get. Kevin always read right through me. He'd greet me and immediately know something was wrong. I couldn't tell him everything. I feared being judged and kept much of the discrimination that had happened secret. "Come on in, Huda," Kevin invited me. "What's up?"

"I'm interested in the CBSA secondment and wanted to ask you a few questions," I said.

"That's great. Rebecca is there now. She's due back in a month. Oh, Huda, they'd love to have someone like you with all your CT experience, your languages, and your travel background. Wow, you'd blow them away. Talk to Rebecca. I can arrange it."

As Kevin spoke, I noticed that he didn't have any certificates or awards on his wall, just like I didn't.

"Great, Kevin. I'll fire her an email and see when she's available. I like your office."

Kevin smiled. "Yeah, I don't hang certificates and stuff like everyone," he said.

"I don't either. I had a manager who refused to issue me one. When I asked for it, they delivered it with broken glass. I never like to go over that, I guess. I don't ask for them now. I don't care for them. But I care about my work and my colleagues. That's what it's all about."

Kevin's phone rang. He indicated I should pause. "Yes, hello." Pause. "Yes, I am." Pause. "Oh, that's great." Pause. "Certainly. Yeah, for sure. Yep. I'll be there." Kevin hung up and looked at me in disbelief. "I can't believe this is happening while we're just talking about this," he said. "The director's executive assistant just let me know I'll be receiving recognition for my work in Afghanistan years back." Kevin's eyes were rolling with excitement, disbelief, and humble gratitude.

"Better late than never, I guess, eh, Kev?" I said.

"Talk to Rebecca. I hope you put your name in. You and I working together would be great, Huda," he shouted as I left his office.

Leslie must've felt my lack of motivation and distraction and thought Counter Intelligence files were the problem. She sent me some Counter Terrorism files, one on Afghan security force members who'd crossed into Canada from the US. The Americans had cleared the Afghan soldiers' travel into the country and their training with the US military, yet eight out of forty-five had gone AWOL. One of those eight had made his way into Canada and was being held by the CBSA, who'd flagged him to us. As I plugged away on the file, I also filled out my CBSA secondment application.

Adam, the service's first Arab Muslim intelligence officer, was much younger than me and had six years less experience. He'd been to the Toronto Region, was an excellent investigator, but had returned to headquarters and was posted to the same Security Screening branch as I. Adam was a military reservist familiar with misogyny and group mentality culture. We'd each experienced racism, discrimination, and Internal Security targeting. But we'd never opened up to each other about it – we didn't want to break down together. We understood that we needed to rise above these challenges. Our conversations were thus about threats we'd identified but that others had missed or interviews in the community that had exceeded our expectations. It was about our devotion to the mission, which we saw as more vigorous than others'.

Adam wasn't qualified to apply for foreign postings, but he indicated his interest in doing so in the future. When I told him about the formal grievances that I'd submitted regarding lack of transparency, bias for white males, and lack of diversity in the International Region, he wasn't surprised. He also wasn't surprised that my claim wasn't upheld. Nevertheless, he thanked me by saying that he admired my courage, adding that I was paving the way for him and others to be treated with equity. "At least, it sends the message," he said. He spoke to me as if I was his older sister. I was touched, and it made me feel that I had a purpose beyond my own career ambitions. It wasn't just Adam: every service minority I spoke with felt that I, as a senior intelligence officer with so many years of service, had gone further than imagined. They would look up to me. I counselled many on how to negotiate their identities at this very peculiar workplace.

In November 2016, I was as surprised as anyone when Trump was elected president. That morning, I knew that life was about to change for my family as Western Muslims, even more than it had after 9/11. I'd argued with Ali, who said Hillary Clinton might not win because she was a woman. I had faith in the American people. I'd told Ali that he was wrong and that she could win given her superior intellect in comparison. One didn't need to watch the presidential debates to know that.

The morning that he won, I was rushing to go work. Mariam, my grade school daughter who was attuned to politics like I was and equally as shocked, asked, "Mom, does this mean we can't go to New York to visit my cousins?" My quick answer was that her cousins could come visit Ottawa. Driving to work, I kept thinking that I should've taken time to comfort Mariam and better explain that the world wouldn't change overnight. But then I realized my world and and my family's had already changed. It disgusts me how Trump hates and targets women, queer people, Mexicans, African Americans, and Muslims – you name it. I walked up to my office with a heavy heart. I was disillusioned and wondered whether Mariam and my other kids were all right. I hoped that their teachers would take time to explain that being Muslim is okay.

The brilliant Mr Robert Forest of IRCC was giving a presentation on the Immigration and Refugee Protection Act to Security Screening's immigration staff the next week. The deputy director general, with whom I had a friendly relationship, attended. I hoped some face time with her would help my application for the CBSA secondment. I'd be representing the service and wanted her to see I was confident and amicable enough to be sent out. I approached her and told her that I'd put my name in for the CBSA secondment. I mentioned Kevin and Rebecca and said that I hoped she'd consider me.

"Oh, I didn't know you applied. Great. I'm going to let you head upstairs. I'm grabbing lunch," she said, touching her stomach. She was a lousy liar, and I was an intelligence officer. I knew something was up and that she didn't want to discuss the secondment. I went to the washroom. Lo and behold, when I came out, she was waiting for the elevator without lunch.

Later, I learned that I wasn't being considered for the position at all. I was upset, less about the secondment and more about the lack of transparency. I wondered what in my file they didn't like. I couldn't just speak to my deputy director general since she was avoiding me. I couldn't file another grievance or count on the Employee Association. I had to know what was in my file. I recalled one of my last conversations with Stacey back in 2015. She had told me that Counter Terrorism's director general had spoken negatively about me, especially about my hijab. She said that there was written evidence in Internal Security holdings. I wondered how many managers and colleagues had spoken negatively about me. I didn't know how to stop worrying. I had to know everything in my Internal Security file. *Maybe there's a reason I've been unable to progress in my career.*

In December 2016, the inception of my lawsuit started with a meeting in the private office of the Access to Information and Privacy (ATIP) CSIS analyst at CSIS headquarters. It wasn't the first time I filed a request to access my Internal Security file. I had done it twice: once in 2004 and then again in 2011, but I quickly cancelled both requests, fearful of the consequences of such a move. I had been warned that this would be an affront to CSIS management. I had changed over the years. Now closer to my forties, I was mature, confident, and in the driver's seat of my life. The allure of the service had completely worn off, now that I had known and witnessed so much more than I could ever write in this book without facing jail time. I was determined to fight back through the Canadian Human Rights Commission (CHRC) and the federal courts; I felt I had exhausted all internal grievance processes and had lost trust in CSIS completely. I was inspired by women of the RCMP who had launched a class action civil lawsuit alleging systemic sexual and gender harassment and discrimination and were still fighting through the media and in court. CSIS was a branch within the RCMP until 1984, and I knew that with many RCMP officers still transferring into CSIS, the same culture of misogyny, racism, and homophobia came with them.

The friendly ATIP analyst looked energized as I walked into his office carrying my clear half-full water bottle. The windowless room had hardly any space and was limited to a computer desk and a large yellowy-beige cabinet with a mechanical combination lock. I reflected on how the windows at CSIS can't be opened for air. I closed the door limiting the air circulation further. "I'd like to get a sense of what you want, which databases you want prioritized, and any keywords that you may have for us at ATIP to narrow down our search and also make sure you gain access to what you are looking for," he said.

"I would like for you to prioritize my Internal Security files, including access to videos and audio recordings, as well as my Human Resources files including grievances," I said. "Incremental access, if possible, would be great," I added.

He looked disappointed as he replied, "You want it all, but keep in mind that you can't take out classified documents. We can arrange an empty office for you to review the material." I now wonder if he knew all along that I would not get access to my classified files.

"Yes, I understand," I said, imaging myself sifting through documents, taking mental notes of the information that would matter for my case. I guess we both had competing and alternative motives.

And so I waited. The ATIP office missed the thirty-day statutory time limit and requested a three-month extension while I actively continued to seek outside legal advice.

I ended up calling a downtown lawyer who I knew from the University of Ottawa. When I stepped out of his office, I received a call from my supervisor indicating that she had good news for me. The next day, she told me that I'd been granted the secondment. "What? They didn't run the competition. There was no selection process and no interviews."

"Yes, well, there were no other applicants, so it's yours," she said.

I was intrigued that I'd received her call immediately after leaving the law firm. I was as paranoid as some of the service targets I'd investigated. I felt the offer was meant to disarm me, but I had been down that road before, and I wasn't going to just stop and be a good little girl. I decided that I was going to challenge the service on what I believed was systemic racism and gender, racial, and religious discrimination. I didn't realize that this meant I'd have to relive every painful memory over and over, but I judged I was going to be okay. I was armed with information from the Canadian Human Rights Commission's Employment Equity report, the director's response to questions about diversity, my experience of harassment and discrimination, and the experiences of other minorities. I had to do something, but I still didn't know what.

22 | DON'T BE A MARTYR

In December 2016, like David to Goliath, I elected to stand up and challenge the entire organization at the risk of my losing my career, financial stability, and mental health. I'd spent my entire adult life as an intelligence officer with the spy service and had been fighting terrorists, spies, and systemic racism. Somewhere deep in my heart I knew that if I didn't challenge CSIS, I'd lose my self-respect and a large part of myself. I wouldn't be me, the daughter my parents had raised with strong values, dignity, and pride. I'd remain loyal to the CSIS mandate, the law, and my country by creating necessary change resulting in, hopefully, an equitable, diverse, modern, dynamic, and robust workplace where everyone felt included and part of the mission. I elected to do this without divulging any classified operational information.

Following the Christmas holidays, in January 2017, I contacted Paul Cavalluzzo, a constitutional lawyer with top-secret clearance and experience in national security. He'd represented Maher Arar. To my surprise, he answered my call himself. He told me that suing an employer was no small matter and that I should exhaust internal mechanisms first. I concluded that he was too busy to take on a blazing fire. I'd already, exhaustively, tried the service's internal mechanisms – the Employee Association, Labour Relations, the diversity coordinator, Human Resources – but nothing worked. The managers knew me on a first-name basis. Out of fear of reprisal, few CSIS employees file complaints, so I stood out. I believed that these internal mechanisms didn't have independent decision making. Even if they addressed individual claims of wrongdoing and discrimination, they were ill-prepared to tackle systemic racism and discrimination. I knew that I wasn't the only person who was disheartened by the lack of support and resources at the service.

The same evening, I called my former colleague from Toronto Region, Cemal, a practising Muslim man of Turkish descent. I expressed my frustrations and asked for my old friend and colleague Alex's number. Cemal was sympathetic. We spoke for hours. I learned that he'd desperately tried to advance his own career, to no avail, for more than twenty-three years. He told me that he'd excelled at a technical exam required for a promotional opportunity but that his candidacy was rejected following a subjective interview process. When he filed a grievance, his manager told him to "go complain to Allah."[1] Cemal also felt that he was unfairly targeted by Internal Security. Investigators in that branch asked how often he prayed and where and what his personal views on Islam were. It must have trickled up to executive managers because they refer to him as "Muslim brotherhood" during Friday drinking parties at the office. We agreed that whatever Internal Security had on us must be full of bias, given their questions about religiosity and especially how little the interviewers understood our lives as Canadian Muslims.

The following day, I called Alex. We hadn't spoken since 2010, when I left Toronto. Back then, he was one of the shining stars, part of the regional director general's inner circle and not one to miss the three o'clock Friday office drinking party. He was sharp, ambitious, and he understood the need to network on Fridays at the director general's office. The gatherings, where racialized service employees like Cemal and I were not invited, were "the single most important factor in getting ahead at the Service."[2]

Though Alex was a few classes after me, he had already been promoted to supervisor and had been running a unit in Toronto for seven years. After seeking to become chief of a division, the promotion was derailed when he fell from grace with management through no fault of his own. At a private work party outside the office, Simon, the region's second-in-command executive manager, verbally attacked Alex's Muslim partner by shouting "All Muslims are terrorists."[3] Alex's partner was offended and walked out of the party in protest. Alex followed but first asked Simon to apologize. The following day, after searching Alex's Facebook page for Muslim friends, Simon "berate[d] Alex for having a [Facebook] relationship with a terrorist," a familiar accusation.[4] After the incident, Alex lost access to operational information, received poor evaluation results, and was excluded by his colleagues, similar to the campaign against me in 2005. Alex tried to defuse the mounting tension by speaking with the regional director general. He received no support and was warned by colleagues that there would be no turning back if he filed an official complaint. He filed anyway.

"But Huda, even though the third-party investigation found harassment, they gave me a letter stating there was no harassment finding. Once I got a lawyer, at cost, who demanded the investigation's findings, CSIS revealed a harassment finding had been made. I had to go outside the service to get CSIS to do the right thing," he said. This was unsurprising yet earth shattering. Service managers and Labour Relations had colluded to prevent wrong from being addressed. They covered up facts to protect the organization against an employee. I felt betrayed. I judged that this was also why my own official complaints had been dismissed. Alex added that in November 2016 there'd been a town hall meeting, during which Toronto's regional director general invited all employees and in no uncertain terms told employees that there were no reprisals, merely the perception of reprisals by some. Alex was upset that no one would apologize and that management had been indifferent about what happened to him.

"I'm sorry, Alex. I don't know what to say. I've had a tough time going to work lately. In fact, I'm having a hard time thinking about anything other than harassment and discrimination at CSIS. Ever since I decided to challenge them and fight for my rights and self-dignity, I've been feeling like I'm doing something wrong. I can't sleep well. When I enter through the glass doors and key in my pin number, I feel worthless, less dignified than anyone else – like I'm not equal. Doesn't that mean I'm letting them do that to me?" I asked.

"I know, Huda. I know that for you this has been happening for a long time. I can only imagine. Take a leave if you need to. I mean, you have your children to take care of," he said.

"Can I speak with your lawyer? I contacted the Canadian Human Rights Commission. They're evaluating my submission now, but I'd really like to consult a lawyer." Alex kindly provided his lawyer's number.

In January 2017, I stopped going to work. I couldn't go back, but I didn't know for how long. I wondered what my parents would say if they found out I was off work. They would be concerned about my well-being, to my annoyance, and frightened about what it would mean for me, a daughter of immigrants, to challenge the service. My brothers wouldn't understand how severe this had been for me. They didn't have the full story, and my sisters were too far away. I didn't want to bother them with the uncertain situation that I found myself in. I didn't like not going to work. I'd had a job ever since high school. Being home and not knowing whether I could keep going at CSIS was too much. I felt ashamed. I told the kids to not tell anyone that I was home. I worried about being seen. I panicked when a friend saw me grocery shopping during the day. Maybe it was the sleeping pills, which left me lightheaded in the morning, but I didn't feel like myself at all.

I was glad for Ali's support. He was equally outraged and fiercely empathetic. He provided the extra fortitude that I needed. Despite the financial risk, including a mortgage Ali couldn't pay for, Ali was determined to see me through this. He instructed me not to speak about any of it to my family, friends, or colleagues, outside of Alex and Cemal.

In late January 2017, I called Emran, one of my Muslim colleagues in Toronto, after learning he'd had a falling out with Toronto Region management. He was also on leave. Six years earlier, when Emran was training at headquarters, he'd pulled me aside to seek my advice on a conflict he was having with an intelligence officer in his class. He was a communication analyst and they had ganged up on him and insulted his partner. An officer, favoured by powerful managers, said things like "Muslims and armed weapons are a bad mix," "Please, don't shoot me," and "Let's go before the Muslims get us" to get under Emran's skin. He felt belittled, humiliated, and uncomfortable bringing his concerns to his trainers.

Emran had sought support from his member of Parliament, who advised him that it took at least five similar instances of harassment and discrimination to prove systemic harassment. We had Alex, Cemal, Emran, and me. We needed a fifth to demonstrate systemic racism. Dina, the service's first African Canadian woman, instantly came to mind. Following her promotion to supervisor, she'd often complained of discrimination. Managers and junior intelligence officers, following managers' examples, undermined her at every step of the way. She felt it important to address racism in the service, so she committed to our cause.

The five of us began speaking to each other often. We decided that we'd all sign up with Alex's law firm. We sent the following communication to our lawyer:

> Our group has convened, discussed, and unanimously agreed to begin working together. Together we now represent various CSIS regions, offices, and ranks. We represent women, LGBT, Muslims, and visible minorities. We are all exemplary employees that have been forced on medical leave, all suffering and medicated for severe depression, anxiety, and stress – and in some cases already diagnosed with PTSD. We've all been discriminated against, had reprisals made against us, and even ridiculed for being who we are by the senior most cadre of the Service in breach of Human Rights in Canada. Our confidence has effectively been made shallow. Our harassers, meanwhile, who are wide-ranging senior managers remain secure at work and protected by publicly funded government lawyers – at no cost to themselves. Our evidence is hard and damning, and it is further corroborated by a committed inventory of witnesses willing to come forward, in addition to a third-party harassment investigation.

Our lawyer, Andrea, held meetings with us individually to get hard evidence and facts. Before our scheduled telephone appointment, she asked that I write down every instance of harassment and discrimination that I'd faced at the service. As I did, my difficulty sleeping worsened. I had vivid dreams about my past that forced me to finally face my feelings about what had transpired. This drained me mentally, physically, and emotionally. I stopped wanting to leave my house, I didn't want to visit my parents, and I didn't enjoy spending time with Ali or the kids. I just wanted to be alone all the time. Ali couldn't believe the pain in my heart and the loneliness, fear, and despair that I'd been living with.

Alex and I talked independently of those in our group. He was forthcoming about the mental health toll that he'd endured over the last year and a half. I asked whether he wanted to read what I'd prepared for our lawyer. After reading it, he texted me: "Huda!!! I am so repulsed. I am so sorry! I read your full story!!! This needs to go public!!!!! I am shaking, angry!!!!"

Our stories and evidence prompted our lawyer to write CSIS a letter informing them that we would be acting as a group, we were preparing to go public with our complaints with the Canadian Human Rights Commission, and we would be calling immediately, through media channels, for an independent public inquiry. This set off alarm bells at CSIS and every manager that was on our complaint was summoned to Ottawa for a meeting at higher levels. My colleagues, the few that knew of our pending lawsuit, enjoyed watching them hover over coffee at the CSIS cafeteria.

Days after our letter was sent, the Quebec mosque attack was carried out. Alexandre Bissonnette entered the Islamic Cultural Centre mosque and shot worshippers, killing six and injuring many. It was truly shocking for this violence to occur in Canada. I'd recently walked to the entrance of the Al Rahma mosque near my house and found glass on the ground. The door had been broken in a hate attack. I realized that such attacks could happen anywhere. Islamophobia had become far more intense since Trump's election than it had been following 9/11. I felt sad for the families who'd lost a father, a son, or a husband. Lives had been shattered because of hate.

I worried how my children would internalize all the hate being directed at Muslims and immigrants. I still worry about this. My children asked why someone would kill Muslims at a mosque. "Because they're Muslims?"

"Yes, but not everyone hates Muslims," I explained.

"Mom, could this happen at our mosque?"

"No, not here," I answered, uncertain.

"Did they catch the bad guy?"

"Yes, don't worry. You're safe." I struggled to find the right answers to their questions. I never thought I'd have to, and then came Trump. I try to shield them from hate by not letting them watch the news or Hollywood movies in which Muslims are often villains and terrorists. After seeing such movies, they were always quick to ask who the villain and good guys were. I hated having to point out that the villain was, yet again, a Muslim.

Ali was just as shocked as me about the attack. "Why? Because they fear immigrants and Muslims. I'm a Muslim and immigrant. I work hard every day and serve my community as a clinical pharmacist in a Canadian hospital's cancer centre. I never took a dime from the government.

I pay my taxes, unlike Trump. Yet they want us to feel like we don't belong. They want us to live in fear."

Ali and I felt bad for the victims of the hideous crime. We were touched by the vigils and sympathy Quebecers and the rest of the country held for victims' families. I spent the next weeks wondering whether CSIS's Montreal and Quebec branches were conducting interviews and community outreach with as many people as possible to understand how Bissonnette had been radicalized. I was certain Quebecers wouldn't have to declare their stances on hate the way Muslims had to after 9/11. My lawsuit group communicated daily. We were all shocked and upset by the attack, just as many Quebecers and Canadians were. The togetherness of Quebecers and other Canadians against hate over the following weeks was moving. Prime Minister Trudeau attended the funeral service in Montreal's Olympic Park.

My group hoped that CSIS would try to resolve our complaints quickly. They responded via letter, forwarded by Department of Justice lawyers: "The Service takes allegations of harassment and discrimination in the workplace seriously. We will engage the services of a third party to conduct an investigation into the specific allegations raised in the letter. We will also not insist on the usual policy requiring complaints filed within one year of an alleged harassment complaint." The service also hired a third party to perform a climate assessment of the Toronto Region to ensure the workplace was healthy and safe for all employees.

The service's investigations were meant to discourage us from moving forward with a civil claim and to buy time for CSIS lawyers to strategize. Our lawyer also gave us the cold shoulder. Our emails went unanswered, and our suggestions weren't followed up on. We decided to hire a different lawyer who'd fight for underdogs and go public with our case. It had to be a Toronto firm. Alex and Cemal shopped around and struck gold.

John Kingman Phillips, an experienced litigator, welcomed our group to a meeting at his downtown law firm. John's snow-white beard and charming warm smile put me at ease. His record on holding powerful entities accountable was impressive, having represented Indian residential school survivors and Omar Khadr. John would be working with Laura Young, who represented the former RCMP officer Peter Merrifield in leading the unionization of the force. The two made an incredible team. I took the train and found myself, amongst my colleagues, at his boutique law firm. "Huda, welcome, please sit down," he said eagerly.

John had a board laid out with our legal options: a third-party investigation, the Canadian Human Rights Commission, and a civil lawsuit. We decided to move full speed ahead with all three, with John only representing us in the lawsuit.

Before John could draft the civil claim, though, several developments took place. On 23 May 2017, citing its own earlier internal Toronto Region workplace climate assessment, the service refused the Canadian Human Rights Commission's mediation offer to meet with us away from public scrutiny. This move surprised all of us. Why would CSIS refuse an opportunity to solve our dispute privately and to thereby avoid headlines about racism, Islamophobia, and xenophobia in the service? CSIS's work relied on public trust. Even if they didn't care about our group, surely bad publicity would hinder CSIS's mission. I then learned from Labour Relations that CSIS wouldn't be providing us with the results or reports from either the workplace climate assessment or the investigation into our allegations. We'd be mere "witnesses" in our complaints. We found this dubious.

Early that summer, and after I had stopped going to work, the results of my ATIP request were mailed to my home address containing only unclassified documents. When I contacted the ATIP office, they refused to have me come in and view the classified material, even though I still held a top-secret clearance and had filed the proper requests.

When I finally calmed my nerves enough to open the package, I started reading: "We neither confirm nor deny that the records you requested exist. We are however advising you, as required by paragraph 10 (1) (b) of the Act that such records, if they existed, could reasonably be expected to be exempted under one or more of section 15 (1) (as it relates to the efforts of Canada toward detecting, preventing, or suppressing subversive or hostile activities), (16) (1) (a) or (c) of the Act." My heart sank as I read these words. *Subversive? Really? How rich!* I sat down and wondered how I would ever prove my case against the service without access to my personal information, mindful that so many others from marginalized communities have faced and continue to face a similar challenge. That list includes refugee applicants, permanent residents, and Canadian citizens who must fight the security service that deemed their activities a threat in federal court without access to the evidence presented against them. Alone in the silence of my suburban Ottawa home, I wondered if this legal challenge I had launched could help unveil the racial bias that operates with impunity and limited accountability on a national level.

My memories took me to early 2003, while on my first assignment outside headquarters, when I was asked to review the hard drive of a civil servant whose colleagues and management thought he was accessing extremist material at work. He was not. I was able to make a conclusive report on the situation, helping to ensure government information didn't make it into the wrong hands to keep this unsuspecting Canadian from being labelled an extremist and seeing his career derail much like mine had. Sifting through the ATIP document, yet another truth was revealed that would seal any doubt that I should continue to fight for my rights. This one truly crushed me. I tried to fight back my tears, but they fell speedily down my face. It was an email exchange from an executive manager to Internal Security that took place on 31 January 2017. The same man who attempted to pacify me with a promotion before my leave of absence sent an email to Internal Security that read, "Will see if I need to put in place some kind of aftercare for when Huda returns to work." The term aftercare in the security and intelligence world means constant surveillance and a reassessment of a person's reliability and loyalty. Aftercare would include monitoring my work computers and personal mobile, physical surveillance, and other investigative tools the service uses against subjects of investigation. I thought fifteen years and ten months were long enough to live under constant CSIS surveillance. I wiped my tears and couldn't wait to pick up my children from school. Surely at that point they had become accustomed to my sadness, but the moment that I heard "hey, mom," I felt a relief and love that I hadn't been able to properly register in months with the weight of the lawsuit on my shoulders. I was full of energy and ready to put away my career and life challenges, at least until silence of night. *I will be all right to finally leave CSIS*, I reckoned.

Eventually, I did end up receiving some of the unclassified material in a package mailed to my house, most of which was very useful for my legal challenge. I found two letters indicating my grievances for being passed over for promotional opportunities on the grounds that the service overwhelmingly favours white males for foreign service: one letter was upheld and the other was partially upheld. This meant that the service felt I had grounds for my complaints but had decided it was preferable to prevent me from advancing my career rather than investigating my complaints further. I fired it off to my lawyers, John and Laura. They asked who I thought might've been able to tamper with the results, a question I couldn't answer.

I also read through my Internal Security interview results and found bias all over them, even by interviewers whom I hadn't assessed as biased. One report said that I read the Quran daily. I was a busy working mom always on the road and making dinner for five – as if I had time to read the Quran every day! Besides, there's nothing wrong with reading the Quran every day, and doing so is hardly a national security concern. The report also said that my children attended Saturday Islamic school. I was livid. Why would they find this information noteworthy in a service report? What impact could my children's school attendance have on my work in the federal government? It made me sick to my stomach.

I'd stopped going to work, but I called the Employee Association president and asked her to meet with me in a restaurant close to headquarters. She expressed outrage and sympathy for me and was apologetic for how things had gone down. I told her that it wasn't just my group. Other people were being bullied, harassed, and discriminated against at CSIS. I told her that several others have called me directly, expressing the anguish they've experienced throughout their careers. She looked me straight in the eyes and said, "Huda, I can see this is very upsetting for you. I've spoken to management about the lack of transparency – the reprisals and all. But please don't be a martyr for everyone. Take care of yourself." I couldn't believe my ears. *Martyr*, the irony of it all.

On 13 July, John and Laura called to say that they'd successfully filed the civil lawsuit under pseudonyms, following approvals from CSIS and Department of Justice Lawyers (DoJ). I would be called Bahira in the civil claim and in media reports. Though we'd wanted this for some time, I panicked. The suit was going to be public. My family, friends who knew where I worked, colleagues, and other national security providers would know that "Bahira" was me. I was the only CSIS employee of fifteen years who'd worn a hijab. Later, there was one other intelligence officer in the service who wore one, but she started years after me and hadn't had the same exposure in the intelligence community that I had.

That evening, I parked my van and rushed my eldest daughter to her soccer game. "Out you go! I'll come watch in a few minutes," I said. She ran out. I sat in the car and read the headline of the *Toronto Star* article: "Five CSIS Employees Are Accusing the Spy Agency of Islamophobia, Racism and Homophobia in a $35-Million Lawsuit."[5] I read the article. Everything that I'd held secret was in a national online newspaper for the public to read. I was ashamed. Everyone in the service would know the deep secrets that I'd held for so long. I couldn't even watch my daughter's soccer game. What if my sources gave my name or business card to the media? What if people I'd interviewed came after me or discovered where I lived? I was concerned for my and my family's safety.

I called Emran and, later, Cemal and told them that I was feeling terrible on a regular basis. They said they felt the same and reassured me that things would work out. This would be it, they each said. The government will be pressured to act. I caught the last ten minutes of the game. Mariam was, by then, used to my distance and distractedness. She was sensitive and old enough to be a bit less demanding than my younger children. By the time I got home, Alex had sent everyone in the group all the articles from the various newspapers. Ali kept reassuring me that no news media would print my name because it was against the law – I'd told him that. He trusted that no newspaper would be so irresponsible.

On the same day, the International Civil Liberties Monitoring Group, a coalition of more than forty Canadian organizations, expressed extreme concern over the shocking allegations of Islamophobia, homophobia, racism, and sexism in CSIS. The National Council of Canadian Muslims called for action, and the public safety critic for the official opposition, Matthew Dubé, demanded an investigation. The next morning, Trudeau stated the alleged harassment in CSIS was being investigated and was "unacceptable."[6] Surprised and overwhelmed by the government and human rights groups' reactions, we met with our lawyer. I feared that there'd be media around John's office, and though there wasn't, John conveyed his surprise that he'd received calls from international and Canadian media outlets asking for interviews.

We could have used the media attention, but we were saddened it had come to this. Going public and discrediting CSIS wasn't our goal. We all declined interviews. We felt that the resulting damage and lack of trust in CSIS, especially by the Muslim community, would be irreparable. If CSIS had merely agreed to mediation, nothing would have gone public. We were also afraid that in speaking with a journalist, we might accidentally go beyond what was before the courts and thus violate our oaths of secrecy, thereby committing an illegal act. John, anticipating that CSIS might soon call him to arrange for mediation, wanted to know our settlement terms.

In early August 2017, our group, with John's support, booked a meeting with the new CSIS director, David Vigneault. Michel Coulombe was the one who'd earlier refused mediation, but he had stepped down in May. We hoped that Vigneault, who wasn't a career CSIS man like Coulombe, might be open to a resolution and to changing CSIS work culture. When we met him at headquarters, he and his lawyers were sympathetic. They received us warmly, listened to our concerns, and agreed to work towards a fair resolution. Then we heard nothing for two months.

Adding to our pressure, Alex and I finally decided to go to the media, scheduling an interview with reporter Michelle Shephard. I travelled to Toronto to meet Alex, and together we walked to the meeting, reassuring each other that we'd be using our aliases. "Huda, everything we're doing is counter to how we've been living our lives in the shadows. We haven't even told close friends where we work. I get it. This feels weird." I agreed. Alex's hands were shaking – he was clearly under a lot of pressure. I had to reassure him: "I believe in what we're doing. It's the right thing to do." Alex agreed.

In the presence of our lawyer John, we spoke for an hour with Michelle at a downtown coffee shop. She didn't understand why the service didn't want to resolve things quickly. Her newsroom co-workers wondered how on earth such comments against gays, Muslims, and other minorities could be made openly in our day and age and at the spy service of all places. Sitting across from her, having read her book, *Guantanamo Bay*, an accurate account of the life of Omar Khadr's family, I felt certain she must have had a source at CSIS. I recalled the service warning us intelligence officers about speaking with reporters. Looking at her inquisitive demeanour, her recorder, and John, I wondered just how many people Omar and I had both met – three at least, I counted. *Will he ever be able to clear his name?* I thought. Then, I wondered the same about me: *Will I ever be successful in challenging the service?*

In October 2017, CSIS reached out to our lawyers via the Department of Justice, and scheduled a mediation session with a high-profile former Supreme Court judge. Our group asked that the service first share with us the Toronto Region workplace climate assessment findings. CSIS and the Department of Justice initially denied that the assessment had concluded, but when the judge and mediator asked for it, the Department of Justice panicked and produced the report. I was running errands when I was emailed the unclassified copy. I dropped what I was doing, got in my car, and began reading. Amid a flood of tears, I felt anguish, panic, and relief all at once. The report found that an old boy's culture prevailed at CSIS, where yelling, swearing, and disrespectful, demeaning, misogynistic, offensive, and inappropriate comments and jokes took place. The report described CSIS as permeated by its militaristic past and stated that fear of reprisal was very present in employees. It revealed that decisions, including staffing decisions, were sometimes made at weekly in-group drinking parties at the office or a pub. A third of the workforce trusted neither CSIS management nor its decision making. They said that inappropriate behaviour was left unchecked because of management inaction and that leadership was lacking. Employees reported being drained by workplace negativity and that they felt disheartened and disillusioned. CSIS employees were also concerned about a lack of workplace diversity. They described the work environment as being unthoughtful of cultural differences and sensitivities. More disturbingly, they revealed discriminatory comments and jokes about ethnicities, including communities CSIS was monitoring. They also discussed a prevalent bias against women.

I wasn't surprised by the findings as much as I was surprised that a third of my Toronto colleagues had participated in the investigation and spoken so candidly to the third-party investigators. I was *really* proud of them. Finally, employees were standing up. My group and I saw this as the first step towards acknowledging and correcting wrongs. By participating in the investigation, my colleagues had risked the wrath of CSIS executives, who I'm sure wanted to limit or bury all of it. CSIS now had to acknowledge that some senior managers were racist, homophobic, and bigoted. The service would have to explain to the public and the minister of public safety how they planned to solve the problem, which was the outcome my group sought.

I showed the judge running mediation the many official complaints I'd made. I also showed the judge the documents that I'd received through the Access to Information and Privacy Act, including my upheld grievances and the falsified documents saying that my grievances hadn't been upheld. I wondered who'd changed them, when, and why. *Was it easier to dismiss my complaints than admit systemic racism was holding back qualified, motivated visible minorities like me?* Despite many hours of conversation, which I'm not at liberty to discuss, we couldn't come to an agreement. But while we were in that meeting, Michelle Shephard's article hit the press, angering CSIS and adding fuel to the fire. The five of us had walked into that meeting feeling confident especially given the results of the climate assessment report. But we walked out disappointed at not having found common ground with CSIS. We each returned to our families. It had been a long day.

The next morning on the train, as Dina and I discussed the failed mediation session, we learned that CSIS had released the climate assessment report on its public website. Buggers, I thought. "They probably thought Alex and I were going public with the report's findings," I said to Dina, though we weren't planning to do so. The media interest and cycle would be short, so I contacted Alex. He and I decided to give statements to the *Toronto Star*, hoping they'd publish at least one of them. We ran them by John and sent them off. Then, still on the train back to Ottawa, I called public safety critic Matthew Dubé and informed him of the now-declassified Toronto Region workplace assessment report corroborating allegations made in our civil claim.

The headline of the *Toronto Star* article read, "Head of Spy Agency CSIS Admits 'Retribution, Favouritism, Bullying' in Workplace."[7] In the article, Vigneault acknowledged that CSIS suffered from a climate rife with problems that he said were categorically unacceptable. He also said, "Only by putting these kinds of issues on the table, and dealing with them directly, will the service be able to continue to evolve as a strong, mission focused, and unified organization."[8] The same article quoted me, "Bahira," as a Muslim intelligence officer who'd worked in Canada and abroad. I thanked my Toronto colleagues for their candour in participating in the assessment and thereby risking "the wrath of their senior management." I also praised Vigneault for his transparency at what was one of Canada's most secretive organizations:

> For 15 years as I was working to advance national security investigations, I was also fighting racism and bigotry. Today, I feel somewhat vindicated. I believe CSIS needs a workforce that is strong, engaged, and diverse at all levels. Canadians deserve that. We have been harassed and bullied and beaten down for so long while CSIS managers denied that was a problem, that it is hard to believe that CSIS is finally admitting the truth. I hope it means that real change is possible, but I'm cynical now. I know too much about the organization to trust that anything will be done.[9]

Following the director's statements, Matthew Dubé repeated his demand for a full investigation of CSIS.[10] During a House of Commons question period, Dubé stood up and asked the minister of public safety, Ralph Goodale, to respond to the Toronto Region report's findings and my group's civil law claim. The minister responded, "The matter is extremely serious and the government will take the necessary steps to stop such abuses," adding that "there will be consequences when employees harass or bully colleagues."[11] Especially given CSIS's mandate against Islamist extremism, I was astonished that neither Goodale nor the director ever used the words *discrimination, racism,* or *Islamophobia*. The climate assessment report said that "discriminatory comments were still being made about ethnicity and the communities being monitored."

Back home in Ottawa, I felt at ease. At least there'd been public acknowledgment of the wrongs that I'd experienced, and my Toronto Region colleagues had spoken up against toxic workplace culture. I felt hopeful. I hadn't deserved what I'd experienced at CSIS, and this was being affirmed – it wasn't just all in my head. I was tired from long-term anxiety, but that night, I slept better than I had in a month, despite the failure of the mediation session.

In the following few weeks, I was regularly in touch with my group. We were all mentally and emotionally drained but felt CSIS and the Department of Justice would reach out again to find a resolution outside the courts. We figured that any further negative media attention would discredit the service and erode public trust, including in the Muslim community, which was essential to CSIS and its community outreach. We waited for CSIS to reply to our civil lawsuit – it had a thirty-day deadline. They didn't. To pressure CSIS, our lawyers demanded that they respond in a federal court. In a telephone conference with our lawyers and the Department of Justice, Justice Simon Noël told CSIS, "there is a course of action to be followed and you are no different from any other parties in Canada ... It is not because you are the Attorney General of Canada that you can act as if the rules do not apply. This is not acceptable."[12]

On 27 October 2017, in its defence statement, CSIS urged the court to dismiss our lawsuit, denying that it had engaged in or tolerated religious bigotry and racism and that it had subjected us to reprisals.[13] They said, "No organization can ensure that its employees and managers will never act inappropriately. Organizations cannot be held to such a standard. Rather, organizations must be measured by whether they have procedures in place to address issues as they arise."[14] Further, CSIS's lawyers wrote, "the five plaintiffs had their complaints addressed by the Service in a fair, reasonable and timely manner, and should not be entitled to compensation."[15] Then they argued that "any scrutiny or direction given to Bahira over the course of her employment with the Service, was reasonable, justified and wholly consistent."[16]

Our lawyers sent my group CSIS's defence statement before it hit the media. I was livid when I read the denials, the justification for the wrongs I'd endured, and CSIS's determination to slander my group, especially after CSIS employees had reported discrimination, bias, lack of trust in management, and fear of reprisals in the climate assessment results. The only thing I could do to quell my anger was vent with Alex, Emran, Cemal, and Dina. It meant the world to me that I was no longer alone in my struggle for justice. We felt that CSIS's statement exactly reflected how CSIS's harassing managers still controlled service decision making. We learned that a manager in discussion with the Department of Justice was a long-time close friend of the manager who'd yelled at Alex that all Muslims are terrorists and that his Muslim in-laws would behead him in his sleep for being gay. This was, clearly, a conflict of interest, and this manager should have recused himself from investigating a close colleague. We wrote a letter to the director advising him of this conflict of interest and bias. Even after revelations of CSIS's widespread toxic workplace culture, the service, appallingly, continued to deny its culpability. What message was that sending harassers and victims?

Thirty days later, our lawyers replied to CSIS's defence statement, citing that CSIS had not taken responsibility for its failure to ensure a diverse and harassment-free work environment. They argued that CSIS policies and procedures hadn't produced real change in CSIS's workplace culture. They also countered CSIS's claim that Internal Security's scrutiny of me was justified. The reply reaffirmed that I was never in violation of service policy and that the extraordinary direction given to obtain preclearance for all religious activity was unreasonable, unjustified, and wholly inconsistent with service policies. It accused CSIS of religious discrimination when its members had harassed and manipulated me, an openly practising Muslim woman.

When the Department of Justice and our lawyers began discussing a second mediation, our group unanimously felt that this mediation would be our last attempt to resolve the case. I didn't want to settle, though, even if all my colleagues did. The night before the mediation, I took the train to Toronto to meet two other law firms to assess the likelihood of the service having our case dismissed in court. The lawyers recommended, given John's expertise and reputation, that I follow his advice. Assured that I had the best representation possible, I walked into mediation with a heavy heart and an open mind.

The session was long. Both sides compromised a great deal and reached a settlement. I signed the non-disclosure agreement and therefore am legally forbidden from discussing the settlement's terms. Still, I think it is vital that I speak my truth, to share my experience with the public for progress's sake. My love and duty to Canada, to the CSIS mandate of public safety and national security, compelled me to write this memoir. It's what has propelled me through my mission to be an agent of change. The journey was more taxing than I can explain. While writing, I relived the memories and emotional exhaustion in order to ensure my story was told as clearly as possible for you, the reader. Patriotism demands courage, an unending thread in my spirit.

The director announced the settlement internally at CSIS and then publicly on 14 December 2017, through the CSIS website. His post indicated that the settlement was in the best interest of both parties. He further added, "I strongly believe in leading an organization where each employee promotes a workplace that is free from harassment and conducive to the equitable treatment of all individuals."

Submitting my resignation letter after the settlement was the hardest thing I've ever had to do. I'd fought for years not to quit. Still, I knew I didn't want to live a life of surveillance and scrutiny, and I had lost faith in CSIS's leadership.

A month after my resignation from CSIS, on my way to Toronto to meet our lawyers, I stepped into an Uber in front of my Ottawa house. The driver said "good morning" in a friendly Caribbean accent.

"I feel guilty every time I take an Uber," I confessed. "My dad was a Blue Line cab driver for twenty years."

"Ahh, well, times have changed. Good thing he's no longer on the road. It's more competitive now."

"He still owns a plate and leases it out. That was his retirement plan. The plate isn't worth half of what he paid for it, so you're right – times have changed."

"Where's he from? Where are you from – Guyana?" he asked.

I smiled. "No, that's the first time I got that."

"Trinidad Tobago?" he asked, convinced I was from the Caribbean too. He kept looking back at me and examining my face.

"I used to get Jamaica before I started wearing a hijab. But lately, it's always Somalia or Sudan. You know, an old Somali woman once yelled at me for not replying to her in Somali and then shouted I shouldn't be ashamed of my language. I'm Arab and African, Yemeni and Ethiopian. But I grew up in Egypt and married an Egyptian. It's all so confusing, I know. Story of my life."

"You speak good English," he said, puzzled.

"I guess I came to Canada young enough not to have an accent. I also speak French, Arabic, and Harari. People think I'm a native speaker in most of them," I added.

"That's really amazing. You should work for the CIA or something. No one will know where you're from."

"In Canada, it's called CSIS – the Canadian Security Intelligence Service. Maybe someday," I said, before getting out of the car.

AFTERWORD

In August 2018, my family and I visited Ground Zero and the 9/11 Memorial Museum in New York City. Waiting in line on that hot summer afternoon, we stood out from the crowd. We were one of the few visibly Muslim families – I was wearing my hijab and Ali had trimmed facial hair. I leaned over and whispered to Ali and the kids to stand with their shoulders straight. I pleaded with the kids to be on their best behaviour. We were there to remember and honour the thousands of lives lost. The children were restless and excitable as they played with the black stanchion post and the attached retractable belt. One of them detached it, and I gave them all a stern stare. I wanted everyone to know that we, a Muslim family, were at Ground Zero to show our respect, to honour those we'd lost, to learn, and to reflect. Many others, tourists or perhaps New Yorkers, smiled back at me. Maybe they sensed my anxiety. Their kind gestures eased my soul.

At the museum, I pulled my eldest daughter, Mariam, a little closer and encouraged her to pay attention. "Maybe you could use this information in a school project." She nodded, understanding the site was historic and significant. She whispered, "Why did some Muslims do this, Mom?"

"Because there are good and bad people, like in every religion. You mustn't trust blindly, and you must make your own decisions about what's right and wrong." I reflected for a minute on how my parents had taught me that one should never question people of faith: "Assume the best," they told me. Maybe that applied years ago, but today's naïve and blind trust in religious institutions, organizations, and governments is worrisome. It's best to be critical and to question.

Today, as a civilian, I continue to demand equity, transparency, and accountability from our national security and law enforcement organizations. I do so by sharing my story in community centres, engaging with the public (particularly future practitioners across universities), and with Canadian change-makers and politicians. As a national security expert, I am trained to imagine the worst and take measures to prevent it. Systemic racism is a threat to our national security. Failure to tackle it decreases trust in government and it can compromise our ability to fight terrorism, political interference, and cyber threats. It has become crystal clear that trust in government is quickly eroding and the result is an eruption of violence. It is also evident that while technology connects us, it can be a multiplying force in misinformation and divisions, challenging critical pillars of democracy. More than ever, we need a collective resurgence of pluralism. We also need to hold government and technology companies accountable. We need individual responsibility and collective effort to prevent political violence.

Once at a dinner party I asked a German intelligence officer from the Bundesnachrichtendienst (BND) how his organization could be so precise with threat analysis – understand what they know and be honest about what they don't know – when other organizations weren't as transparent. He said that individual moral responsibility is ingrained in Germans as a lesson of the Holocaust. After the war, Adolf Eichmann and other low-level military officers defended themselves as merely carrying out superiors' orders. To shift their culpability in the killing of millions of Jews, they claimed that they were forced to serve as instruments. That didn't fly, and they were rightly held accountable. "Germans," he said, "even at the lowest levels of public service, must be prepared to take responsibility for our actions and accept the consequences."

This degree of individual moral consciousness is what we need today. It's our individual *responsibility* and *duty* to correct wrongs and not stand idle in our workplaces, in our places of worship, in government positions, during political elections, in the private sector, and in international relations. Democracy depends on citizens being informed and people being transparently and forcefully held to account. It *always* takes courage for one person to speak up for truth, but others will always follow. I spoke my truth and I hope you can one day speak yours too.

ACKNOWLEDGMENTS

I want to thank McGill-Queen's University Press and my editor, Emily Andrew, for enthusiastically endorsing this book. Emily brought the depth of her editorial experience and provided invaluable insights, rigorous reading, a selection of expert peer reviewers, and an excitement for this book that has made every tear dropped while writing worth the journey.

I am also enormously grateful to my friend and outstanding editor Sasha Fury who helped me craft this book from the onset a couple of years ago. When I thought it was ridiculous to write a book that included way too much *I*, they believed in my voice. They urged me to speak my truth as it would provide a perspective that isn't otherwise available to marginalized people in Canada. I include those wanting to serve the country in law enforcement and national security work in that. "You have to keep at it because no one else has been through what you have been through; no one else can write this," she said. She gave me a sense of purpose and a mission for the greater good, a formula that has always motivated me. I am equally grateful to my friend Tori Dudys for coming into this project and contributing immensely. Her thorough and insightful attention to detail helped me push through the many drafts it took to get here.

I also want to thank British and Canadian security and intelligence expert Dr Steve Hewitt of the University of Birmingham, United Kingdom, and Dr Anver Emon, director of the Institute of Islamic Studies at the University of Toronto, for their advice and recommendations and for inspiring me to start my own academic journey in surveillance and race at the

University of Ottawa. Many others provided me with support and guidance along the way but have chosen to be anonymous in this book about spies and secrets. You know who you are, thank you!

NOTES

PROLOGUE

1 Andrew Russel, "Canada's Spy Agency Faces $35-Million Lawsuit over Allegations of Islamophobia, Homophobia," Global News, 14 January 2017, https://globalnews.ca/news/3598968/canadas-spy-agency-lawsuit-allegations-islamophobia-homophobia/.
2 "Trudeau Says Alleged Harassment in CSIS Is Unacceptable," Global News, 14 July 2017, https://globalnews.ca/video/3600306/trudeau-says-alleged-harassment-in-csis-is-unacceptable.
3 Matthew Dubé, "Liberals Must End the 'Old Boys' Club' Culture of CSIS," New Democratic Party of Canada, 26 October 2017, https://www.ndp.ca/news/liberals-must-end-old-boys-club-culture-csis.
4 Devin Dwyer and Cindy Smith, "US Spy Agencies Face 'Shocking' Lack of Diversity," ABC News, 6 October 2020, https://abcnews.go.com/Politics/us-spy-agencies-face-shocking-lack-diversity/story?id=72915850.
5 "GCHQ Had a 'Colour Bar' Banning the Hiring of Non-white Staff for Over 30 Years, New Book Reveals," BNH News, 19 October 2020, https://bonnewshaiti.com/gchq-had-a-colour-bar-banning-the-hiring-of-non-white-staff-for-30-years-new-book-reveals/.
6 *National Security and Intelligence Committee of Parliamentarians Annual Report 2019* (Ottawa: Her Majesty the Queen in Right of Canada, 2020), https://www.nsicop-cpsnr.ca/reports/rp-2020-03-12-ar/annual_report_2019_public_en.pdf.
7 National Council on Canadian Muslim Relations (NCCM), "Recommendations: National Action Summit on Islamophobia," accessed 12 June 2022, https://www.nccm.ca/islamophobiasummit/.
8 Amanda Coletta, "Quebec City Mosque Shooter Scoured Twitter for Trump, Right-Wing Figures before Attack," *The Washington Post*, 18 April 2018, https://www.washingtonpost.com/news/worldviews/

wp/2018/04/18/quebec-city-mosque-shooter-scoured-twitter-for-trump-right-wing-figures-before-attack/; Wendy Gillis, "With the Accused in Etobicoke Mosque Slaying Linked to Neo-Nazi Social Media Accounts, It's Time for Canada to Act against Far Right Extremists, Muslims and Others Say," *Toronto Star*, 22 September 2020, https://www.thestar.com/news/gta/2020/09/22/with-the-accused-in-etobicoke-mosque-slaying-linked-to-neo-nazi-social-media-accounts-its-time-for-canada-to-act-against-far-right-extremists-muslims-and-others-say.html; Tom Yun, "Suspect in Killing of Muslim Family in London, Ont., May Have Accessed Neo-Nazi Site on Dark Web: Documents," *CP24*, 15 March 2022, https://www.cp24.com/news/suspect-in-killing-of-muslim-family-in-london-ont-may-have-accessed-neo-nazi-site-on-dark-web-documents-1.5819477.
9 Stewart Bell, "Documents Reveal Internal Debate over Threat of Canadian Right Wing Extremism," Global News, 7 May 2018, https://globalnews.ca/news/4188139/far-right-extremely-small-csis/.

CHAPTER ONE

1 Kjetil Tronvoll, Charles Schaefer, and Girmachew Alemu Aneme, "The History of the Red Terror Contexts & Consequences," in *The Ethiopian Red Terror Trials: Transitional Justice Challenged*, (Rochester: Boydell & Brewer, 2009), 25, https://www.jstor.org/stable/10.7722/j.ctt81gzd.
2 Ibid., 28.

CHAPTER SEVEN

1 Todd H. Green, *The Fear of Islam: An Introduction to Islamophobia in the West* (Minneapolis: Fortress Press, 2019), 123.
2 The Holy Quran (trans. Alī, A. Yūsuf), 5:32.

CHAPTER EIGHT

1 *Security Intelligence Review Committee Annual Report 1986–1987* (Ottawa: Minister of Supply and Services Canada, 1987), http://www.sirc-csars.gc.ca/pdfs/ar_1986-1987-eng.pdf.
2 *Security Intelligence Review Committee Annual Report 1984–1985* (Ottawa: Minister of Supply and Services Canada, 1985), http://www.sirc-csars.gc.ca/pdfs/ar_1984-1985-eng.pdf.

3 Ibid.
4 *Security Intelligence Review Committee Annual Report 1988–1989* (Ottawa: Minister of Supply and Services Canada, 1989), http://www.sirc-csars.gc.ca/pdfs/ar_1988-1989-eng.pdf.
5 *Security Intelligence Review Committee Annual Report 1989–1990* (Ottawa: Minister of Supply and Services Canada, 1990), http://www.sirc-csars.gc.ca/pdfs/ar_1989-1990-eng.pdf.
6 Royal Canadian Mounted Police, "Historically Relevant Dates to the RCMP," 10 November 2021, https://www.rcmp-grc.gc.ca/en/historically-relevant-dates-rcmp.
7 Government of Canada, "Remarks by Prime Minister Justin Trudeau to Apologize to LGBTQ2 Canadians," 28 November 2017, https://pm.gc.ca/en/news/speeches/2017/11/28/remarks-prime-minister-justin-trudeau-apologize-lgbtq2-canadians.
8 *Security Intelligence Review Committee Annual Report 1993–1994* (Ottawa: Minister of Supply and Services Canada, 1990), http://www.sirc-csars.gc.ca/pdfs/ar_1993-1994-eng.pdf.

CHAPTER NINE

1 Bruce Livesay, "Torture and Interrogation the CSIS and RCMP Way," *Canada's National Observer*, 20 September 2017, https://www.nationalobserver.com/2017/09/20/news/torture-and-interrogation-csis-and-rcmp-way.
2 Colin Freeze, "Arar Freed after Appeal from Chrétien," *Globe and Mail*, 10 November 2004, https://www.theglobeandmail.com/news/national/arar-freed-after-appeal-from-chretien/article4091468/.
3 Jeff Sallot, "How Canada Failed Citizen Maher Arar," *Globe and Mail*, 12 September 2006, https://www.theglobeandmail.com/news/national/how-canada-failed-citizen-maher-arar/article1103562/.
4 Michael Den Tandt and Brian Laghi, "CSIS Wanted Arar Kept in Syria, Memo Shows," *Globe and Mail*, 4 June 2005, https://www.theglobeandmail.com/news/national/csis-wanted-arar-kept-in-syria-memo-shows/article4118179/.
5 *Commission of Inquiry into the Actions of Canadian Officials in Relation to Maher Arar, Report of the Events Relating to Maher Arar: Factual Background: Volume 2* (Ottawa: Public Works and Government Services Canada, 2006), http://epe.lac-bac.gc.ca/100/206/301/pco-bcp/commissions/maher_arar/07-09-13/www.ararcommission.ca/eng/Vol_II_English.pdf.

CHAPTER ELEVEN

1. "Former MI5 Head: Iraq War 'Radicalised a Generation,'" BBC, 20 July 2010, video, 2:17, https://www.bbc.com/news/av/uk-10697083/former-m15-head-iraq-war-radicalised-a-generation.
2. "Canadian Muslims Complain of CSIS Harassment," CBC, 2 July 2004, https://www.cbc.ca/news/canada/canadian-muslims-complain-of-csis-harassment-1.518363.
3. Ibid.
4. Ibid.
5. Michelle Shephard, "Canada's Maverick Spy Dies," *Toronto Star*, 18 November 2010, https://www.thestar.com/news/canada/2010/11/13/canadas_maverick_spy_dies.html.
6. Stewart Bell, "Eulogizing a Life of Secrets," *National Post*, 18 November 2010, https://www.pressreader.com/canada/national-post-latest-edition/20101118/283171489920840.

CHAPTER EIGHTEEN

1. "'You Don't Care about Me' Omar Khadr Sobs in Interview Tapes," CBC News, 15 July 2008, https://www.cbc.ca/news/canada/you-don-t-care-about-me-omar-khadr-sobs-in-interview-tapes-1.709736.
2. Federal Public Sector Labour Relations and Employment Board, *FPSLREB Decisions: Bergeron v. Canadian Security Intelligence Service*, 12 August 2011, https://decisions.fpslreb-crtespf.gc.ca/fpslreb-crtespf/d/en/item/358613/index.do?q=CSIS.

CHAPTER NINETEEN

1. Sheryl Sandberg, *Lean In: Women, Work, and the Will to Lead* (New York: Alfred A. Knopf, 2018), 27.

CHAPTER TWENTY

1. Vaughn Hillyard, "Donald Trump's Plan for a Muslim Database Draws Comparison to Nazi Germany," *NBC News*, 20 November 2015, https://www.nbcnews.com/politics/2016-election/trump-says-he-would-certainly-implement-muslim-database-n466716.

2 Gleen Kessler, "Trump's Outrageous Claim That 'Thousands' of New Jersey Muslims Celebrated the 9/11 Attacks," *Washington Post*, 22 November 2015, https://www.washingtonpost.com/news/fact-checker/wp/2015/11/22/donald-trumps-outrageous-claim-that-thousands-of-new-jersey-muslims-celebrated-the-911-attacks/.
3 Laura Payton, "Muslim Groups 'Troubled' by Stephen Harper's Mosque Remark," *CBC*, 2 February 2015, https://www.cbc.ca/news/politics/muslim-groups-troubled-by-stephen-harper-s-mosque-remark-1.2940488.
4 Ibid.
5 "'A Canadian Is a Canadian Is a Canadian': Harper, Trudeau Spar over Right to Revoke Citizenship," *Globe and Mail*, 28 September 2015, video, 1:10, https://www.theglobeandmail.com/canada/video-video-a-canadian-is-a-canadian-is-a-canadian-harper-trudeau-spar/.

CHAPTER TWENTY-TWO

1 John Doe #1, Jane Doe #1, John Doe #2, John Doe #3, Jane Doe #2 (Plaintiffs) v. Her Majesty the Queen in Right of Canada (Defendant), Federal Court File Number T-1032-19, 13 July 2017.
2 Ibid.
3 Ibid.
4 Ibid.
5 Michelle Shepherd, "Five CSIS Employees Are Accusing the Spy Agency of Islamophobia, Racism and Homophobia in a $35-Million Lawsuit," *Toronto Star*, 13 July 2017, https://www.thestar.com/news/canada/2017/07/13/five-employees-accuse-canadas-spy-agency-of-islamophobia-racism-and-homophobia-in-35-million-lawsuit.html.
6 "Trudeau Says Alleged Harassment in CSIS Is Unacceptable," *Global News*, 14 July 2017, https://globalnews.ca/video/3600306/trudeau-says-alleged-harassment-in-csis-is-unacceptable.
7 Michelle Shephard, "Head of Spy Agency CSIS Admits 'Retribution, Favouritism, Bullying' in Workplace," *Toronto Star*, 25 October 2017, https://www.thestar.com/news/canada/2017/10/25/csis-director-calls-behaviour-unacceptable-after-report-uncovers-bullying-reprisals-at-canadas-spy-agency.html.
8 Ibid.
9 Ibid.

10 "Bullying Must Have Consequences, Says Goodale, Following Reports of Abuse inside CSIS," CBC News, 27 October 2017, https://www.cbc.ca/news/canada/toronto/csis-goodale-harassment-bullying-1.4375889.
11 Ibid.
12 Michelle Shephard, "Judge Slams Ottawa for Delays over $35-Million CSIS Lawsuit Alleging Workplace Islamophobia, Racism and Homophobia," *Toronto Star*, 24 October 2017, https://www.thestar.com/news/canada/2017/10/24/judge-slams-ottawa-for-delays-over-35-million-csis-lawsuit-alleging-workplace-islamophobia-racism-and-homophobia.html.
13 Jim Bronskill, "CSIS Asks Court to Dismiss Lawsuit Alleging Workplace Harassment," *Globe and Mail*, 27 October 2017, https://www.theglobeandmail.com/news/politics/goodale-says-harassment-must-bring-consequences-amid-calls-for-csis-investigation/article36751772/.
14 Ibid.
15 Ibid.
16 Michelle Shephard, "CSIS Says Harassment Complainants Don't Deserve $35 Million as Goodale Calls Bullying at Spy Agency 'Unacceptable,'" *Toronto Star*, 27 October 2017, https://www.thestar.com/news/canada/2017/10/27/csis-says-harassment-complaints-dont-deserve-35-million-as-goodale-calls-bullying-at-spy-agency-unacceptable.html.